EDUCATION RESEARCH AND THE MEDIA

Universities around the world now actively encourage academics to engage in public scholarship, publishing in traditional and new media – newspapers, television, radio, blogs and social media. *Education Research and the Media* addresses this situation, using empirical and reflexive accounts, to interrogate and advance the ways in which this shift is usually discussed.

Drawing on Australian and international scholars and contexts, this edited collection probes the effects of these engagements. Taken together, the book offers new conceptualisations of the junctures and disjunctures of local, national and transnational mediascapes in education research, working across both traditional media and social media platforms. The book takes as its starting point that traditional national media, while still significant, are now embedded in practices and discourses that transcend geographic and spatial boundaries. Global media logics challenge the profitability and operations of media corporations, as the production of news and information is paradoxically both democratised and fragmented.

There is a limited body of research about how this mediatised landscape impacts on public scholarship. This is the first book in the field of education to systematically investigate this landscape, using empirical examples and analysis, as well as a range of theoretical and conceptual approaches.

Aspa Baroutsis is a Postdoctoral Research Fellow at the Griffith Institute for Educational Research, Griffith University, Australia. Her research interests include social justice and education; education policy and mediatisation; teachers' work and identity; and children's voice and agency. Her most recent publication is about media mentalities and logics in *Discourse: Studies in the Cultural Politics of Education*.

Stewart Riddle is a Senior Lecturer in the School of Education at the University of Southern Queensland. His research interests include social justice and equity in education, music-based research practices and research methodologies.

Pat Thomson is Professor of Education in the School of Education, The University of Nottingham. Her research agenda is to further understandings about and practices of socially just pedagogies in schools and communities; she often focuses inquiry on the arts and alternative education. She writes, blogs and tweets about academic writing and doctoral education on patthomson.net

EDUCATION RESEARCH AND THE MEDIA

Challenges and Possibilities

Edited by Aspa Baroutsis, Stewart Riddle
and Pat Thomson

LONDON AND NEW YORK

First published 2019
by Routledge
2 Park Square, Milton Park, Abingdon, Oxon OX14 4RN

and by Routledge
52 Vanderbilt Avenue, New York, NY 10017

Routledge is an imprint of the Taylor & Francis Group, an informa business

© 2019 selection and editorial matter, Aspa Baroutsis, Stewart Riddle and Pat Thomson; individual chapters, the contributors

The right of Aspa Baroutsis, Stewart Riddle and Pat Thomson to be identified as the authors of the editorial material, and of the authors for their individual chapters, has been asserted in accordance with sections 77 and 78 of the Copyright, Designs and Patents Act 1988.

All rights reserved. No part of this book may be reprinted or reproduced or utilised in any form or by any electronic, mechanical, or other means, now known or hereafter invented, including photocopying and recording, or in any information storage or retrieval system, without permission in writing from the publishers.

Trademark notice: Product or corporate names may be trademarks or registered trademarks, and are used only for identification and explanation without intent to infringe.

British Library Cataloguing in Publication Data
A catalogue record for this book is available from the British Library

Library of Congress Cataloging-in-Publication Data
A catalog record has been requested for this book

ISBN: 978-0-8153-5586-1 (hbk)
ISBN: 978-0-8153-5588-5 (pbk)
ISBN: 978-1-351-12911-4 (ebk)

Typeset in Bembo
by Taylor & Francis Books

CONTENTS

List of illustrations vii
About this book ix

1 Mapping the field of education research and media 1
   Aspa Baroutsis

PART I
Conducting education research with traditional and social media **25**

2 Headlines and hashtags herald new 'damaging effects': Media and Australia's declining PISA performance 27
   Aspa Baroutsis and Bob Lingard

3 Televising the revolution? #RevolutionSchool and representations of education across traditional and social media 47
   Nicole Mockler

4 Re-mattering media affects: Pedagogical interference into pre-emptive counter-terrorism culture 66
   Shiva Zarabadi and Jessica Ringrose

5 Examining media discourses of diversity and 'indoctrination': Public perceptions of the intended screening of *Gayby Baby* in schools 80
Michelle Jeffries

PART II
Communicating education research using traditional and social media 97

6 Entering the political fray: The role of public education scholars in media debates 99
Cynthia Gerstl-Pepin and Cynthia Reyes

7 Who speaks for teachers? Social media and teacher voice 119
Pat Thomson and Stewart Riddle

8 Muddling through with the media: Lessons from the introduction of Kiwi Standards 135
Martin Thrupp

9 Tweet the 'phallic teacher': Early career feminist education research, Altmetrics and alternative peer review 148
Lucinda McKnight and Linda Graham

10 Scholarship of the cyborg: Productivities and undercurrents 165
Deborah M. Netolicky and Naomi Barnes

11 Concluding thoughts, provocations and speculations on education research and media 180
Aspa Baroutsis, Pat Thomson and Stewart Riddle

List of contributors 190
Index 193

ILLUSTRATIONS

Figures

1.1 Distribution of education research and media publications by decade	5
1.2 Distribution of journal articles based on journal rank	5
1.3 Distribution of publications based on country	6
1.4 Distribution of education research publications based on thematic groups	9
2.1 Heat map of clustered concepts based on newspaper texts	35
2.2 Heat map of clustered concepts based on tweets	36
2.3 Comparative findings of newspaper and Twitter commentary on PISA	42
3.1 Articles by type and media ownership	51
3.2 Distribution of articles by time frame	51
3.3 Users by group	56
3.4 #revolutionschool network map	57
3.5 Initial content coding of #revolutionschool tweets	58
3.6 Promoting/affirming tweets	59
3.7 Critiquing tweets	59
4.1 Terror jarring assemblage	73
4.2 Quiltingveil assemblage	74
7.1 Antagonism in, through and with social media	128

Tables

1.1 Inclusion criteria for literature searches	3
1.2 Distribution of publications based on media sources	4
1.3 Representative examples of publications by country and theme	10
2.1 Common categories across newspaper texts and tweets	34
2.2 Ranked concepts across newspaper texts and tweets	34
3.1 Categorisation of users	55
3.2 Observed vs expected tweets by user group	56
3.3 Observed vs expected critiquing tweets by user group	60
5.1 Conceptions of education and sexuality by orientation	85
6.1 Edu-Scholar rankings from 2010–2018	106

ABOUT THIS BOOK

Universities around the world now actively encourage academics to engage in public scholarship, publishing and sharing their research via traditional and new media – newspapers, television, radio, blogs and social media. This can, at times, be a difficult terrain for academics to navigate. While the 21st century academic is expected to engage in public discourse, little official attention is paid to the challenges and possibilities of engaging in public scholarship and its effects on academics' work and lives.

Many universities employ dedicated communications who publish glossy reports, issue press releases to print media, television and radio and also run in-house blogs, websites and YouTube channels. But academics are also expected to engage in both personal and institutional 'branding'. There are also now a multitude of quasiofficial and university endorsed digitised platforms that encourage academics to promote their work: including sharing papers via Twitter and other social media, ResearchGate, and Academia, to name just a few. Similarly, there are mechanisms used for the identification of academics, such as ORCID, that have linked with academic publishers and now all journal articles through many of the leading publishers require academics to include an ORCID identification number to track and help 'promote' scholarly outputs more widely. The effects of these mediatised shifts in academic work require ongoing documentation and investigation.

This book had its genesis at a symposium held in Melbourne in December 2016 at the Annual Australian Association for Education Research Conference (www.aare.edu.au). It has been a while in the making. Initially, we felt that there was a need for a guide for scholars wishing to engage with traditional and social media. However, we quickly realised the impossibility of such a task, given the fast-moving debates about public scholarship and academic media engagement. The struggles for particular forms of educational subjectivities and traditions of research are set against the advocacy of institutions, imperatives of policy and growth of new media-savvy educational actors. As such, we decided to put together a first take in the very broad field of education to systematically investigate the mediatised landscape in which researchers are now working, using empirical examples and analysis, as well as a range of theoretical and conceptual approaches.

The editors and contributors shared the understanding that it was important to offer a wide view of the field of education media research, rather than get bogged down in any particular aspect of it. We were also keen to include a focus on affect and the ways in which the personal in social media engagement is also the professional and the political. True to our focus on knowledge building, we were able to assemble a number of contributions from researchers working at the nexus of education research and media.

This book focuses on the intersection of education research and traditional and social media platforms. It probes the effects of these engagements. Taken together, this edited collection offers new conceptualisations of the junctures and disjunctures of local, national and transnational mediascapes in education research, working across both traditional media and social media platforms. The book takes as its starting point that traditional national print media, while still significant, are now embedded in practices and discourses that transcend geographic and spatial boundaries. Global and networked media logics challenge the profitability and operations of media corporations, as the production of news and information is paradoxically both democratised and fragmented. Authors in this volume were asked to consider public scholarship and the questions: 'How are academics, now expected by policy and their institutions, to take their work to wider publics?' and 'How can education researchers operate in this new and rapidly changing environment?'

Education researchers are not only engaging in mediatised scholarship but also working to understand what these changes mean, both for understandings of mediatisation, policy enactment and resistances, and also what are the implications for our research methods. This innovative collection shows how the national-global are now imbricated, via conventional and social media, with new genres, rules of political engagement and ambiguous consequences for education research, policy and practice. Our book does not focus on methods per se, but offers both evidence and possible theorisations of this emerging imbrication/ecology, highlighting the affordances, both positive and negative, of different media genre. With contributions from Australia, New Zealand, the United Kingdom and the United States of America, the chapters bring a range of methodological and theoretical approaches to the central problem of how education researchers now make their research public.

This book does not offer an exhaustive mapping of all possible forms of education research and media. Rather, we bring together some key examples of the types of media research that are now being undertaken, providing both empirical and theoretical analysis, before concluding with some speculations about what is missing and what might possibly come next. As such, we have decided to present the book in two parts, with the first examining multiple encounters of conducting education research through and with traditional and social media, while the second considers experiences of communicating education research through media.

As an introduction to the collection, Baroutsis situates the emerging field of education research and media in Chapter 1, focusing on public discourse about education issues, in and through traditional and social media. This chapter provides a historical, statistical and thematic account of the archive of publications. Following a systematic review of the literature, the theoretical and methodological contributions to the field are mapped. Drawing on a thematic analysis, a discussion of the empirical conceptualisations of media constructions of education follows. The empirical findings can be categorised into literature about: education policy and politics; student assessments; schools, education systems and reforms; teachers' work; and children and young people. These studies outline the mediatisation of education, describing the messages about education that are being constructed and conveyed by traditional print and social media.

In Chapter 2, Baroutsis and Lingard provide a comparative analysis of print and social media representations of Australia's changing performance on the OECD's Program for International Student Assessment (PISA). Drawing on frame analysis, they suggest social media are putatively more democratic and inclusive of many actors, focusing to a greater extent on issues of equity. In contrast, investigative print and digital newspapers drew on a narrower set of actors and focused on limited aspects of PISA such as rankings and declines; nonetheless, they provided some critical and evidence-informed accounts. Mockler then explores the representations of education crisis and reform across both traditional and social media in Chapter 3. She takes as a case study the Australian Broadcasting Corporation's documentary series *Revolution School*. Using news frame analysis, the chapter explores the similarities and differences in representations of the 'problem frame' and the imagined solutions across the range of texts. The chapter asks questions about the 'bottom up' framing of education reform at the hands of social media and its relationship with the 'top down' news framing represented in traditional media texts.

The next two chapters draw on societal discourses of race and sexualities to address contemporary issues facing education. They demonstrate how these global issues make their way into schooling and education policy debates. In Chapter 4, Zarabadi and Ringrose explore the 'remediated' coverage of three British girls who 'fled' to Syria to marry jihadi fighters. In the contemporary climate of counter-terrorism the authors argue such media events create new temporal and affective relations that make their way into policy initiatives and schooling environments. They demonstrate how a deeper understanding of mediated affects and affective media helps us grasp how perhaps seemingly insignificant media events can re-mediate and shape educational policies, practices and experiences with profound material implications for shaping bodily capacities to affect and be affected. This is followed by Jeffries' examination in Chapter 5 of the discourses employed by digital citizens as they engage with online newspaper and social media commentary regarding the intended school showing of a documentary, *Gayby Baby*. The analysis maps discourses of diversity and 'indoctrination', offering understandings of public debates relating to the representation of sexual diversity and sexuality diverse families in schools.

In Chapter 6, Gerstl-Pepin and Reyes explore multiple ways education researchers can make their work more accessible to policymakers, publics, teachers, parents, students and community members. They define as public scholars those researchers who seek to challenge misconceptions of educational policy issues in news media reports and public arenas. Drawing on media content analysis, the research examines the writings, presentations and biographies of four high-profile US education scholars to inform educational dialogues concerning such topics as social inequity, standardised testing and globalisation. This is followed by Thomson and Riddle's examination of the mediatisation of teacher voice in Chapter 7. They ask, does social media enhance the ways in which the teacher might 'have a say' in decisions that concern them – about curriculum, assessment, pedagogy, working conditions and so on? Or does it promote a highly individualised and antagonistic conversation in which position-taking and celebrity-making are paramount? They identify the three key ways in which teachers use social media to 'speak' and argue that better theorisations of educational social mediatisation are urgently needed.

Chapter 8 sees Thrupp reflect on his own experiences whilst undertaking research on the Kiwi Standards (National Standards) in New Zealand. This policy was heavily contested by many primary teachers, principals and academics. Those opposing Kiwi Standards were subjected to conservative attack blogs in what became known as 'dirty politics'. He raises issues of research 'independence', the tensions between being a researcher and an activist, and the effects of public and media commentary that questions the legitimacy of research. This is followed in Chapter 9 by a discussion of McKnight's and Graham's experiences of the dissemination of feminist education research in a social media landscape dominated by anonymous commentators and alternative metrics. The chapter offers a case study taking a single example of a feminist article submitted to an Australian educational journal to contemplate how the editor and author, an early career researcher, negotiated perceived personal and professional risks in relation to publication. They suggest these risks are a feature of the postfeminist global mediascape, and demonstrate how patriarchal, misogynist, homophobic and alt right discourses play out in this space.

Netolicky and Barnes round off the contributions to the book in Chapter 10, providing a theoretical and duo-ethnographic exploration of the productiveness and possibilities of new media. They share their own digital experiences, providing insights into what new media offers the education scholar, such as empowerment, collaboration and increased productivity, as well as drawing attention to the mess of educators' being and becoming, and the sometimes-dark underbelly of the new media world. They argue that cyborg scholarship, in which researchers operate as merged human-technology amalgams, allows education scholars to at once resist, embrace and influence the system by making transparent the work of being and becoming an educator-scholar.

Finally, we present some speculations. Our concluding chapter is intended to work less as a neat and tidy wrap up for the collection, and more as an extension and extrapolation of some of the key issues, concepts and problems raised throughout the book. We pose some provocations for widening the discussion about the politics, ethics and pragmatics of academic work and engaging with public spheres through traditional and social media. We ask how we might collectively enable ourselves and others to do difficult, and sometimes dangerous, intellectual work in a mediascape that is ever-changing and often unforgiving of missteps. We leave open the question about how academics might productively and proactively work within the assemblage of education research and media.

Aspa Baroutsis
Stewart Riddle
Pat Thomson

1
MAPPING THE FIELD OF EDUCATION RESEARCH AND MEDIA

Aspa Baroutsis

Introduction

An emerging field of education research focuses on public discourse about education issues, in and through traditional and social media. Traditional media refers to scholarship about education in broadcast media such as television and movies; as well as print media such as newspapers, both hardcopy and electronic formats (cf Baroutsis, 2016; Thomson, Blackmore, Sachs, & Tregenza, 2003). More recently, as documented in this book, *Education Research and the Media: Challenges and Possibilities*, there is a growing prominence of the use of social media, such as Facebook and Twitter, in and about education matters. Drawing on systematically retrieved selected literature, this chapter provides a comparative review of education research and media by mapping the theoretical, methodological and empirical elements in the publication archive. The compiled data seeks to identify key research addressing the mediatisation of education, expressing the entanglements and influences between media, education and education research. This timely review provides scholars with an overview of the research as well as significant commentary about the gaps and issues, thereby identifying future research directions.

Some of the first empirical literature in the field of education research and media is found in the early 1990s. Cunningham (1992) analysed how the press portrayed teachers and how this influenced public attitudes. The following year, Wallace (1993) identified the role of mass media in the education policy process. It was not until 2004 when the first journal special issue was published in the *Journal of Education Policy*, edited by Pat Thomson (also see Chapter 7), which focused entirely on education research and media. The introduction to the special issue stated:

> Research is also now tangled up in media. Major funding bodies now expect grantees to make their findings public via media as well as other forms of

publication. Researchers are routinely asked by journalists for their views on a range of government initiatives and social issues. Professional research associations are beginning to find ways to assist their members to deal with an unfamiliar communication genre that depends on the production of binaries, polarities, and condensed 'bytes'. Yet, as an object of research, the knot of policy, governance, and media is still largely the purview of journalism, media studies, cultural studies, and English scholars.

(Thomson, 2004, p. 251)

To date, research and media continue their entanglements. The same text could be used to describe the current situation albeit with a greater degree of intensity as education institutions globally are asked to demonstrate their research engagement and impact.

Four other special issues have followed. In 2006, Michelle Stack and Deirdre Kelly edited a special issue titled 'Popular media, education and resistance' in the *Canadian Journal of Education*. One part of this special issues addressed how children, youth and schools were 'represented' by media. Similarly, in 2007, Michelle Stack and Megan Boler edited another special issue in *Policy Futures in Education*, titled 'Media and policy in education'. While this special issue related to media education, there were a number of articles that focued on policy making and resistance. Also, in 2007, Cynthia Gerstl-Pepin (also see Chapter 6) edited a special issue titled 'Media, democracy, and the politics of education' in the *Peabody Journal of Education*. The introduction stated that the goal of the publication was: 'To draw attention to the important role that media play in educational politics and to make a case for research that is attentive to the intersection of educational politics and media coverage' (Gerstl-Pepin, 2007, p. 1). The importance of understanding the entanglements of politics and media has only increased. The next special issue was in 2015, in *Critical Education* titled, 'News media, education, and the subversion of the neoliberal social imaginary'. The editors of this volume stated: 'This issue will explicate the various ways in which the mainstream media has helped facilitate and legitimate neoliberalism as a universal logic in reforming education, both locally and globally' (Ford, Porfilio, & Goldstein, 2015, p. 2). Additionally, to date, there have been four books about education research and media: *Education policy in the media* by Thomas (2006); *Literacy Wars* by Snyder (2008); *News media & the neoliberal privatization of education*, an edited collection by Wubbena, Ford, and Porfilio (2016), drawn from the *Critical Education* special issue; and *Global university rankings and the mediatization of higher education* by Stack (2016). A detailed overview of these and other volumes follows.

Collecting the literature

The systematic process of collecting literature was framed around the goal of mapping the publications that span education and media. A search of published scholarly literature was conducted using library search engines that draw on education databases and Google Scholar. Additionally, searches were conducted via individual journals where literature was initially located on the topic. A difficulty I encountered here related to the choice of search terms. Often, the terms 'media' and 'education' yielded general publications that related to media arts or the teaching of media. Similarly, the inclusion of 'education research' and 'media' was only marginally more generative. Instead, a number of more advanced searches, utilising Boolean terms, were required that compiled various iterations of key words, for example, 'media representation', 'newspapers', 'twitter', 'school', 'education' or 'teachers'. As a secondary means of identifying publications in the field, a snowball method was used. This included identifying key words in retrieved papers and reviewing the reference list of each publication to help identify supplementary phrases used for searching for additional literature. This highlights one of the difficulties that researchers are likely to face when seeking to systematically collate literature in this field.

Following the retrieval of publications, based on the outlined search term parameters, a refinement process was undertaken. This stage involved the application of four inclusion criteria (see Table 1.1). First, the subject matter was required to combine both an aspect of media and education. While there are many publications in the area of media communication and journalism, unless they related specifically to education, they were not included. Second, traditional print media and/or social media sources had to form the empirical basis of the publication's data set or the publication had to provide a theoretical or methodological discussion about education and media. Other traditional media such as radio or television were not included in this archive. Third, publications had to have undergone a peer-review process; therefore, unpublished works or conference proceedings are not part of this archive. Finally, only publications written in English were included. In all, this literature review process identified 167 publications, with 23 being excluded, leaving 144 publications that form the corpus of data in this chapter.

The selected publications were then categorised based on their media source and focus. First, texts were grouped into either those with traditional print or social media sources with 85% of the publications using traditional print media sources

TABLE 1.1 Inclusion criteria for literature searches

Criteria	Included publications	Excluded publications
Subject matter focus	Related to an aspect of education	General publications about media
Media sources	Print or social media used as data sets and/or Analysed an aspect of media practice	Other sources such as radio, television, movies etc. and/or General media research
Published	Peer-reviewed journal, reviewed professional journals, books	Theses, unpublished works
Language	Written in English	Other languages

TABLE 1.2 Distribution of publications based on media sources (n=144)

Source of publication	Media-related focus of publication		
	Theoretical only	*Theoretical and empirical*	*TOTAL*
Print media	16%	69%	85%
Social media	5%	10%	15%
TOTAL	21%	79%	

while 15% were derived from social media (see Table 1.2). Second, the texts were grouped based on their focus, that is, those that empirically used media sources as their data set and those without an empirical focus that theorised about an aspect of education and media. The empirical publications also frequently provided theoretical framings of these data which are described later in the chapter. The analysis found that 79% of publications had an empirical focus (see Table 1.2). These findings should be viewed in conjunction with the descriptive statistics outlined in the following section.

Descriptive statistical overview of publications

A simple descriptive statistical analysis maps the demographics of the publications in this education research and media archive. This includes: the distribution of publications based on publication dates; the type or format of the publications; the journal rankings; and the country the research was conducted in, if specified in the publication.

First, when compiled into decades, the analysis shows an exponential growth in the number of publications that report on education and media (see Figure 1.1). Based only on the literature derived from the outlined inclusion parameters, one of the first publications about traditional print media and education was in the late 1970s (Gorton, 1979), while one of the first social media publications was almost three decades later (Luehmann, 2008). This gap is understandable given that the inception of print media sources such as newspapers date back to the early seventeenth century (Stephens, 2007), while the World Wide Web was invented centuries later in 1991. The discovery afforded many forms of networked communications including sites such as: 'Blogger (1999), Wikipedia (2001), Myspace (2003), Facebook (2004), Flickr (2004), YouTube (2005), Twitter (2006)' (van Dijck, 2013, p. 7). Therefore, the quantity of academic literature reflects the newness of these social media.

Second, based on the type of publications across both print and social media (n=144), 88% of articles were found in peer-reviewed journals, 6% book chapters, 3% in reviewed professional journals and 3% books. This signals the emerging nature of the education research and media field.

Third, the preponderance of publications is in journals (n=127), with 57% of the articles being published in high ranking journals (see Figure 1.2) based on the SCImago Journal Rank (SJR) indicator (www.scimagojr.com).

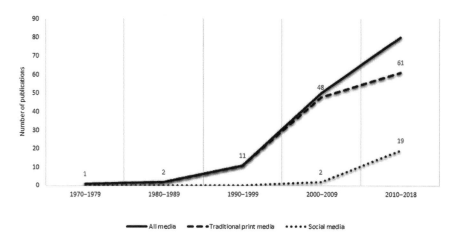

FIGURE 1.1 Distribution of education research and media publications by decade (n=144)

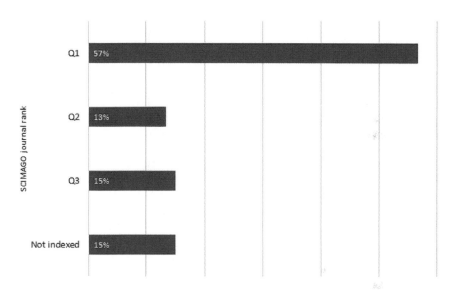

FIGURE 1.2 Distribution of journal articles based on journal rank (n=127)

Finally, of the traditional print and social media-based empirical studies, there were 104 publications that indicated the country associated with the research. The remaining publications were not country-specific due to the nature of these media, that is, social media are global entities. Figure 1.3 identifies the distribution of publications. Of the studies using print media as empirical data, the largest collection of publications, 26%, draws on Australian newspapers and contexts. This is followed by the US with 23% of the publications and the UK with 14%. Of interest here is that the Australian traditional media sector is oligopolistic, compared

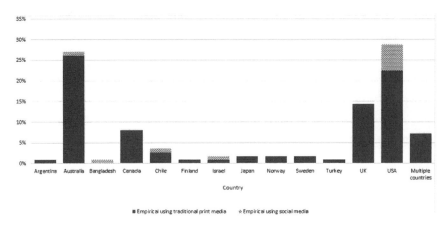

FIGURE 1.3 Distribution of publications based on country (n=111)

to that of the other two nations, and therefore tends to lack a diversity in both perspective and context (Cunningham, 2010). Research publications derived from these traditional print media are likely to reflect this lack of diversity. The studies using social media as empirical data were fewer, but as shown in Figure 1.1, these are increasing. Of those studies where a country was specified, the majority of these publications (6%) were from the US context.

The descriptive statistics outlined in this section map the field of education research and media in simple terms, providing an historical overview of publications.

Mapping education research and media conceptualisations

This section draws on two research frames or conceptualisations to discuss the contributions of this archive to the field of education research and media. The first section maps the theoretical and methodological contributions, followed by a discussion of the empirical conceptualisations of media constructions of education.

Theoretical and methodological conceptualisations of education research and media

Media-focused education research acutely draws on the neologism of mediatisation; a concept that is derived from media and communications research (cf Esser & Stromback, 2014; Hepp, Brieter, & Hasebrink, 2018). The first wave of mediatisation studies was predominantly concerned with 'mechanisation' and 'electrification' with the second wave being concerned with 'digitalisation' (Hepp et al., 2018). With digitisation, there has been a spread of technology-based communication media that permeates many aspects of society, from interacting with family, friends and work colleagues; to engagement with learning and employment; to finance, retail and leisure activities; and governance, administration and politics.

Much of the early work in this area was by a small group of Australian scholars (cf Blackmore & Thomson, 2004; Lingard & Rawolle, 2004; Rawolle, 2005, 2010; Rawolle & Lingard, 2010; Thomas, 1999, 2006) that developed the foundational concept by adopting and adapting understandings of mediatisation, drawing on the perspectives of education systems, stakeholders and practices. Education is a socio-cultural practice and as such, drawing on the work of Mazzoleni (2008), the mediatisation of education can be described as 'ways in which the media, which are vehicles of various types of messages (by which meaning is exchanged and negotiated), and society have made themselves mutually indispensable and unavoidably interrelated' (p. 1).

However, with the shift to digitalisation comes the opportunity for 'datafication'. This is a process that transforms regular information, such as a location or an online social interaction or other intangible aspects of everyday life, 'transforming it into a data format to make it quantified' enabling individuals and organisations to 'use the information in new ways, such as in predictive analysis' (Mayer-Schönberger & Cukier, 2013, np). Take, for example, a book. When this is scanned from a hardcopy format it is digitised, but datafication indexes the book making it searchable (Mayer-Schönberger & Cukier, 2013). In so doing, a user's actions in relation to the book become quantifiable and therefore, the user's habits can be analysed. Through the spread of technology-based communication media, we see the 'moulding force' of media in the social construction of realities (Hepp, 2013). It is this media influence on society that is the subject of mediatisation.

Theorising the influence of media better enables understandings for education stakeholders of this 'global public sphere' (Mazzoleni, 2015). Put simply, mediatisation is a conceptual tool that can interrogate and explain how these media shape public education discourse, both locally and globally. For example, Blackmore and Thorpe (2003) considered why particular education themes become foregrounded as issues and how government stakeholders mobilise media for strategic advantage during periods of education reform (also see Chapter 8). Similarly, Hattam, Prosser and Brady (2009) outlined the tactics used by policy and media actors to spin education news and the constitutive role these media play in the education policy process. In another example, Fenech and Wilkins (2017) considered how parent users of childcare may be differentially influenced by print media depending on type and format of the publication. Finally, Thapliyal (2018) critically analysed the effects of the strategic deployment of digital media to amplify and privilege particular perspectives.

Traditional print and social media inform education discourses; however, these media also create and influence, steer and shape education news and information for public consumption. In the outlined examples, mediatisation is conceptualised as a set of practices that impact the practices of others (Rawolle, 2010, p. 22). Mediatisation foregrounds 'media mentalities' and logics (Baroutsis, 2017) that are used to secure influence and the consequent 'mediatisation effects' (Rawolle & Lingard, 2014), particularly the effects on democratic decision making (Rawolle, 2010). For example, a recent article documented the institutional and journalistic practices of agendisation, accountabilisation, factualisation, emphasisation and sensationalisation in the reporting of teachers' work (Baroutsis, 2017). In other studies

(Franklin, 2004; Gewirtz, Dickson, & Power, 2004), scholars investigated the constitutive role of 'spin', the purposeful management of information, and its complex relationship with education policy which makes it difficult for stakeholders and the public to distinguish the policies from the spin. Lingard and Rawolle (2004) draw on Bourdieu's (2011) critique of television to identify two logics of practice: circular circulation and permanent and structural amnesia, as they relate to education policy. Also drawing on Bourdieu, Phelan and Salter (2017) examined journalistic habitus and neoliberal logics of the marketised education agenda.

Similarly, there are social media logics and effects. In a digital age, the 'communication ecosystem' is shifting and transforming (Mazzoleni, 2017), as 'new media reconfigure and diversify processes of communication and interaction' (p. 142). Klinger and Svensson (2015) note that within this context evolves a 'network media logic[s]' which produces, distributes and uses media differently to mass media logics of practice. That is, for example, within social media networks, 'users are like intermediaries, distributing popular content' and media usage is based on highly selective 'interest-bound and like-minded peer networks' (p. 1246). Adhikary, Lingard, and Hardy (2018) demonstrated how Facebook has become a new platform for policy mediatisation through strategies such as the focus on the audio-visual dissemination of information and the use of emotional stimuli to influence public perceptions.

The review of the methodological conceptualisations of publications in the education research and media archive, identified four main tools for analysis: frame analysis, critical discourse analysis, content analysis and social network analysis. Frame analysis draws on the work of scholars such as Entman (1993) and Goffman (1986), who suggest media 'select some aspects of a perceived reality and make them more salient in a communicating text' (Entman, 1993, p. 53). Critical discourse analysis (CDA), drawing on the work of scholars such as Fairclough (2010), has a more linguistic focus and analyses language as social practice. Content analysis, an umbrella concept of approaches that often include technology-assisted analyses, both qualitative and quantitative, examines patterns in communications (cf Krippendorff, 2013). Social network analysis also draws on technology for large-scale analysis of social networks, and identifies relationship and interactions within social structures, visualised graphically through models and sociograms (also see Chapters 2 and 3).

These theoretical conceptualisations of media in education research, either overtly or surreptitiously, form the basis of many publications. Often, but not always, the theoretical undertones in education research are drawn from understanding and assumptions about media influences and logics of practice and have empirical manifestations within publications. However, it is through precise and detailed methodological work that education researchers can better align with scholarship in media and communication.

Empirical conceptualisations of education research and media

Education research, when reporting on the findings of media analyses, tends to focus on six broad themes: education policy and politics; student assessments;

schooling, education systems and reforms; teachers and their work; children and young people; and education research. Figure 1.4 identifies the distribution of all publications; however, only the first five themes will be discussed in this chapter. The majority of publications (28%) focus on an element of schooling, education systems and reforms; 23% of the archive focuses on teachers and aspects of teachers' work; 19% to international large-scale student assessments; 18% to education policy and politics; while 6% focus on children and young people. The latter, media and children and young people, identifies an area where future research should be considered. Finally, the smallest portion of publications provides a commentary about education research and media; however, these are usually not empirical accounts.

Table 1.3 identifies publications from the archive that are indicative of these themes, with many of the authors being represented in this book. This section provides discussion and examples of these themes, along with identifying the notable exceptions to education research in the field thereby suggesting the scope for further research.

Education policy and politics

In addition to the publications outlined earlier that focus on mediatisation and media logics, a number of other important empirical studies are outlined here that focus on education policy and politics. These publications empirically demonstrate the effects of traditional print media on the education policy process. For example, it is suggested that news media interpret school accountability policies thereby becoming part of the policy enactment process; reinforcing this rather than being

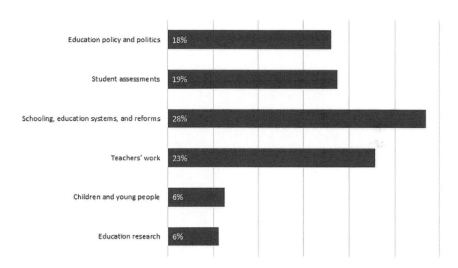

FIGURE 1.4 Distribution of education research publications based on thematic groups (n=144)

TABLE 1.3 Representative examples of publications by country and theme

Country	Education policy and politics	Student assessments	Schooling, education systems and reforms	Teachers' work	Children and young people
Argentina			Robert (2012)		
Australia	Baroutsis (2016) Blackmore and Thomson (2004) Lingard and Rawolle (2004) Rawolle (2005) Thomas (2006)	Baroutsis and Lingard (2017) Mockler (2013)	Thomas (1999)	Baroutsis (2017)	Taylor (2018) Mills (2004)
Canada		Stack (2007)		Greenberg (2004)	Kelly (2006) Gardam and Giles (2016)
Chile			Cabalin (2015)		Cabalin (2014)
France		Pons (2011)			
Germany		Martens and Niemann (2013)			
Israel		Yemini and Gordon (2017)			
Japan		Takayama (2008)			
Nordics: Norway, Finland, Sweden		Fladmoe (2011) Elstad (2009)	Rönnberg, Lindgren and Segerholm (2013)	Edling (2015)	
South Africa				Alhamdan et al. (2014)	

Country	Education policy and politics	Student assessments	Schooling, education systems and reforms	Teachers' work	Children and young people
South Korea		Waldow, Takayama and Sung (2014)			
Turkey		Gur, Celik and Ozoglu (2012)			
UK	Franklin (2004) Pettigrew and MacLure (1997) Wallace (1993)	Grey and Morris (2018) Murphy (2013) Warmington and Murphy (2004)	MacMillan (2002)		
US	Anderson (2007)	Steiner-Khamsi, Appleton and Vellani (2018)	Gerstl-Pepin (2002)	Cohen (2010) Goldstein (2011) Ulmer (2016)	Chesky and Goldstein (2016)

part of policy contestation (Baroutsis, 2016). Elstad (2009) noted the 'negative bias' in the press that draws attention to schools that are performing badly in attainment measurements by naming, shaming and blaming them. Wallace (1993), drawing on the anthropological concept of the 'myth', analysed a debate about traditional and progressive educational practices identified in the UK Plowden Report. He states, 'Myths were created according to the news values of journalists, emphasizing selected messages stripped of the qualifying context set out in the evaluation report' (Wallace, 1993, p. 327). The use of newly released education reviews or reports are examples of common events that are the focus of media, and therefore media analysis. For example, Rawolle (2010) analysed the Batterham Review of Australia's science capability and Thomas (2006) an Australian school curriculum review known as the Wiltshire Review. A similar conceptualisation to the myth is the 'political spectacle'. Anderson (2007) suggested media use this to 'generate points of view, perceptions, anxieties, aspirations, and strategies to strengthen or undermine support for specific education policies, practices, and ideologies' (p. 103). However, Pettigrew and MacLure (1997) provide a word of caution, stating that the 'press reporting of educational issues is frequently unfair are only partially substantiated' suggesting instead that they are more likely to 'inhibit debate through discourses of omission' (p. 392).

Student assessments

International large-scale student assessments frequently provide empirical data for a media analysis. This includes the Programme for International Student Assessment (PISA), the Trends in International Mathematics and Science Study (TIMSS) assessment, and other local student assessments such as the UK General Certificate of Secondary Education (GCSE), the Australian National Assessment Program – Literacy and Numeracy (NAPLAN) and the US Common Core State Standards (CCSS). For example, Berliner and Biddle (1999) analysed the reporting of the US results in the TIMSS assessment by print media, claiming the coverage of US public schools and schooling was biased, negative, simplistic, critical, lacked an understanding of the nature of schools and is ignorant of the effects of poverty and the distribution of opportunities in schooling that lead to student success. Warmington and Murphy (2004) analysed the UK media's concern over perceived falling standards in the A-level examination, finding that reporting tended to be formulaic and prone towards 'producing ritualistic and polarized coverage' (p. 285). Mockler (2013) examined the editorial coverage of Australia's performance in standardised international literacy and numeracy tests and NAPLAN, and identified the narratives of distrust, choice and performance as prevalent in newspaper reportage on the topic. Finally, an analysis by Supovitz (2017), whose team has been engaged in research that tracked Twitter debates on the CCSS in the USA since 2013 (see www.hashtagcommoncore.com), shows that this social media platform is influential in education politics and policies. He states, 'During the

Common Core debates, Twitter was a robust terrain for grassroots activists rather than one dominated by professional advocacy groups' indicating the increasing political influence of these groups and social media (Supovitz, 2017, p. 50).

Of all the student assessments, the PISA test draws the greatest interest in terms of empirical studies analysing media coverage; each with a slightly different focus. Stack (2006, 2007) reviewed the Canadian press coverage of PISA, concluding that 'media interpreted these test results in concert with business and electoral elites as a "failure of marginalized students," rather than a failure of society to address systemic discrimination' (Stack, 2007, p. 100). Similarly, Takayama (2008, 2010, 2013) analysed the role of national Japanese newspapers and the education department in 'mediating the potentially homogenising curricular policy pressure of globalisation exerted through the PISA league tables' (Takayama, 2008, p. 387). Elstad (2009, 2012) explored the press coverage and debate in Norwegian newspapers of the country's PISA performance, identifying blame management strategies deployed by education officials in an effort to 'avoid blame or displace it onto political opponents' (Elstad, 2012, p. 10). Likewise, Gur et al. (2012) critiqued the interpretation and utilisation of PISA results by the Turkish education authorities, suggesting decisions to proceed with curriculum reforms were made prior to the release of the PISA 2003 results, with these being used to justify the changes.

Most Australian media coverage of the country's PISA performance focused on quality, counting and comparing results 'to provide "evidence" that was then used to comparatively position Australia against other countries' (Baroutsis & Lingard, 2017, p. 432). Yemini and Gordon (2017) suggested Israeli newspapers devote most of their attention to international examinations, rather than national examinations which are perceived as redundant. Grey and Morris (2018) demonstrated the distortion of the OECD's original messages by the UK government, and how media:

> framed the results in terms of a narrative of decline, crisis and the need for urgent reform … giving little coverage to either the recommended policy actions or the contrasting interpretations of the PISA results by politicians and the OECD.
>
> (p. 1)

Steiner-Khamsi et al. (2018) analysed business-oriented US newspapers who see 'education as a profitable business opportunity' but perceived education as being in crisis with 'no correlation between spending and education outcome', while also expressing the value of 'school accountability, teacher performance, and decentralisation' for improving the quality of education (p. 190).

Understandably, analyses of a nation's performance in international large-scale student assessments are country based, with a number of scholars offering cross-country comparisons. Examples include: a comparison of PISA performance in Australia, Germany and South Korea (Takayama, Waldow, & Sung, 2013; Waldow et al., 2014); Germany and the US (Martens & Niemann, 2013); Norway, Sweden and Finland (Fladmoe, 2011); France, Scotland and Portugal (Pons, 2011); and Japan, England and France (Yasukawa, Hamilton, & Evans, 2017).

Schools, education systems and reforms

This is a broad category covering numerous topics, and as such, has the largest grouping of publications. Across these publications, there is a focus on how traditional print and social media construct, or 'represent', education. This is not to say that representational ontologies are not problematic (Hayes & Comber, 2017) in that researchers make sense of media data in particular ways through particular positionings. However, analyses of these discourses indicate media portrayals can be 'shallow depictions of educational issues' as Gerstl-Pepin (2002) found in an analysis of the 2000 US presidential election campaign and the candidates' views on education issues. She suggested that media portrayals of education tended to 'reinforce and reflect public assumptions that America's educational system is failing' (Gerstl-Pepin, 2002, p. 37). Similarly, Baker (1994) noted media coverage of education is often 'negative and derisory' (p. 286). This trend is evident in today's media coverage, with my own research finding media coverage of education is often 'negative, critical, oppressive, and reductionist' (Baroutsis, 2016, p. 567) and that there is a focus on the decline of standards and quality in education (Baroutsis & Lingard, 2017).

School standards were covered by a number of publications. For example, Ronnberg et al. (2013) investigated the Swedish school inspection activities, framed within understandings of an audit culture. School standards were sometimes framed around larger social issues. For example, MacMillan (2002) investigated the types of events that attract media attention, suggesting that these followed particular 'recurring patterns and themes' and that these were 'generalized as a feature of all British schools' (p. 36). Robert (2012) suggested newspapers are a 'site of contestation' where debates over global reforms are 'contextualised in "obvious" and "natural" local language' (p. 2). In particular, media attention often reaches a frenzy when there are proposed changes to school practices and reforms. For example, Snyder (2008, 2009) outlined literacy reforms, particularly the phonics debate, that have attracted a multitude of media attention.

At times, these media perceptions are presented as common-sensical and self-evident 'facts' about education. This is not a statement intended to understate the agency of the reader, but as Bernard Cohen (1963) states, 'The press is significantly more than a purveyor of information and opinion', adding, 'It may not be successful much of the time in telling people what to think, but it is stunningly successful in telling its readers what to think about' (p. 13). Alarmingly, such coverage does incite moral panics. As Stanley Cohen (2002) states, mass media are 'carriers' and 'producers' of moral panic. Unfortunately, when moral panic about education in crisis is circulated, 'more moral panics will be generated' (Cohen, 2002, p. 233).

Inevitably, moral panics promote and encourage media to proffer solutions to education-related problems. A number of publications analyse media generated solutions that are often presented as ways of averting these crises, but often become problematic in themselves. For example, Haas (2007), when analysing media constructions of think tanks, suggested 'news media presented all the think tanks as credible sources of research, facts, and figures on education' (p. 63). Other studies include a focus on multinational edu-businesses (Hogan, 2015), the 'Teach for ...' movement (Brewer & Wallis, 2015; Faltin Osborn & Sierk, 2015), marketisation (Goldstein & Chesky, 2016) and privatisation (Shuffelton, 2015).

The publications related to schools, education systems and reform also highlight the included voices, and perhaps more importantly, identify those that are excluded from debates about education (also see Chapter 7). This is an area within the field of education research and media that urgently needs further research. Thomas (1999) noted which stakeholders are given the authority to speak about education; finding it was predominantly ministers of education rather than teachers (p. 41). Similarly, Gill (1994) analysed media roles in curriculum change, suggesting there is an absence of professional voices in the debates, with these voices often being conveyed as the 'drama of dissonant and often acrimonious voices' (p. 111). Other often excluded voices are those of children and young people (also see Chapter 2). For example, Chesky and Goldstein (2016) analysed the presence of girls' voices in news reports about STEM education reform in the US, while Mills (2004) found the press constructed boys as 'the new disadvantaged' (p. 344). It is not surprising, then, that Robert (2012) found that traditional print media pushed particular gendered education agendas (also see Chapter 5). Exclusion can also occur when the perspectives of various cultural and racial minority groups are not identified or when the stereotypical constructions become the normalised (Hall & Smith, 2012; Hussain & Stern, 2015) (also see Chapters 4 and 9).

Drawing on the notion of excluded voices, some publications focused on activism as a means of demonstrating how groups of people and organisations rally together to find a forum to express their concerns and affect change. This is particularly evident in the social media publications. For example, Cabalin (2014) wrote about the 2011 Chilean student movement, identifying these as, 'The most important social protests in Chile's recent history, where young people played a leading role in the discussion over education' (p. 25). Similarly, Avigur-Eshel and Berkovich (2017) analysed middle-class parent activism as a means of addressing political inequality and enabling participation in policy debates.

Teachers' work

The aspects of teachers' work addressed in the publications in this thematic group include: constructions of teachers and teachers' social media usage.

First, publications that addressed constructions of teachers and their work are predominantly covered through traditional print media articles. These covered a range of topics. For example, Hansen (2009) investigated UK regional newspapers' reporting of teachers suggesting portrayals move from a 'negative view of teachers as troublesome to a more positive emphasis on teachers as a hardworking profession besieged by mounting pressures' (p. 335). In the US, Cohen (2010) found that teachers are portrayed in terms of discourses of accountability and caring, while Ulmer (2016) found the press reinforced that teacher quality is in crisis. In Australia, Keogh and Garrick (2011) found media discourses contributed towards negative public opinion about teacher quality. In Sweden, Edling (2015) indicated that the press generally spoke about teachers in over-simplified stereotypes such as the 'good' or 'bad' teacher, ignoring the relational and job complexity of teachers' work. Zemke (2007) found a similar situation in the UK where the press exaggerated the positive and negative aspects of teachers' work. Punakallio and Dervin (2015) identified counternarratives to international perceptions of Finnish teachers being 'the best' suggesting these discourses were 'overly positive, uncritical and somewhat naïve' (p. 318). Constructions of teachers also extended to unionism and industrial action. For example, Greenberg (2004) investigated the 1997 Ontario teachers' strike; Goldstein (2011) analysed media perceptions of teachers' unions finding media reporting about these to be immensely negative.

The second aspect of teachers' work is evident predominantly through studies drawing on or about social media, and investigating teachers' use of social media (also see Chapter 10). For example, research by Carpenter and Krutka (2014, 2015); Goodyear, Casey, and Kirk (2014); Holmes, Preston, Shaw, and Buchanan (2013); Moreillon (2015); Visser, Evering, and Barrett (2014) found that teachers used microblogging environments, such as Twitter, as professional development, enabling them to 'access novel ideas and stay abreast of education advances and trends, particularly regarding educational technology' (Carpenter & Krutka, 2015, p. 707). Sauers and Richardson (2015) analysed school leaders' use of Twitter, finding that it tends to be used for 'educational purposes and as a way to create communities of practice focused on educational issues' (p. 127). Other than investigating teachers' professional development usage of social media, other studies such as Shiller (2015) analysed the utility of social media, particularly teacher-authored blogs, finding these enabled 'individuals to speak back to neoliberal discourses by providing a space to critique media and to present a counter-narrative to what media has presented' thereby reframing the teacher quality debates (p. 1). However, Veletsianos and Kimmons (2016) suggest that researchers' focus on social media has 'only examined a fragment of scholars' online activities, possibly ignoring other areas of online presence' (p. 1).

Children and young people

This thematic group is one of the smallest and demonstrates an area where further research is required. The most recent of these publications is by Taylor (2018) who conducted a content analysis of Australian newspaper reporting on drug testing in schools, framed through discourses of 'public good'. A Canadian study by Gardam and Giles (2016) compared the framing of the deaths of seven First Nations students in non-First Nations and First Nations news sources. In another study, Kelly (2006) considered mainstream media frames of 'troubled and troubling youth' and the imagery conveyed through discourses of 'inner-city youth as "gang bangers"; teen mothers as "children having children" and "welfare bums"; and girls as fashion obsessed and impressionable' (p. 27).

Future considerations

This archive of literature about education research and media was systematically generated drawing on specific inclusion criteria. Even so, it is a vast and complex corpus, drawing on both traditional print and social media across the globe. I have chosen to review these publications drawing on the standard research frames of the theoretical, methodological and empirical aspects of research in an effort to identify the progress in the field. While it is difficult to write a conclusion that summarises this corpus of literature, I have elected to provide some insights and propose future directions for research in the field of education research and media, drawing on three aspects: critique, representation and voice.

First, as an emerging field of research, it is understandable that there is a focus on exploring and understanding the media logics of practice and the mediatisation of education, and as such, much of the literature has focused on *critique*. Unfortunately, such critique can take on a problematic approach that focuses on evaluative judgments intent on 'fault finding' (Williams, 1976, p. 75) or essentialist perspectives that incorporate notions of the 'good' and the 'bad'. Foucault (1997) suggests, 'there is something in critique which is akin to virtue' (p. 43) and as such, there is scope within such understandings to take up a more radical approach that takes a critical stance towards pre-established norms (Butler, 2001). Therefore, research critique of media reporting and practices provides valuable insights into journalistic practices for both educators and those in areas of media communication. However, it is timely for scholars to consider moving beyond simply a critique of media reporting of education and consider the more generative and productive aspects of research in this area. That is, moving from deconstruction to construction. Therefore, rather than an analysis of 'the problem', future research could expand to consider solutions and interventions; counter-narratives and approaches; and resistance and activism; thereby providing pathways for improvement and change.

Second, established scholarship in the field of education research and media tends to draw on the problematic notion of *representation*. From a research perspective, researchers are inevitably part of the research process and therefore even the most critical and reflexive researcher makes sense of data in particular ways (Hayes & Comber, 2017) and these interpretations become part of the phenomena being studied. At times, this may privilege certain understandings and perspectives over others (Barad, 2007). Instead of understanding media practices through representations of education, other approaches include 'discourses' (Foucault, 1972) or 'performances' (Barad, 2007). Barad (2007) suggests that performative approaches 'call into question the basic premises of representationalism and focus inquiry on the practices or performances of representing, as well as on the productive effects of those practices and the conditions for their efficacy' (Barad, 2007, p. 28). While I suspect that many of the articles in this archive do focus on discourses and performative approaches, the use of terms such as 'representation', without providing a detailed explanation of the theoretical and/or methodological perspectives, means there is scope for misunderstanding and conjecture.

Finally, there is scope for scholarship in education research and media to more actively focus on the excluded *voices* and practices that can promote inclusion. Couldry (2010) suggests that 'voice is undermined by rationalities which take no account of voice and by practices that exclude voice or undermine forms for its expression' (p. 15). Representational thinking often overlooks those excluded in traditional and social media, making this aspect, by far, the most difficult to implement. Additionally, both education and media research are unlikely to be able to sway institutional and organisation-specific practices in journalism, given this is a profit-driven industry. However, a momentum in research that provides recommendations and solutions to policy makers is more likely to gain outcomes, particularly when these practices of inclusion are modelled by governments, education jurisdictions and schools.

In this chapter, I have provided an historical, statistical and thematic account of the archive of publications in this emerging field of education research and media. As scholarship moves forward, there must be a move beyond critique and representation to more generative approaches that incorporate inclusive solutions, resistances and voices. Therefore, I end this chapter by again drawing on a quote by Pat Thomson as it appeared in the first special issue on the topic as it is a fitting close to this chapter. Thomson (2004, p. 252) states: 'Bringing a corpus together begins to mark out a territory, a specific topology of research … It is a landscape waiting further exploration'. As evidenced by this review of the literature, scholarship in the field of education research and media has certainly marked out a territory.

References

Adhikary, R. W., Lingard, B., & Hardy, I. (2018). A critical examination of Teach for Bangladesh's Facebook page: 'Social-mediatisation' of global education reforms in the 'post-truth' era. *Journal of Education Policy*, 33(5), 632–661.

Alhamdan, B., Al-Saadi, K., Baroutsis, A., du Plessis, A., Hamid, O. M., & Honan, E. (2014). Media representation of teachers across cultures in a globalised world. *Comparative Education*, 50(4), 490–505.

Anderson, G. L. (2007). Media's impact on educational policies and practices: Political spectacle and social control. *Peabody Journal of Education*, 82(1), 103–120.

Avigur-Eshel, A., & Berkovich, I. (2017). Who 'likes' public education: Social media activism, middle-class parents, and education policy in Israel. *British Journal of Sociology of Education*, 0(0). doi:10.1080/01425692.2017.1418294

Baker, M. (1994). Media coverage of education. *British Journal of Educational Studies*, 42(3), 286–297.

Barad, K. (2007). *Meeting the universe halfway: Quantum physics and the entanglement of matter and meaning*. Durham: Duke University Press.

Baroutsis, A. (2016). Media accounts of school performance: Reinforcing dominant practices of accountability. *Journal of Education Policy*, 31(5), 567–582.

Baroutsis, A. (2017). Understanding media mentalities and logics: Institutional and journalistic practices, and the reporting of teachers' work. *Discourse: Studies in the Cultural Politics of Education*, 0(0), 1–15. doi:10.1080/01596306.2017.1399861

Baroutsis, A., & Lingard, B. (2017). Counting and comparing school performance: an analysis of media coverage of PISA in Australia, 2000–2014. *Journal of Education Policy*, 32(4), 432–449.

Berliner, D. C., & Biddle, B. J. (1999). The awful alliance of the media and public-school critics. *The Education Digest*, 64(5), 4–10.

Blackmore, J., & Thomson, P. (2004). Just 'good and bad news'? Disciplinary imaginaries of head teachers in Australian and English print media. *Journal of Education Policy*, 19(3), 301–320.

Blackmore, J., & Thorpe, S. (2003). Media/ting change: The print media's role in mediating education policy in a period of radical reform in Victoria, Australia. *Journal of Education Policy*, 18(6), 577–595.

Bourdieu, P. (2011). *On television*. Cambridge, UK: Polity.

Brewer, J. T., & Wallis, M. (2015). #TFA: The intersection of social media and education reform. *Critical Education*, 6(13), 1–17.

Butler, J. (2001). What is critique? An essay on Foucault's virtue. *European Institute for Progressive Cultural Policies*. Retrieved from http://eipcp.net/transversal/0806/butler/en/#_ftnref2

Cabalin, C. (2014). Online and mobilized students: The use of Facebook in the Chilean student protests. *Comunicar*, 43(XXII), 25–33.

Cabalin, C. (2015). Mediatizing higher education policies: Discourses about quality education in the media. *Critical Studies in Education*, 56(2), 224–240.

Carpenter, J. P., & Krutka, D. G. (2014). How and why educators use Twitter: A survey of the field. *Journal of Research on Technology in Education*, 46(4), 414–434.

Carpenter, J. P., & Krutka, D. G. (2015). Engagement through microblogging: Educator professional development via Twitter. *Professional Development in Education*, 41(4), 707–728.

Chesky, N. Z., & Goldstein, R. A. (2016). Whispers that echo: Girls' experiences and voices in news media reports about STEM education reform. *Journal for Critical Education Policy Studies*, 14(2), 130–157.

Cohen, B. (1963). *The press and foreign policy*. Princeton, NJ: Princeton University Press.

Cohen, J. L. (2010). Teachers in the news: A critical analysis of one US newspaper's discourse on education, 2006–2007. *Discourse: Studies in the Cultural Politics of Education*, 31(1), 105–119.

Cohen, S. (2002). *Folk devils and moral panics: The creation of the Mods and Rockers*. London: Routledge.

Couldry, N. (2010). *Why voice matters: Culture and politics after neoliberalism*. Los Angeles: SAGE.

Cunningham, P. (1992). Teachers' professional image and the press 1950–1990. *History of Education*, 21(1), 37–56.

Cunningham, S. (2010). Policy. In S. Cunningham & G. Turner (Eds.), *The media and communications in Australia* (3 ed., pp. 31–48). Crows Nest: Allen & Unwin.

Edling, S. (2015). Between curriculum complexity and stereotypes: Exploring stereotypes of teachers and education in media as a question of structural violence. *Journal of Curriculum Studies*, 47(3), 399–415.

Elstad, E. (2009). Schools which are named, shamed and blamed by the media: school accountability in Norway. *Educational Assessment, Evaluation and Accountability*, 21(2), 173–189.

Elstad, E. (2012). PISA debates and blame management among the Norwegian educational authorities: Press coverage and debate intensity in the newspapers. *Problems of Education in the 21st century*, 48, 10–22.

Entman, R. M. (1993). Framing: Toward clarification of a fractured paradigm. *Journal of Communication*, 43(4), 51–58.

Esser, F., & Stromback, J. (Eds.). (2014). *Mediatization of politics: Understanding the transformation of Western democracies*. Houndmills, UK: Palgrave Macmillan.

Fairclough, N. (2010). *Critical Discourse Analysis: The critical study of language*. London: Routledge.
Faltin Osborn, S. R., & Sierk, J. L. (2015). Teach For America in the media: A multimodal semiotic analysis. *Critical Education*, 6(16), 1–18.
Fenech, M., & Wilkins, D. P. (2017). Representations of childcare in the Australian print media: An exploratory corpus-assisted discourse analysis. *Australian Educational Researcher*, 44(2), 161–190.
Fladmoe, A. (2011). Education in the news and in the mind: PISA, news media and public opinion in Norway, Sweden and Finland. *Nordicom Review*, 32(2), 99–116.
Ford, D. R., Porfilio, B., & Goldstein, R. A. (2015). The news media, education and the subversion of the neoliberal social imaginary. *Critical Education*, 6(7), 1–24.
Foucault, M. (1972). *The archaeology of knowledge and the discourse on language* (A. M. Sheridan-Smith, Trans.). New York: Vintage Books.
Foucault, M. (1997). What is critique? In S. Lotringer & L. Hochroth (Eds.), *The politics of truth: Michel Foucault* (pp. 23–82). New York: Semiotext(e).
Franklin, B. (2004). Education, education and indoctrination! Packaging politics and the three 'Rs'. *Journal of Education Policy*, 19(3), 255–270.
Gardam, K., & Giles, A. R. (2016). Media representations of policies concerning education access and their roles in seven First Nations students' deaths in Northern Ontario. *The International Indigenous Policy Journal*, 7(1), np.
Gerstl-Pepin, C. I. (2002). Media (mis)representations of education in the 2000 presidential election. *Educational Policy*, 16(1), 37–55.
Gerstl-Pepin, C. I. (2007). Introduction to the special issue on the media, democracy, and the politics of education. *Peabody Journal of Education*, 82(1), 1–9.
Gewirtz, S., Dickson, M., & Power, S. (2004). Unravelling a 'spun' policy: A case study of the constitutive role of 'spin' in the education policy process. *Journal of Education Policy*, 19 (3), 321–342.
Gill, M. (1994). Who framed english? A case study of the media's role in curriculum change. *Critical Studies in Education*, 35(1), 96–113.
Goffman, E. (1986). *Frame analysis: An essay on the organization of experience*. Boston: Northeastern University Press.
Goldstein, R. A. (2011). Imaging the frame: Media representations of teachers, their unions, NCLB, and education reform. *Educational Policy*, 25(4), 543–576.
Goldstein, R. A., & Chesky, N. Z. (2016). A twenty-first century education: The marketization and mediatization of school reform discourses. In Z. C. Wubbena, D. R. Ford, & B. Porfilio (Eds.), *News media and the neoliberal privatization of education* (pp. 25–44). Charlotte, NC: Information Age Publishing.
Goodyear, V. A., Casey, A., & Kirk, D. (2014). Tweet me, message me, like me: Using social media to facilitate pedagogical change within an emerging community of practice. *Sport, Education and Society*, 19(7), 927–943.
Gorton, R. (1979). What do Principals think of news media coverage? *NASSP Bulletin*, 63 (431), 116–118.
Greenberg, J. (2004). Tories, teachers and the media politics of education reform: News discourse and the 1997 Ontario teachers' strike. *Journalism Studies*, 5(3), 353–371.
Grey, S., & Morris, P. (2018). PISA: multiple 'truths' and mediatised global governance. *Comparative Education*, 54(2), 109–131.
Gur, B. S., Celik, Z., & Ozoglu, M. (2012). Policy options for Turkey: A critique of the interpretation and utilization of PISA results in Turkey. *Journal of Education Policy*, 27(1), 1–21.
Haas, E. (2007). False equivalency: Think tank references on education in the news media. *Peabody Journal of Education*, 82(1), 63–102.

Hall, H. R., & Smith, E. L. (2012). 'This is not reality … it's only TV': African American girls respond to media (mis)representations. *The New Educator*, 8(3), 222–242.

Hansen, A. (2009). Researching 'teachers in the news': The portrayal of teachers in the British national and regional press. *Education 3–13*, 37(4), 335–347.

Hattam, R., Prosser, B., & Brady, K. (2009). Revolution or backlash? The mediatisation of education policy in Australia. *Critical Studies in Education*, 50(2), 159–172.

Hayes, D., & Comber, B. (2017). Researching pedagogy in high poverty contexts: Implications of non-representational ontology. *International Journal of Research & Method in Education*, 0(0). doi:10.1080/1743727X.2017.1395409

Hepp, A. (2013). *Cultures of mediatization*. Cambridge, UK: Polity.

Hepp, A., Brieter, A., & Hasebrink, U. (Eds.). (2018). *Communicative figurations: Transforming communications in times of deep mediatization*. Gewerbestrasse, Switzerland: Palgrave Macmillan.

Hogan, A. (2015). Boundary spanners, network capital and the rise of edu-businesses: The case of News Corporation and its emerging education agenda. *Critical Studies in Education*, 56(3), 301–314.

Holmes, K., Preston, G., Shaw, K., & Buchanan, R. (2013). 'Follow' me: Networked professional learning for teachers. *Australian Journal of Teacher Education*, 38(12), 55–65.

Hussain, K., & Stern, M. (2015). Lessons from the 'Pen alongside the sword': School reform through the lens of radical Black press. *Critical Education*, 6(7), 25–43.

Kelly, D. M. (2006). Frame work: Helping youth counter their misrepresentations in media. *Canadian Journal of Education*, 29(1), 27–48.

Keogh, J., & Garrick, B. (2011). Creating catch 22: Zooming in and zooming out on the discursive constructions of teachers in a news article. *International Journal of Qualitative Studies in Education*, 24(4), 419–434.

Klinger, U., & Svensson, J. (2015). The emergence of network media logic in political communication: A theoretical approach. *New Media & Society*, 17(8), 1241–1257.

Krippendorff, K. (2013). *Content analysis: An introduction to its methodology*. London: SAGE.

Lingard, B., & Rawolle, S. (2004). Mediatizing educational policy: The journalistic field, science policy, and cross-field effects. *Journal of Education Policy*, 19(3), 361–380.

Luehmann, A. L. (2008). Blogs' affordances for identity work: Insights gained from an urban teacher's blog. *The New Educator*, 4(3), 175–198.

MacMillan, K. (2002). Narratives of social disruption: Education news in the British tabloid press. *Discourse: Studies in the Cultural Politics of Education*, 23(1), 27–38.

Martens, K., & Niemann, D. (2013). When do numbers count? The differential impact of the PISA rating and ranking on education policy in Germany and the US. *German Politics*, 22(3), 314–332.

Mayer-Schönberger, V., & Cukier, K. N. (2013). *Big data: A revolution that will transform how we live, work, and think*. Boston: Houghton Mifflin Harcourt.

Mazzoleni, G. (2008). Mediatization of society. In W. Donsbach (Ed.), *The international encyclopedia of communication* (pp. 1–5). Malden, MA: Blackwell.

Mazzoleni, G. (2015). Towards an inclusive digital public sphere. In S. Coleman, G. Moss, & K. Parry (Eds.), *Can the media serve democracy* (pp. 174–183). New York: Palgrave Macmillan.

Mazzoleni, G. (2017). Changes in contemporary communication ecosystems ask for a 'new look' at the concept of mediatisation. *Javnost – The Public*, 24(2), 136–145.

Mills, M. (2004). The media, marketing, and single sex schooling. *Journal of Education Policy*, 19(3), 343–360.

Mockler, N. (2013). Reporting the 'education revolution': MySchool.edu.au in the print media. *Discourse: Studies in the Cultural Politics of Education*, 34(1), 1–16.

Moreillon, J. (2015). #schoollibrarians Tweet for professional development: A netnographic case study of #txlchat. *School Libraries Worldwide*, 21(2), 127–137.

Murphy, R. (2013). Media roles in influencing the public understanding of educational assessment issues. *Oxford Review of Education*, 39(1), 139–150.

Pettigrew, M., & MacLure, M. (1997). The press, public knowledge and the grant maintained schools policy. *British Journal of Educational Studies*, 45(4), 392–405.

Phelan, S., & Salter, L. A. (2017). The journalistic habitus, neoliberal(ized) logics, and the politics of public education. *Journalism Studies*, 0(0), 1–19. doi:10.1080/1461670X.2017.1370976

Pons, X. (2011). What do we really learn from PISA? The sociology of its reception in three European countries (2001–2008). *European Journal of Education*, 46(4), 540–548.

Punakallio, E., & Dervin, F. (2015). The best and most respected teachers in the world? Counternarratives about the 'Finnish miracle of education' in the press. *Power & Education*, 7(3), 306–321.

Rawolle, S. (2005). Cross-field effects and temporary social fields: A case study of the mediatization of recent Australian knowledge economy policies. *Journal of Education Policy*, 20(6), 705–724.

Rawolle, S. (2010). Understanding the mediatisation of educational policy as practice. *Critical Studies in Education*, 51(1), 21–39.

Rawolle, S., & Lingard, B. (2010). The mediatization of the knowledge based economy: An Australian field based account. *Communications: The European Journal of Communication Research*, 35(3), 269–286.

Rawolle, S., & Lingard, B. (2014). Mediatization and education: A sociological account. In K. Lundby (Ed.), *Mediatization of communication* (Vol. 21, pp. 595–614). Berlin: De Gruyter.

Robert, S. A. (2012). (En)gendering responsibility: A critical news analysis of Argentina's education reform, 2001–2002. *Discourse: Studies in the Cultural Politics of Education*, 33(4), 485–498.

Ronnberg, L., Lindgren, J., & Segerholm, C. (2013). In the public eye: Swedish school inspection and local newspapers: exploring the audit–media relationship. *Journal of Education Policy*, 28(2), 178–197.

Sauers, N. J., & Richardson, J. W. (2015). Leading by following: An analysis of how K-12 school leaders use Twitter. *NASSP Bulletin*, 99(2), 127–146.

Shiller, J. (2015). Speaking back to the neoliberal discourse on teaching: How U.S. teachers use social media to redefine teaching. *Critical Education*, 6(9), 1–17.

Shuffelton, A. (2015). Re-privatizing the family: How 'opt-out' and 'parental involvement' media narratives support school privatization. *Critical Education*, 6(12), 1–15.

Snyder, I. (2008). *Literacy Wars: Why teaching children to read and write is a battleground in Australia*. Crows Nest, AU: Allen & Unwin.

Snyder, I. (2009). The stories that divide us: Media (mis)representations of literacy education. *English in Australia*, 44(1), 13–23.

Stack, M. (2006). Testing, testing, read all about it: Canadian press coverage of the PISA results. *Canadian Journal of Education*, 29(1), 49–69.

Stack, M. (2007). Representing school success and failure: Media coverage of international tests. *Policy Futures in Education*, 5(1), 100–110.

Stack, M. (2016). *Global university rankings and the mediatization of higher education*. Houndmills, UK: Palgrave Macmillan.

Steiner-Khamsi, G., Appleton, M., & Vellani, S. (2018). Understanding business interests in international large-scale student assessments: A media analysis of The Economist, Financial Times, and Wall Street Journal. *Oxford Review of Education*, 44(2), 190–203.

Stephens, M. (2007). *A history of news* (3 ed.). New York: Oxford University Press.

Supovitz, J. (2017). Social media is the new player in the politics of education. *Kappan*, 99(3), 50–55.

Takayama, K. (2008). The politics of international league tables: PISA in Japan's achievement crisis debate. *Comparative Education*, 44(4), 387–407.

Takayama, K. (2010). Politics of externalization in reflexive times: Reinventing Japanese education reform discourses through 'Finnish PISA success'. *Comparative Education Review*, 54(1), 51–75.

Takayama, K. (2013). Untangling the global-distant-local knot: The politics of national academic achievement testing in Japan. *Journal of Education Policy*, 28(5), 657–675.

Takayama, K., Waldow, F., & Sung, Y.-K. (2013). Finland has it all? Examining the media accentuation of 'Finnish Education' in Australia, Germany and South Korea. *Research in Comparative and International Education*, 8(3), 307–325.

Taylor, E. (2018). Student drug testing and the surveillance school economy: An analysis of media representation and policy transfer in Australian schools. *Journal of Education Policy*, 33(3), 383–397.

Thapliyal, N. (2018). #Eduresistance: A critical analysis of the role of digital media in collective struggles for public education in the USA. *Globalisation, Societies and Education*, 16(1), 49–65.

Thomas, S. (1999). Who speaks for education? One newspaper's reporting of a review of the Queensland school curriculum. *Discourse: Studies in the Cultural Politics of Education*, 20(1), 41–56.

Thomas, S. (2006). *Education policy in the media: Public discourses on education.* Teneriffe, AU: Post Pressed.

Thomson, P. (2004). Introduction. *Journal of Education Policy*, 19(3), 251–253.

Thomson, P., Blackmore, J., Sachs, J., & Tregenza, K. (2003). High stakes principalship-sleepless nights, heart attacks and sudden death accountabilities: Reading media representations of the United States principal shortage. *Australian Journal of Education*, 47(2), 118–132.

Ulmer, J. B. (2016). Re-framing teacher evaluation discourse in the media: An analysis and narrative-based proposal. *Discourse: Studies in the Cultural Politics of Education*, 37(1), 43–55.

van Dijck, J. (2013). *The culture of connectivity: A critical history of social media.* New York, NY: Oxford University Press.

Veletsianos, G., & Kimmons, R. (2016). Scholars in an increasingly open and digital world: How do education professors and students use Twitter? *Internet and Higher Education*, 30 (July), 1–10.

Visser, R. D., Evering, L. C., & Barrett, D. E. (2014). #TwitterforTeachers: The implications of Twitter as a self-directed professional development tool for K–12 teachers. *Journal of Research on Technology in Education*, 46(4), 396–413.

Waldow, F., Takayama, K., & Sung, Y.-K. (2014). Rethinking the pattern of external policy referencing: Media discourses over the 'Asian Tigers'' PISA success in Australia, Germany and South Korea. *Comparative Education*, 50(3), 302–321.

Wallace, M. (1993). Discourse of derision: The role of the mass media within the education policy process. *Journal of Education Policy*, 8(4), 321–337.

Warmington, P., & Murphy, R. (2004). Could do better? Media depictions of UK educational assessment results. *Journal of Education Policy*, 19(3), 285–299.

Williams, R. (1976). *Keywords.* New York: Oxford University Press.

Wubbena, Z. C., Ford, D. R., & Porfilio, B. J. (Eds.). (2016). *News media & the neoliberal privatization of education.* Charlotte, NC: Information Age Publishing.

Yasukawa, K., Hamilton, M., & Evans, J. (2017). A comparative analysis of national media responses to the OECD Survey of Adult Skills: policy making from the global to the local? *Compare: A Journal of Comparative and International Education*, 47(2), 271–285.

Yemini, M., & Gordon, N. (2017). Media representations of national and international standardized testing in the Israeli education system. *Discourse: Studies in the Cultural Politics of Education*, 38(2), 262–276.

Zemke, E. (2007). Embracing complexity: Findings from a comparative analysis of representations of teachers in the British press and research literature. *Education Research and Perspectives*, 34(1), 27–56.

PART I
Conducting education research with traditional and social media

2

HEADLINES AND HASHTAGS HERALD NEW 'DAMAGING EFFECTS': MEDIA AND AUSTRALIA'S DECLINING PISA PERFORMANCE

Aspa Baroutsis and Bob Lingard

Introduction

This chapter provides a comparative analysis of print and social media coverage of Australia's changing performance on the triennial Organisation for Economic Co-operation and Development's (OECD) Program for International Student Assessment (PISA)[1]. The purpose of our analysis is to offer an empirical base for considerations of how policy might be developed in more democratic and inclusive ways. We comparatively analyse the different ways print and social media discussed and portrayed Australia's 2015 PISA performance in December 2016, when the results of the 2015 test were reported.

PISA results reference two aspects of performance, both of which will be addressed in this chapter. The first is referred to as quality and reports a nation's results in relation to international mean scores and the performance of other nations; and the second called equity, provides a measure of the strength of the correlation in a given nation between students' socio-economic backgrounds and performance. Since the first test in 2000, OECD analysis of performance has indicated that top performing systems, such as Finland and Shanghai, have both high quality and high equity. This is an important finding of PISA which suggests that there is no quality/equity trade-off (Condron, 2011).

In what follows, we first contextualise global media coverage, identifying the different media logics of practice in the United Kingdom (UK), the United States (US), and Australia. This comparison of media logics enables us to grasp the idiosyncratic specificities of the Australian media context when reporting on PISA. We then outline our theoretical and methodological approaches, followed by documentation of our analyses of newspaper (print and digital) and Twitter coverage of Australia's 2015 PISA performance. We also consider the methodological issues we faced when dealing with our social media data and in relation to defensible comparisons between social and legacy media data. The newspaper and Twitter data were collected for a 26-day period in December 2016. The print media analysis focuses on the major Australian dailies in each of the capital cities and two national newspapers. While the newspaper data were collected by the authors, the Twitter data were provided by a commissioned third-party. Another distinction in these data sources was that the newspapers were all Australian based, while the Twitter data were global, with the restriction that only English language tweets were chosen. A comparative analysis of the similarities and differences between these modes of coverage is then provided. We conclude with a summative account of our findings.

Contextualising global media PISA coverage

There is an expanding interest in social media in contemporary politics where more attention is being paid to issues raised via social media (Mellon & Prosser, 2017). For example, if we contemplate a recent UK election we see the significance that social media played in the campaigns of both major parties, with the *The Guardian* (Australian edition: 10 June 2017, np) referring to it as a 'social media election'. This article, amongst others, argues that the surprisingly good performance of the UK Labour party might be attributed to their very effective use of social media[2]. Similarly, we also note the significance of social media to the successful electoral campaigns of former US President Obama and the New Zealand Prime Minister, Jacinda Ardern. More pertinently, perhaps, is the case of US President Trump and his ongoing use of Twitter to bypass traditional legacy media (print and broadcast).

In this use of social media, the President was seeking to communicate directly with his loyal supporters and seeking to avoid interrogation of his ideas by investigative journalists. This is where we might see the 'echo chamber effect' through the alignment of views between the President and his social media followers. President Trump's regular references to 'fake news' and usage of social media are situated in what some have called our 'post-truth' era (Sismondo, 2017). This period has seen attacks by the President on expertise and an emphasis on 'affect' rather than empirical knowledge in framing politics. The latter was evidenced by the ongoing loyalty of the President's followers despite the inadequacies of his presidency.

Alongside this use of social media, computational propaganda is also used in politics (cf The Computational Data Project, http://comprop.oii.ox.ac.uk/). There is evidence to suggest that social media internet bots[3] have also been used to frame the issues in the Common Core debate in the US (cf #CommonCore, www.hashtagcommoncore.com). This heralds an era of 'robot journalism', where social media are being used to saturate the public sphere with a particular point of view, thereby attempting to manipulate public opinion. What this shows is that all is not what it seems with social media communications and it is in this context that we analyse our gathered data.

None of this is to say that print media is no longer relevant to contemporary politics. We also note that some newspapers also have complementary online versions, where access is not restricted through paywalls, while some newspapers such as *The Guardian* Australia are online only publications. In terms of political influence, we would suggest that in the UK context, progressive print media such as *The Guardian* and the *Independent*, and investigative journalists associated with these publications, have played a significant role in critiquing the privatisation and destruction of government schooling. Similarly, some sections of legacy media in the US (e.g. *The New York Times* and CNN) have played an important oppositional role to the Trump presidency and provide a beacon for democracy and freedom of speech. In contrast to the UK and US situations, the Australian context has concentrated ownership of legacy media (Murdoch and Fairfax) and an apparent comparative lack of voices of critique (Baroutsis & Lingard, 2017), particularly as Fairfax-owned media have downsized and reduced the numbers of investigative journalists.

This brief commentary about the differences in media practices in the UK, US, and Australia suggests that the logics of practice (Bourdieu, 2011) of media frames are vastly different in each context, including education reporting. However, in the current context of the global flows of ideas, what Appadurai (1996) refers to as 'mediascapes', we are not denying the movement of media stories across the globe and across media types. We might see these, in Bourdieu's (2011) terms, as 'circular circulation' across media types and in and across nations, particularly evident in the reporting of nations' PISA performance.

Against the backdrop of the global context and our previous print media analysis of Australia's changing PISA performance, in this chapter we focus specifically on PISA 2015 and both traditional and social media coverage of Australia's performance. Our earlier research (Baroutsis & Lingard, 2017) showed that there has been an increase in media coverage of PISA results since 2000, with the mediatisation of the political reception of PISA having real policy effects. This has occurred as test performance comparisons across nations have become more significant in policy making (Sellar & Lingard, 2014). Another central finding of the earlier analysis is that instead of focusing on both quality and equity, print media coverage focused almost entirely on national mean scores in respect of quality and on Australia's declining comparative performance since 2009. For example, overall 68% of the content of the news articles focused on evidence of educational quality, that is, a nation's mean scores on PISA (Baroutsis & Lingard, 2017). Furthermore, as Australia's performance apparently declined, a resultant 'PISA shock' occurred, particularly after Shanghai's exceptional performance on PISA 2009, leading to much greater media coverage. Thus, we found coverage of Australia's performance in PISA spiked following this period with 46% of all newspaper articles from this study being published in the two-year period (2012–2013). We note here that this print media coverage takes for granted the legitimacy of PISA tests and that it is the views of politicians and policy makers that are reported in these stories with the voices of teachers, teacher unions, and students largely excluded.

Theorising networks and mediascapes

We have mentioned the significance of circular circulation to contemporary mediascapes that flow across the globe and are mediated to some extent by the specificities of the media field in a given nation. The OECD, through PISA, has also constituted the globe as a commensurate space of measurement with a related network of policy makers and experts working with the same epistemological assumptions (Lingard, Sellar & Baroutsis, 2015). Mobilities and networks are central concepts in our analysis in this chapter, as they facilitate understanding of legacy and social mediascapes. We draw on the concept of 'mobilities' (Thrift, 1996; Urry, 2007) and networks (Castells, 2010) as our theoretical and methodological approaches. Bauman (2000) refers to various mobilities that function within nations and across the globe today as elements of 'liquid modernity'.

Here, we are interested in movements and flows of ideas or information about a nation's PISA performance. Urry (2007) suggests this concept of mobilities provides a means for interpreting 'how chaotic, unintended and non-linear social consequences can be generated which are distant in time and/or space from where they originate and which are of a quite different and unpredictable scale' (p. 10). As noted earlier, PISA as an international large-scale assessment constructs the globe as a single commensurate space of measurement. In Rose's (1999) words, utilising the thinking of Latour, 'that which is distant' is represented 'in a single plane, visible, cognizable, amenable to deliberation and decision' (p. 211). Furthermore, reporting of PISA results is done in a globally comparative way through a single global league table of national performances. We also see different mobilities across the print and digital media platforms and traditional and social media formats, where the pace and scope of the production of information are different. Here Bauman (2000) suggests that:

> The game of domination in the era of liquid modernity is not played between the "bigger" and the "smaller", but between the quicker and the slower. Those who are able to accelerate beyond the catching power of their opponents [sic] rule.
>
> (p. 188)

Social media platforms such as Twitter are much faster-paced than legacy media, operating in real-time and with an ephemeral character; and are more pervasive than legacy media. There is another difference in relation to speed between traditional and social media in relation to their conditions of production. Quality journalism in legacy media has often taken time to properly investigate an issue as against the sometimes capricious and unconsidered production through social media. We see here a 'media manifold' (Couldry & Hepp, 2016, p. 53) driving social, economic, and political changes, rather than one type of media influencing society. This contemporary context refers to cross-platform media, with influences being played out through both technology and content, representing a contemporary reality which is categorised as 'deep mediatisation' (Hepp & Hasebrink, 2018). This is change itself, as well as providing a platform for comments on change. Deep mediatisation signifies that what we have is the provision of a space for the free rein of expression and surveillance of participants at the same time.

When focusing on the movements and flows of information, it is helpful to consider what Castells (2010) refers to as a 'network society', the 'new social morphology of our societies' (p. 500). The suggestion is that 'networks' have a central role in societies of the Information Age (Castells, 2010). Put very simply, 'a network is a set of interconnected nodes' with the typology of these nodes varying in distance, frequency, length, structure, and networks they belong to and are excluded from (Castells, 2010, p. 501). Networks could include news teams, newspaper owners, private groups and public organisations, and government departments, operating both locally and globally. One manifestation is the emergence of what has been called 'network governance', which sees the inclusion of private sector actors inside the state in horizontal and vertical relationships, with these relationships also stretched globally (Rhodes, 1997; Ball & Junemann, 2012). To some extent, the latter sees the eliding of national borders or at least such national borders are made more porous. Additionally, 'networking logic substantially modifies the operation and outcomes in processes of production, experience, power, and culture' (Castells, 2010, p. 500). As such, we need to be careful not to accept a flat network ontology, which elides consideration of power differentials (Hepp & Hasebrink, 2018); rather, we need to connect content, 'data traces' (Breiter & Hepp, 2018), and meta data to different actors and power relations.

Intertextuality is another useful concept that 'foregrounds notions of relationality, interconnectedness and interdependence in modern cultural life' (Allen, 2000, p. 5). Foucault (1972) refers to the intertwining (intertextuality) of a network through analogy, stating:

> The frontiers of a book are never clear-cut: beyond the title, the first lines, and the last full stop, beyond its internal configuration and its autonomous form, it is caught up in a system of references to other books, other texts, other sentences: it is a node within a network.
>
> (p. 23)

This statement provides us with an example of the intertextuality within and between networks. Here, drawing on Barthes (1986), starting with a print or digital 'text' as the central unit, we can weave a web of interrelated 'threads', demonstrating the relation of text to other texts, or data traces to other traces. In this sense, the interweaving is not only about the 'sources' or 'origins' of textual material, but also the 'intertext of another text' that has previously been written and those 'already read' (Barthes, 1986, p. 60). In the digital age of deep mediatisation, we can develop Barthes' concept so as to speak of 'interdata', that is, data threads of other data traces and the already read.

Networks can also be used to theorise movements and flows, particularly as mediascapes. Appadurai's (1996) framework of various 'scapes' is helpful for exploring disjunctive global cultural flows and is closely related to the global imaginary created by contemporary media and politics. Mediascapes refer to the 'distribution of the electronic capabilities to produce and disseminate information' and to the flows of media thus enabled (Appadurai, 1996, p. 35). Appadurai (1996) indicates that what is offered through a theorising of mediascapes are 'image-centred, narrative-based accounts of strips of reality' (p. 35), which are often governed by both private and public interests. Mediascapes offer accounts of local understandings that constitute the global Other. These accounts or narratives may in time constitute a desired or preferred personal or national situation (Appadurai, 1996). However, experiences of media are complex and interrelated, as with the examples we present in this chapter, where we see interconnections between the print media and social media that can, at times, blur 'realities' and 'fictions'. With today's deep mediatisation, we argue that there is another new and significant mediascape: namely, a 'datascape'[4], referring to the flows of statistics and numbers globally across national borders. The drawing together of mediascapes and datascapes results in what we see and refer to as a 'deep mediascape'. This deep mediascape is enabling and constraining, providing a medium for the expression of opinions and ideas of all, but also simultaneously functioning as an almost global panopticon of surveillance (Lingard, 2015).

Documenting newspaper and Twitter coverage of Australia's 2015 PISA performance

Previous studies have shown that the month of December is the most active time for analysis of PISA coverage, as this period generates most news articles and discussion about PISA performance (Baroutsis & Lingard, 2017). We draw on two data sets for the period 6–31 December 2016, which aligned with the release of PISA 2015 results on 6 December: the first is newspaper text (print and digital) and the second is Twitter text (digital). The newspaper data were gathered through the Factiva database using the Boolean search terms 'pisa' AND 'school' from ten newspapers in both digital and print formats[5]. The Twitter data were data mined by a professional company as part of a larger project[6], using the search term 'pisa' and the December data were provided to us in a spreadsheet. Both the newspaper and Twitter data were 'cleaned' to remove irrelevant references, for example, travel to Pisa, Italy. Additionally, with the Twitter data, only posts written in English were retained. These searches yielded 35 newspaper articles, approximately 30% of the total number of articles about Australia's PISA performance that were published in 2016, and 36,672 tweets. Comparatively, the newspaper data consisted of 29,585 words (186,811 characters), while the Twitter data amounted to a significantly larger volume of text consisting of 617,773 words (4,411,878 characters).

There are some methodological issues traversed here, so as to problematise our analysis and make transparent the difficulties we faced. These are in relation to Twitter data and comparisons with legacy data. There are also some specific features of the Twitter data that raise analytical and methodological issues. For example, there is a huge amount of such data raising questions about selectivity for analysis. Our data show that from 19 November–31 December 2016, there were 200,022 tweets returned through the search term 'pisa'. There is an immediacy about Twitter data; it being instantaneous in one respect and short-lived in another. There are also issues with authorship with Twitter data, in that, without deep investigation it is not known if bots have been used to produce the posts. There is also an implicit epistemological equivalence between tweets, that is, there is no curation of the veracity or otherwise, of the views expressed. Indeed, at any time curation might also be considered censorship. In comparing the legacy media data and the Twitter data, we need to acknowledge that we are using data located in different places and spaces. The legacy media data were largely situated in Australia and dealt mainly with national issues regarding Australia's PISA performance. In contrast, the Twitter data were situated in a global space with only some of these data focused explicitly on PISA in Australia. As such, there are inherent difficulties with the comparative analysis in this chapter and for any future research that uses social media as empirical data.

A separate content analysis was undertaken on each data set using Leximancer software, a text analytics tool that analyses the context of textual documents and extracts visual representations such as conceptual heat maps and quadrant graphs. These analyses were used to facilitate comparisons and to identify key concepts within the texts. In order to be able to provide a cross-case comparison, 16 specific category words related to the PISA testing were used that were common to both data sets (see Table 2.1). Based on these concept rankings, we selected four categories for investigation that were ranked highly across both data sets: 'result', 'performance', 'test', and 'achievement' (see Table 2.1 *). The concepts 'rank' and 'findings' were classified higher in Twitter texts, but not in newspaper articles (see Table 2.1 +) and while 'equity' and 'quality' ranked low across both data sets (see Table 2.1 ^ and #), 'equity' ranked higher in Twitter text, while 'quality' ranked higher in newspaper texts.

In addition to the categories, relevant concepts were identified using the Leximancer software. The newspaper texts yielded 40 concepts, while the Twitter texts identified 56 concepts. The concepts were included in the analysis parameters if they were deemed to be an evaluative term that denoted a positive, negative, or neutral description of Australia's performance on PISA. These varied across the two data sets and Table 2.2 identifies the top-ranking concepts based on frequency counts. The cut-off point was decided where a 'natural' break occurred in the numeric values. The two common top-ranking concepts across both data sets were 'behind' and 'drop' (see Table 2.2 =). We note also that while the concept 'decline' was ranked highest in the newspaper texts (see Table 2.2 @), it appeared three points lower than the last ranked concept in the Twitter texts with a count of 1,935, therefore it is not displayed in Table 2.2.

Finally, for each data set, the related concepts were clustered into broader themes and displayed on a conceptual heat map of the social network that identified Australia's PISA performance. Figure 2.1 identifies the clustered themes and

TABLE 2.1 Common categories across newspaper texts and tweets

Ranked newspapers categories (word counts)	Ranked Twitter categories (word counts)
result (120) ★	test (12,864) ★
performance (100) ★	result (12,863) ★
test (41) ★	rank (12,844) +
achievement (18) ★	findings (12,260) +
data (18)	performance (11,917) ★
comparison (17)	achievement (11,665) ★
measure (12)	measure (1,120)
quality (12) #	standards (1,045)
rank (10) +	data (911)
standards (7)	equity (863) ^
change (6)	reasons (685)
evidence (6)	comparison (537)
outcomes (5)	evidence (422)
reasons (4)	change (318)
equity (3) ^	quality (280) #
findings (3) +	outcomes (236)

TABLE 2.2 Ranked concepts across newspaper texts and tweets

Ranked newspapers concepts (word counts)	Ranked Twitter concepts (word counts)
decline (33) @	indictment (12,980)
improve (24)	regret (12,977)
behind (22) =	lags (12,890)
falling (20)	bottom (12,866)
drop (18) =	insufficient (12,865)
backwards (16)	damaging (12,865)
problem (15)	latest (12,864)
highest (15)	strong (12,862)
lift (15)	damning (12,860)
	top (12,830)
	drop (12,720) =
	lagging (12,400)
	informed (11,725)
	behind (11,649) =
	exaggerating (11,530)
	hammering (11,530)
	ruin (11,418)

Headlines and hashtags   35

hot concepts based on the newspaper texts, while Figure 2.2 does this for the Twitter texts. The heat maps display related or connected concepts in close proximity on the map. The maps were adjusted to include 100% of the concepts and a 70% theme size, which means that there were fewer, broader themes, enabling us to gain a better understanding of the main content associated with Australia's PISA performance. The themes are algorithmically determined by the Leximancer software. That is, the 'hottest' or most relevant concepts are clustered into themes that appear as the largest circles in Figures 2.1 and 2.2.

The thematic group identified as 'damage' on the heat maps (see Figures 2.1 and 2.2) classifies the prevalent evaluative terms that were used across traditional and social media platforms. Here, as with Table 2.2, we note the most prevalent concepts were the negative evaluative terms in both newspaper and Twitter texts (see

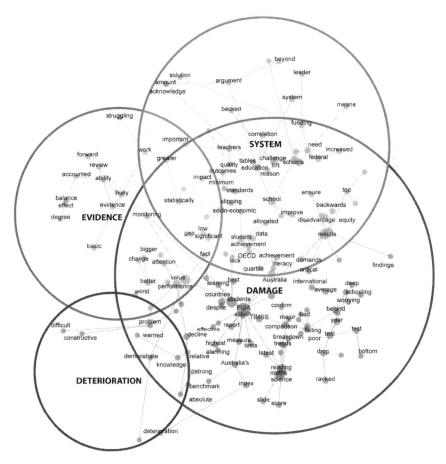

FIGURE 2.1 Heat map of clustered concepts based on newspaper texts[7]

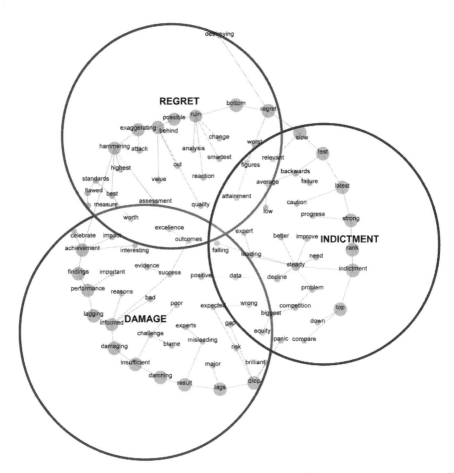

FIGURE 2.2 Heat map of clustered concepts based on tweets[8]

Figures 2.1 and 2.2). Our analysis is not the first instance where the practices and structures of schooling have been characterised as damaging (Francis & Mills, 2012) or even violent and capable of harming children and society (Harber, 2004).

In the comparative analysis in the next section, as well as our concluding comments in the final section, we outline these traditional and social media understandings of the damaging effects of PISA testing. In particular, our findings suggest that newspaper texts reinforce test legitimacy through a focus on the damaging effects of declining results on a nation's future economic prospects. In these accounts, the legitimacy of the tests and of cross-national comparisons are taken for granted. While this is also evident in Twitter texts, social media tends to demonstrate more opinions from multiple voices and perspectives. There is a tendency for social media, in our case Twitter, to provide a space to question test legitimacy and comparison through a greater focus on the damaging effects of testing on the future, focusing on socio-economic consequences.

Comparative analysis of media

We next provide a comparative analysis of the similarities and differences between these modes of media coverage.

Traditional media reinforce test legitimacy

There is a propensity within the logics of legacy media practice to push particular agendas when framing news coverage (Baroutsis, 2017). One such push across both the Australian national and metropolitan newspapers is to reinforce PISA test legitimacy and to focus on PISA test results using agendas related to the nation's economic outcomes and future prosperity. This approach is seen elsewhere, where traditional media outlets tend toward policy reinforcement rather than policy contestation (Baroutsis, 2016). Here, we provide examples of this reinforcement in the news coverage through news articles by journalists, editorials, and opinion pieces across a number of newspapers.

The framing of news coverage about Australia's PISA performance in mainstream media reporting by journalists reinforces test legitimacy by linking test performance with economic outcomes. Many of the news articles, for example Wade (2016) and other articles in our data set and elsewhere (Baroutsis & Lingard, 2017), commence with a comparative analysis of the PISA mean scores over time that serves to highlight Australia's declining PISA performance. Often, this is followed with the article highlighting the economic costs associated with the decline. For example, this news article in *The Age* titled, 'Falling school standards are costing us billions', states:

> The deterioration in the performance of school students has slashed billions from Australia's economic wellbeing. The release of data this week showing Australian teenagers are falling behind many of their international peers has slashed the value of the Fairfax-Lateral Economics wellbeing... The latest PISA result, released on Tuesday, showed Australia's reading score dropped from 512 to 503 between 2012 and 2015. ... That deterioration has sliced $15.2 billion from Australia's wellbeing since 2012.
>
> *(Wade, 2016, p. 10)*

This article reports on a Fairfax analysis that seeks to measure Australia's 'wellbeing' by representing the Gross Domestic Product (GDP), an economic measure, in relation to PISA performance. By linking the PISA results, which are measures of school systems, to GDP, a measure of economic performance, there is a legitimation of the value of the test. The outcome of this is to state that just over $15 billion has been lost due to Australia's poor PISA performance.

PISA test legitimacy is also reinforced through editorials, again through a focus on economic outcomes and score slippage. In particular, the focus expands to provide a commentary about economic mismanagement by government and education systems, suggesting more could be achieved with less funding. For example, this editorial critiques approaches governed by 'heavy spending with sloppy targeting and poor policy', lamenting that despite the significant economic input, Australia has 'slipped steadily' in PISA rankings (*The Australian Financial Review,* 2016, p. 38). This is a prevalent theme, for example, another editorial in the online version of *The Australian* titled, 'Rebuild education from basics' states:

> Money is not the main problem. While commonwealth school funding has increased by 50 per cent from 2003 and will rise from $16 billion to more than $20bn by 2020, 15-year-olds have fallen an entire school year behind their counterparts in maths just 12 years ago.
>
> *(The Australian, 2016a, np)*

The editor suggests that 'a stronger curriculum and better teaching' are the answer (*The Australian,* 2016a, np). This absurd 'funding does not matter' stance ties with the views of conservative politicians.

Finally, hired opinion writers also tend to have a focus on the economic outcomes of Australia's declining PISA performance. For example, this op-ed piece published in *The Advertiser* states:

> In the 2000 PISA reading test, our students scored 528 points; by 2015 the figure fell to 503. Notwithstanding we are a First World country with an advanced economy and record levels of expenditure, our results are going backwards and generations of students are leaving school ill-prepared for the demands and challenges of the 21st century.
>
> *(Donnelly, 2016, p. 22)*

Here, the link with the economic imperatives of a developed country is juxtaposed with declining PISA performance. Additionally, even though there is mention of the next generation of young people being poorly prepared for their future lives, the argument presents young people as homogenous without references being made to equity and socio-economic differences. This is not surprising, as of the 35 newspaper articles on PISA published in December 2016, only two articles, both by the same journalist in *The Courier Mail* (Martyn-Jones, 2016a; Martyn-Jones, 2016b), are supportive of and comment on equity issues in relation to schooling. Additionally, an editorial in *The Australian* titled 'Economic status has little bearing' outright states that 'the claim that SES is the significant determinant of educational outcomes is a furphy[9]' (*The Australian,* 2016b, np). In contrast, Australia's PISA performance since 2000 unequivocally shows a strengthening correlation between students' socio-economic background and performance. Equity has declined along with the decline in quality, but is denied in this newspaper report and remains unreported in most print media coverage. Here, we see that the newspaper framing of PISA performance tended toward an economics-based argument rather than a socio-economic-based one.

Social media questions test legitimacy

A popular perception of the role of social media suggests that it is able to promote political activism and bring about social change. However, we note, as does Miller (2017), that while social media does connect people across spaces, enriching the potential to mobilise political resistance or change, this tends to be 'based on limited forms of expressive solidarity as opposed to an engaged, content-driven, dialogic public sphere' (p. 251); that is, the pejorative of 'clicktivism', governed by a logic of practice often referred to as 'low investment politics' that does not take a lot of time nor much sacrifice on the part of the activist (Miller, 2017, p. 254). Additionally, research has shown that social media users, particularly Twitter users, are not typically representative of the general population (Mellon & Prosser, 2017).

Social media enables individuals to express their perspectives about current issues or debates. This is mostly formulaic; taking the form of statement followed by a supporting link to another text on the internet. This practice is potentially due to the assistive buttons on many websites that encourage readers to share the page on social media. For example, see this post by *The Guardian*:

> @Guardian: The Guardian 2014 'OECD and PISA tests are damaging education worldwide – academics' https://t.co/lC5633omjl

This hyperlink takes the reader of the post to an open letter, with the same headline as the tweet, written to Andreas Schleicher, the director of the OECD's PISA. The letter was written by academics two years earlier. This post was tweeted and retweeted 382 times during the month of December 2016. Additionally, this is an example of a modernised version of the circular circulation of information. In this example, there is cross-fertilisation between traditional and social media and across time; that is, where a newspaper article written in 2014 resurfaces in tweets two years later in 2016.

While acknowledging the current limitations of political activism within social media, that is not to say that such practices are not important, and on one level, there is the future potential for this logic to evolve and become 'an important transformational political force' (Miller, 2017, p. 266). Indeed, we note that while newspaper texts in this study implicitly tend to take for granted the legitimacy of the PISA test and results, Twitter posts are more inclined to question the legitimacy of both the test results and the test regime. If, as we hypothesise, legacy media have greater impact on actual policy making and on policy makers, this then excludes certain perspectives from entering political debate. This in itself represents a significant shift in communicative practice and focus of media debate around PISA. For example, the following tweet shared 94 times in December 2016 also references the open letter to Andreas Schleicher, and also highlights the damaging effects of PISA:

> @ACADEMIC1[10]: 2yrs ago, academics said OECD and Pisa tests are damaging education worldwide https://t.co/Apn3ltagjX It's time to #endpisa

This post is by an academic, @ACADEMIC1, who is opposed to PISA testing, and references the hashtag, 'endpisa'. Similarly, another academic from the US, @ACADEMIC2, links to an article by a journalist in the *Times Educational Supplement* that quotes @ACADEMIC1:

> @ACADEMIC2: Pause on PISA – read results with caution warn @ACADEMIC1 https://t.co/yomQMWSJb8

This post was retweeted 52 times in December 2016. Combined, these two examples demonstrate how social media crosses geographic and national boundaries in questioning the legitimacy of the testing regime on a global scale.

Another aspect of the Twitter data for December 2016 was the greater focus on equity, which also was presented as a reason to question test legitimacy and the potentially damaging effects of PISA. Broadly, these perspectives appeared across both individual posts and those from teacher organisations invested in the consequences of the test outcomes. For example:

> @PERSON1: Equity and quality in education go together. See Japan Finland, Estonia, Canada in 15 year old science results in PISA @OECDeduSkills
> @PERSON2: Equity requires a shift in how we talk about Australia's results. Shocking disparity highlighted again in analysis… https://t.co/J0h6celPxs

The first post references an OECD working paper titled, 'Education policy implementation: A literature review and proposed framework' (Number 162) and was retweeted 16 times. While the second post, linking to a *Guardian* Australia article titled, 'If there's a magic bullet to fix education outcomes, it starts with equity', was not retweeted at all during December 2016.

In other examples from peak bodies or teacher organisations, we again see that sometimes the scope of the reach of the equity message is limited, if not picked up by followers and retweeted. For example,

> @TeachForAU: #TeachForAll reports that the #PISA results highlight the link between socio-economic advantage and performance: https://t.co/DaPFMjGSjE
> @TeachersFed: p.206 of #PISA report defines success in education as high achievement AND high equity – this is why Australia needs #Gonski funding https://t.co/F9y8GrB4W8

Both tweets reference the then newly released PISA reports in December 2016. The first post from Teach for Australia was retweeted twice, while the second from the New South Wales Teachers' Federation, a trade union representing teachers, was retweeted eight times. In other examples, the equity message was rejected outright. For example:

@PERSON3: NEW TODAY: The narrative about PISA and equity is flawed https://t.co/ecv8DT8fNu #aussieED

This post was retweeted 19 times in December 2016 and provided a link to the individual's own blog that outlines their perspective.

We note that Andreas Schleicher, the Director of the Education and Skills Directorate at the OECD, and perhaps the central and most powerful actor in relation to PISA, also uses Twitter. His Twitter posts seek to be educative to the extent that they try to explain what PISA is, what the results mean, and how they might be used for productive policy purposes. For example:

@SchleicherOECD: PISA 2015 results now available: Get the full package https://t.co/3eFQGKCNAB Programme for International Student Assessment

Thus, the OECD, as embodied in Schleicher, uses social media as another mode of communicating the OECD's desired message in respect of PISA. Elsewhere, we have noted the OECD's usage of various national print media to disseminate the OECD's desired message and policy implications of PISA results (Baroutsis & Lingard, 2017).

In contrast to legacy media, there is more scope for multiple voices on social media. For example, the voices of teacher unions and academics are much more prevalent on social media than in the legacy media coverage of PISA. Yet we note that this more inclusive potential does not mean these are representative of the population or that any expressed voices will necessarily be listened to by politicians and policy makers, nor do we suggest that they are always worthy contributions. Legacy media have a much stronger framing of coverage of PISA test results and a closer management of voices, which tend to be aligned with the editorial stance and thus restrict the range of views expressed (Baroutsis, 2017).

Conclusions

Figure 2.3 represents our summative comparative analysis of similarities and differences between the two data sets (print and digital newspapers and Twitter posts) commenting on Australia's 2015 PISA performance reported in 2016. We note though, as with all abstractions, the figure simplifies the reality. However, we need to explain that in the diagrammatic representation, the strength of the arrow (solid or broken) signifies the magnitude of the relationship between the elements.

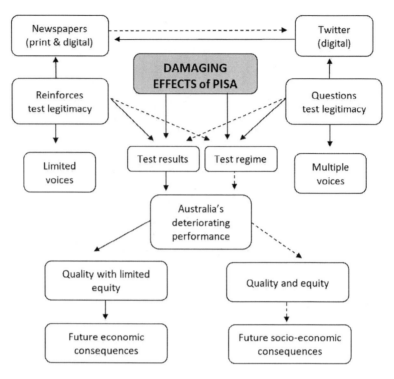

FIGURE 2.3 Comparative findings of newspaper and Twitter commentary on PISA

While Twitter is often seen as enabling multiple voices to express opinions, we note in our analysis that much Twitter commentary actually references newspaper articles. We also note that digital newspaper reporting, in contrast with print newspaper texts, also often references Twitter posts; sometimes, these include the entire screenshot of a tweet. Also, often included is the location referencing (URL) of the digital media text, and more specifically the location of this text within the network, thereby increasing the complexity and density of the data network. These actions leave digital traces, which 'are not just made by the users themselves but also by others when they interact online with reference to them' (Breiter & Hepp, 2018, p. 388).

Our analysis has shown that newspaper reporting on PISA in Australia takes as given the purposes, technical quality, and legitimacy of PISA; rarely are these problematised. In contrast, some of the Twitter commentary actually questions the purposes, quality, and legitimacy of PISA. The Twitter posts also draw attention to the negative impact on school systems, and to the PISA test practice of 'gaming' by some national systems in relation to the test. The focus of newspaper reporting is on test results, while much of the Twitter commentary is broader, focusing on what we might see as the PISA test regime. Here, test regime means much more than simply test results; rather, it includes broader purposes, the nature of the tests, analyses of test data, related policy recommendations, policy implications, and national responses and usages of PISA testing data.

We note that the two data sets are different in content, contexts, and authoring voices. The newspaper data set deals specifically with Australia's PISA performance (test results), while the Twitter data deal more with the PISA testing regime, rather than specific national test results. The newspaper articles are basically national in focus, but there is some referencing to high performing systems (Baroutsis & Lingard, 2017). The Twitter commentary acknowledges the reality of a 'global education policy field' (Lingard & Rawolle, 2011) and is thus more global in coverage. The newspaper articles are written by professional Australian journalists, as well as opinion writers and newspaper editors, who largely reference Australian policy makers and politicians in their stories. In contrast, a wider range of voices are represented on Twitter, including academics, teachers, teacher union representatives, interested public, stakeholder organisations, and activists within them, while the student voice is not included[11]. Thus, we would argue that there are multiple voices on Twitter and limited voices reported in newspapers.

Our analysis of Australian newspapers in December 2016 also demonstrates a focus on Australia's deteriorating comparative performance on PISA. This reporting gives much more emphasis to quality with limited attention paid to equity. It is the case, however, that for Australia, as for other OECD member nations, the correlation between socio-economic background and PISA performance has strengthened since the first PISA was administered in 2000. This growing inequality remains largely unreported in Australian newspaper coverage of PISA. At times, coverage denies the significance of socio-economic background. Twitter posts also give emphasis to quality, but pay more attention to equity matters than print media. The latter includes some commentary on the need for additional and redistributive funding to schools serving the poorest communities. Both sets of accounts see future consequences of declining quality, particularly in relation to future economic prosperity. Twitter posts pay more attention to a broader set of socio-economic consequences of declining quality and growing inequality. Both data sets thus speak of the damaging effects of PISA, but some of the Twitter posts also include in these damaging effects some negative and reductive impacts of the PISA testing regime on the quality of schooling provided. The newspaper accounts, in contrast, simply emphasise the damaging future economic consequences of Australia's declining PISA performance.

Media researchers (Breiter & Hepp, 2018; Hepp & Hasebrink, 2018) have recognised the danger of accepting a flat network ontology when exploring media trends and effects. This means we need to ascertain which voices in which media have most policy and political effects, thus acknowledging power differentials. Here we can only speculate. We have noted the differences in national media fields, but there are also significant differences in national political fields. In Australia, we do not have a national 'tweeter-in-chief' as is the case in the contemporary US, where the President has used social media to massage, mobilise, and manipulate his constituency and to bypass quality print media. The impact of social media including

Twitter is of course not simply either 'good' or 'bad' and remains an empirical question that requires research and further investigation. Indeed, Howard (2015) has argued we are now in an era of 'Pax Technica' to acknowledge the substantial interconnectedness of the world today, which he argues provides some stability in the context of what we see as destabilising events such as Brexit and the election of President Trump. We have seen this global interconnectedness in our analysis of Twitter posts of PISA 2015 results.

Our comparative analysis has provoked a number of important questions. While social media is putatively more democratic and inclusive, for example, in our case, expressing a range of opinions from a range of authors about both quality and equity on PISA, it manifests what we might see as epistemological equivalences, that is, that any and all points of view are treated as equally valid. In contrast, high quality investigative print and digital newspapers, which focus on narrower aspects of PISA, nonetheless putatively provide critical and evidence-informed accounts. Here, we might see social media opinions as non-curated, while traditional investigative media reporting is curated. One could possibly speculate that, at times, the more inclusive character of social media might function as a form of 'repressive tolerance', that is, noise without effect, allowing all in a seemingly democratic way to express their opinions.

The question remains, and this is an empirical question for future research: What comparative impact do traditional and social media have on actual policy making in education, both separately and interactively? There is an additional normative, political question about how both traditional and social media might be mobilised in more democratic ways in policy making and to ensure greater quality and equity in Australian schooling? In our view, research is required to answer these empirical questions and such research needs to be tightly focused in terms of place and space, time and duration, all of which would contextualise the policy impacts of specific media coverage. We hypothesise that in Australia, print media still function as opinion leaders and continue to have influence with policy makers and politicians, with a complex interplay between print and digital newspapers and social media.

Notes

1. The OECD's PISA has been conducted every three years since 2000 and assesses the reading, mathematical, and scientific literacies of a national sample of 15-year-olds. In 2015, approximately 75 nations participated in the test. There are currently 35 OECD member nations.
2. As an example, we are thinking in particular of the YouTube film clips (www.youtube.com/watch?v=zpSVVgZyUBs) produced by the distinguished progressive film producer, Ken Loach, and distributed exclusively through this channel.
3. These are internet robots that run automated processes. This can include posting tweets through individual using user accounts, with the account holder's permission.
4. Data infrastructures are centrally important here and important in the workings of contemporary globalisation (see Easterling, 2014).
5. The newspapers are: *The Australian, The Courier Mail, The Advertiser*, the *Hobart Mercury*, the *Northern Territory News* (News Corp Australia), *The Australian Financial Review, The Sydney Morning Herald, The Age, The Canberra Times* (Fairfax Media), and *The West Australian* (Seven West Media).

6 The Twitter data were mined as part of an Australian Research Council Discovery Project, DP150102098, entitled, *Data in Schools and Systems: An International Study*.
7 Heat map shows theme clusters (from most relevant to least relevant): damage, system, evidence, and deterioration.
8 Heat map shows these clusters (from most relevant to least relevant): damage, indictment, and regret.
9 'Furphy' is Australian slang for an erroneous story that is claimed to be factual.
10 For ethical reasons, a pseudonym is used here and for all other non-public figures.
11 This raises the question of whether students are excluded or are just not present on this social media platform.

References

Allen, G. (2000). *Intertextuality: The new critical idiom*. London: Routledge.
Appadurai, A. (1996). *Modernity at large: Cultural dimensions of globalization* (Vol. 1). Minneapolis: University of Minnesota Press.
Ball, S. J., and Junemann, C. (2012). *Networks, new governance and education*. Bristol, UK: The Policy Press.
Barthes, R. (1986). *The rustle of language*. New York: Hill and Wang.
Baroutsis, A. (2016). Media accounts of school performance: Reinforcing dominant practices of accountability. *Journal of Education Policy*, 31(5), 567–582.
Baroutsis, A. (2017). Understanding media mentalities and logics: Institutional and journalistic practices, and the reporting of teachers' work. *Discourse: Studies in the Cultural Politics of Education*, 0(0), 1–15. doi:10.1080/01596306.2017.1399861
Baroutsis, A., and Lingard, B. (2017). Counting and comparing school performance: An analysis of media coverage of PISA in Australia, 2000–2014. *Journal of Education Policy*, 32(4), 432–449.
Bauman, Z. (2000). *Liquid modernity*. Cambridge, UK: Polity Press.
Bourdieu, P. (2011). *On television*. Cambridge, UK: Polity Press.
Breiter, A., and Hepp, A. (2018). The complexity of datafication: Putting digital traces in context. In A. Hepp, A. Brieter, and U. Hasebrink (Eds.), *Communicative figurations: Transforming communications in times of deep mediatization* (pp. 387–405). Gewerbestrasse, Switzerland: Palgrave Macmillan.
Castells, M. (2010). *The rise of the network society* (2 ed.). Oxford, UK: Wiley-Blackwell.
Condron, D. J. (2011). Egalitarianism and educational excellence: Compatible goals for affluent societies? *Educational Researcher*, 40(2), 47–55.
Couldry, N., and Hepp, A. (2016). *The mediated construction of reality: Society, culture, mediatization*. Cambridge, UK: Polity Press.
Donnelly, K. (2016, December 8). Meritocracy and competition have been replaced by the belief that all are winners and success is elitist. *The Advertiser*, p. 22.
Easterling, K. (2014). *Extra state craft: The power of infrastructure space*. London: Verso.
Foucault, M. (1972). *The archaeology of knowledge and the discourse on language* (A. M. Sheridan-Smith, Trans.). New York: Vintage Books.
Francis, B., and Mills, M. (2012). Schools as damaging organisations: Investigating a dialogue concerning alternative models of schooling. *Pedagogy, Culture & Society*, 20(2), 251–271.
Harber, C. (2004). *Schooling as violence: How schools harm pupils and societies*. London: RoutledgeFalmer.
Hepp, A., and Hasebrink, U. (2018). Researching transforming communications in times of deep mediatization: A figurational approach. In A. Hepp, A. Brieter, and U. Hasebrink

(Eds.), *Communicative figurations: Transforming communications in times of deep mediatization* (pp. 15–48). Gewerbestrasse, Switzerland: Palgrave Macmillan.

Howard, P. N. (2015). *Pax Technica: How the internet of things may set us free or lock us up*. New Haven: Yale University Press.

Lingard, B. (2015). Le panoptisme global: I'nfluence des tests internationaux et des infrastructurtes de donnees en education. *Administration & Education*, 145(1), 127–132.

Lingard, B., and Rawolle, S. (2011). New scalar politics: Implications for education policy. *Comparative Education*, 47(4), 489–582.

Lingard, B., Sellar, S., and Baroutsis, A. (2015). Researching the habitus of global policy actors in education. *Cambridge Journal of Education*, 45(1), 25–42.

Martyn-Jones, L. (2016a, December 11). The class divide is very real. *The Courier Mail*, p. 68.

Martyn-Jones, L. (2016b, December 18). It's a tale of two students. *The Courier Mail*, p. 68.

Mellon, J., and Prosser, C. (2017). Twitter and Facebook are not representative of the general population: Political attitudes and demographics of British social media users. *Research and Politics*, 4(3), 1–9.

Miller, V. (2017). Phatic culture and the status quo: Reconsidering the purpose of social media activism. *Convergence: The International Journal of Research into New Media Technologies*, 23(3), 251–269.

Rhodes, R. A. W. (1997). *Understanding governance: Policy networks, governance, reflexivity, and accountability*. Buckingham: Open University Press.

Rose, N. (1999). *Powers of Freedom: Reframing political thought*. Cambridge, UK: Cambridge University Press.

Sellar, S., and Lingard, B. (2014). The OECD and the expansion of PISA: New global modes of governance in education. *British Educational Research Journal*, 40(6), 917–936.

Sismondo, S. (2017). Post-truth? *Social Studies of Science*, 47(1), 3–6.

Smith, K. (2016, December 6). Corridors. *The Australian*, np.

The Australian Financial Review. (2016, December 9). Good schools start with good teachers. *The Australian Financial Review*, p. 38.

The Australian. (2016a, December 7). Rebuild education from basics. *The Australian*, np.

The Australian. (2016b, December 21). Economic status has little bearing. *The Australian*, np.

Thrift, N. (1996). *Spatial formations*. London: SAGE.

Urry, J. (2007). *Mobilities*. Cambridge, UK: Polity Press.

Wade, M. (2016, December 10). Falling school standards are costing us billions. *The Age*, p. 10.

3

TELEVISING THE REVOLUTION? #REVOLUTIONSCHOOL AND REPRESENTATIONS OF EDUCATION ACROSS TRADITIONAL AND SOCIAL MEDIA

Nicole Mockler

Introduction

In June 2016, *Revolution School*, a four-part documentary series produced by Cornell Jigsaw-Zapruder Productions, aired on the Australian Broadcasting Corporation's (ABC) TV1 channel. Far from being an occasion for the audience to 'plug in, turn on and cop out', as per Gil Scott-Heron's warning in his 1970s song *The Revolution will not be Televised*, the documentary spawned 33 articles in national and capital city daily newspapers and a lively Twitter backchannel[1] which, using the hashtag #revolutionschool, included over 8300 tweets. This chapter explores representations of education across these mainstream and social media sources, mapping the dominant frames in use in the mainstream and social media texts and exploring their similarities and differences. It thus aims to use the particular example of *Revolution School* to explore the relationship between social and mainstream media in the context of education, and to extend the discussion about representations of education in the public space from one that to date has been centred on mainstream media to one that recognises the contribution of social media to these representations. It works from the position that such representations matter, as they both reflect and reinforce public attitudes toward education, which impact in various and significant ways on the work of schools, teachers and students.

The chapter is presented in four parts. The first locates the project within the field, foregrounds the approach taken in the research and provides an overview of *Revolution School*. The second presents the analysis of the print media texts, identifying three dominant framing packages in use across the 33 articles. The third section presents the analysis of the Twitter backchannel, with a particular emphasis on understanding who was tweeting, whose voices dominated and users' attitudes to the representations of education presented in the documentary series. The chapter concludes by exploring the similarities and differences between the two groups of texts in terms of the frames in use, and highlighting further possibilities for research around the discursive construction of education across 'mainstream' and 'new' media spaces.

Background and approach: Understanding media representations of education

Research on media representations of education is a well-established field utilising a range of conceptual and methodological tools to explore the role of these media in shaping public understandings of education and teachers' work (see, for example: Baroutsis, 2016; Blackmore & Thorpe, 2003; Fenech & Wilkins, 2017; Mills & Keddie, 2010). This work shares a focus on mainstream media (mostly print media) texts, and generally takes as a starting point the argument, articulated by Mills & Keddie (2010), that media are a primary source of public knowledge about education, and consequently, that how educational matters are reported in these media *matters*.

Studies exploring education and 'new' or social media are less common, and tend to focus on the use of platforms such as Twitter for professional networking and learning in education (see, for example: Goodyear, Casey, & Kirk, 2014; Holmes, Preston, Shaw, & Buchanan, 2013; Moreillon, 2015). In media and communication studies, a burgeoning field of research explores the varying uses of social media, including the 'ad hoc emergence of issue publics' (Bruns & Burgess, 2011, p. 38) and 'hashtag publics' (Bruns, Moon, Paul, & Münch, 2016), mobilised around particular issues and events. This research tends to work with very large data sets (for example, Bruns & Burgess' 2011 work on the #ausvotes Twitter hashtag drew on over 415,000 tweets from over 36,000 users), and tends to be limited, therefore, to quantitative, software-assisted analysis.

This chapter seeks to 'borrow' from both of these fields. Building on previous work that used framing analysis to explore the discursive construction of education through print media texts (e.g. Mockler, 2014, 2016), it works with Nisbet's notion of social media and 'bottom up' framing:

> New forms of interactive digital media . . . shift the focus away from a transmission model of traditional news framing effects to a more interactive, social constructivist, and "bottom up" model of framing. As lay citizens become active contributors, creators, commentators, sorters, and archivers of digital news content, new possibilities and new demands arise for framing research . . .
>
> *(Nisbet, 2010, p. 75)*

A key concern in this chapter is to explore the resonances and dissonances between the mainstream media 'conversation' and that encapsulated in the Twitter backchannel, asking whether, in this case at least, the 'top down' and 'bottom up' framing share more in common than sets them apart. In considering discussions of education in the public domain, media events such as *Revolution School* provide useful opportunities to explore not only how 'the media' frames and presents educational issues through mainstream channels, but also how these representations resonate with audiences.

Revolution School

Revolution School originally aired over four weeks, starting on 31 May 2016. The documentary follows the 2015 school year at Kambrya College, a public secondary school in the eastern suburbs of Melbourne. In the opening sequence of the first episode, the voice-over sets the scene for what is to come over the next four hours of viewing:

> Australia's education system is falling behind. 15 years ago, our schools were ranked sixth in the world, but now we're struggling to make the top 20. We're letting down our children and the nation. This is the story of one high school's attempt to arrest that decline.

The discourse of crisis is thus invoked in *Revolution School* prior to any significant introduction to the school itself or the documentary's protagonists. These include the school principal, Michael Muscat, 'education guru', according to the Revolution School voice over, John Hattie, from the Melbourne Graduate School of Education (MGSE) at the University of Melbourne, and an array of other staff members and students from the school and external academic consultants. The four-part documentary charts aspects of the school's improvement over the course of 2015, a 'quest to be the best it can be'. Episodes focus variously on classroom management, teacher talk, reading and literacy, wellbeing and the importance of teachers understanding their impact, with the personal stories of a number of students threaded through the school improvement narrative.

Two key messages are strongly conveyed to the audience over the course of the series, held in a constant tension that contributes to the documentary's appeal. First, 21st century schooling is portrayed as highly complex. The challenges of catering to the academic, intellectual, social and emotional needs of a large student body are finely drawn, through extended footage of classroom interaction, one-on-one teacher–student interactions and parent-teacher-student meetings. Teachers are represented as hard working, adaptable and committed to their work and to the best interests of their students. In direct-to-camera interviews, Kambrya teachers frequently reflect on the demands of their work, their successes and challenges, their learning needs and achievements. Extra-curricular activities such as the school musical and an 'outward bound' camp highlight the beyond-the-classroom dimensions of school life. The many tasks associated with school improvement are portrayed as a team effort, although very much the brainchild of a respected and highly effective principal, who takes responsibility for its initiation and carriage.

The second key message relates to simplicity. Clear and 'sure fire' solutions to educational problems are portrayed as available and implementable with the right level of will and hard work within schools. A strong sense of 'what works', incontrovertible proof of how schools can be 'fixed', pervades the documentary. Hattie is said to be 'provocative' and 'shaking up conventional views about education' with his clear-cut views, formed when he 'number crunched data from over 70,000 education studies around the world' about what matters and what does not matter in relation to improving student learning. Hattie's ideas about impact, along with those of Bill Rogers about classroom management; Lea Waters about student wellbeing; Diane Snowball about reading and literacy, are presented as simple solutions available to schools. Much is made in the first episode about pervasive misconceptions regarding 'what matters' in improving student learning. Hattie notes that:

> the majority of debates in the policy arena, in the press, amongst the parents and, critically, amongst the teaching profession, are about things that don't matter much. Class sizes, facilities, private schools, they truly don't make much of a difference to the grades. What really matters is the interaction you have with the teacher.

Many of the strategies employed by the external experts within the series aim to contribute to improving the quality of teacher–student interaction, advanced in a way that appears to regard such interactions as separate from rather than integral to the human dimensions of education and learning.

This tension between complexity and simplicity in the quest for school improvement is central to all four episodes of *Revolution School*, and is also strongly reflected in the associated mainstream media and social media texts examined in this research.

Print media texts

A total of 33 print media texts were collected for examination, generated by a search of the Factiva database for the phrase 'revolution school' over the six-week period from 23 May to 28 June 2016, inclusive. Articles were collected from the 12 national and capital city daily newspapers, with identical articles eliminated. The series was referred to in 13 feature stories, 16 television guide introductions, two opinion pieces and two letters pages. Figure 3.1 highlights the distribution of article types according to media ownership[2].

Furthermore, articles were spread unevenly across the time frame, with 16 of the 33 articles published prior to or on the day of the airing of the first episode, and 15 published between the first and fourth episodes. Only two articles were published after the final episode went to air, as highlighted in Figure 3.2.

NVivo was used to analyse these media texts, with particular reference to the framing devices used to shape the discussion of the documentary. In the first place, basic content analysis (Miles, Huberman, & Saldana, 2013) was conducted, allowing dominant themes to emerge inductively from the texts themselves. Second,

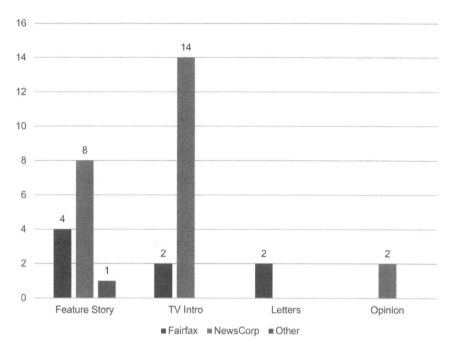

FIGURE 3.1 Articles by type and media ownership

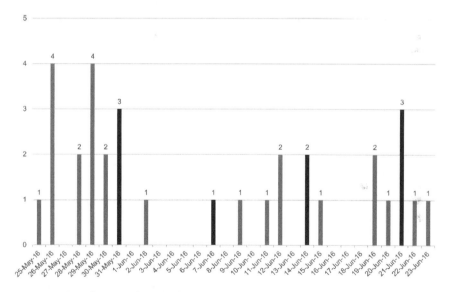

FIGURE 3.2 Distribution of articles by time frame (black columns indicate day of episode airing)

Gamson's approach to framing analysis (Gamson & Lasch, 1983; Gamson & Modigliani, 1989) was employed to identify the frames in use within the texts, and the framing and reasoning devices used to bring these frames to life[3]. Three key framing packages were identified in the print media texts, namely those of *crisis*, *redemption* and *the keys to school improvement*.

Australian education in crisis: 'Now we're struggling to make the top 20'

The print media articles strongly framed the story of Kambrya College with the notion that Australian education is in crisis, with 24 of the 33 articles subscribing in some way to this frame. Three of the 16 'TV intro' articles included in television viewing guides, for example, included the words:

> "15 YEARS ago our schools were ranked sixth in the world. Now we're struggling to make the Top 20. This is the story of one high school's attempt to arrest that decline." So begins this fascinating series, which charts Kambyra College's quest to lift itself from the bottom 10 per cent by using new teaching strategies over one school year.
>
> *(Free-to-air highlights, 2016; Rigden, 2016a, 2016b)*

A further three articles used Australia's declining performance on the Programme for International Student Assessment (PISA) as background to the *Revolution School* story (Cook, 2016; Powley, 2016; Toohey, 2016), again portraying Kambrya as a contrast to the masses contributing to this decline.

On a more local level, crisis is used as a device to frame Kambrya's 'revolution'. Fourteen of the 33 articles referred to the school's former placement in the bottom ten percent of Victorian schools in 2008[4], prior to the arrival of Principal Michael Muscat and the subsequent improvement effort. In one article, 2008 is referred to as 'a kind of ground zero for Kambrya' (Quinn, 2016). In another, the Principal was reported as saying 'It was the wild west. There was blood, there were queues every day outside the first aid office' (Doherty, 2016c).

On both a national and a local level, then, crisis is seized as an important frame for discussion of *Revolution School*. Whether 'bucking the trend' of performance on international tests or 'arresting' its own decline, the school is positioned in these media texts as an underdog succeeding against the odds, drawn with framing devices such as depictions of the school in strife seeking to arrest a national decline and reasoning devices such as statements to the effect that 'something needed to be done' used to contribute to this package.

Redemption: 'A heroic story'

The print media articles strongly frame *Revolution School* as a multifaceted tale of redemption and reversal, with 30 of the 33 articles resonating with this frame.

Kambrya's redemption is linked to the leadership efforts of Principal Michael Muscat, who 'decided to turn things around' (Dunk, 2016) and consequently 'would surely be an early favourite for Australian of the Year' (Cater, 2016). Muscat's role as saviour of the school is closely linked to that of Hattie, as 'with the school grappling with disorder and lack of direction, principal Michael Muscat turned to educational statistician John Hattie' (Back to classroom basics, 2016), finding there 'support for his approach and guidance' (Blundell, 2016).

The redemption frame also champions the teachers within the school, with the Executive Producer of the series noting in one article that 'it really is a heroic story and I would defy anyone to walk away and not have great admiration for the teachers of Kambrya, for what they have achieved' (Back to classroom basics, 2016). Another expands on this notion:

> Confronted with unruly, disrespectful and wilfully disruptive students with scant obvious interest in learning, the temptation to lash out with the occasional backhander must be immense. That they generally resist that urge is testament not only to the fact the law takes a dim view of corporal punishment as a pedagogical tool these days but also to the extraordinary moral fibre the best educators must possess.
> In Revolution School, the scope of that challenge is laid out plainly.
>
> *(Quinn, 2016)*

Finally, in framing Kambrya's story in terms of redemption, the 'bravery' of the school in allowing the 'warts and all' (Doherty, 2016b; Easy on the homework – it's just not worth it, 2016) documentary to be filmed is frequently invoked. Students and teachers are said to be 'brave enough to lay everything bare' (Rigden, 2016a), including 'not the kinds of problems schools usually own up to' (Doherty, 2016c). The redemption frame thus employs framing devices around bravery and heroics, and reasoning devices designed to draw the reader in to the compelling tale of 'revers[al of] fortunes' (Molloy, 2016) presented in *Revolution School*.

Facts and fallacies: The keys to school improvement

The final framing package identified relates to the certainty with which various strategies are said to be integral to or unrelated to school improvement, with 28 of the 33 articles reflecting this frame. 'Common sense' strategies such as setting homework (Doherty, 2016b, 2016c; Easy on the homework – it's just not worth it, 2016) and reducing class sizes (Blundell, 2016; Cater, 2016; Doherty, 2016a) are debunked as ineffective in favour of decisions being 'guided by solid information rather than preconceptions and prejudice' (Blundell, 2016).

> AUSTRALIANS need to dump false beliefs that flash private schools and small class sizes are keys to student success, a leading academic says . . . if Australia is

to arrest its academic decline on the global stage, it needs to stop debating issues of "distraction".

(Doherty, 2016a)

The effect of this is to suggest that there are known solutions that are, for reasons unknown, not generally employed by schools, while Kambrya provides the contrast. Effective teaching is not 'unpacked' within these media texts, but presented as an incontrovertible truth, a strategy that can and should be pursued, that is measurable and verifiable, and that constitutes 'what makes the difference'. 'Impact', one of the key reasoning devices in use within this frame, becomes a proxy for 'certainty' and approved solution. Furthermore, this contributes to the anticipation of compelling television and creates a sense of urgency around the series – here these media texts suggest that the audience is guaranteed to see verified, statistically significant effective teaching in action, the known keys to school improvement.

#Revolution School

There were 8673 tweets containing the #revolutionschool hashtag collected using a plug-in for Google Sheets called *Premium Twitter Archiver*, from the first #revolutionschool tweet, which was made by @ABCTV at 5.15pm on 23 May 2016 (eight days prior to the airing of the first episode), to midnight on 28 June 2016 (seven days after the airing of the final episode). An initial scan of the tweets highlighted 285 tweets that were clearly not related to *Revolution School*, and these tweets were deleted from the dataset, leaving a total of 8388. In exploring the Twitter backchannel, I was most interested in understanding who was tweeting, whose voices were loudest in the backchannel and users' attitudes to the representations of education presented in the documentary series.

Who was tweeting?

There were 2356 individual twitter accounts that contributed to the 8388 tweets, representing a mean of 3.56 tweets per user. The distribution of tweets amongst users is by no means uniform; however, with 1484 users (63%) tweeting into the backchannel only once. At the other end of the spectrum, four users (0.17%) tweeted into the backchannel over 100 times, with one of these users tweeting a total of 488 times. Ninety-three percent of users (2200) tweeted into the backchannel less than ten times. The effect of this is that over 48% (4326) of the tweets in the backchannel were contributed by only 7% of the users in the conversation.

Along with the tweets themselves, the Premium Twitter Archiver collected the 140-character twitter 'bio' for each of the 2356 users, and these were manually examined with the aim of identifying the characteristics and membership groups of those engaged in the discussion. While 1173 users either provided no information in their bio or did not provide information that indicated their relationship to either education or broadcasting, the remaining 1183 users were allocated to one of

11 groups (see Table 3.1 for more details). Where users indicated their membership of more than one of these groups in their bio, they were allocated to the group named first. Figure 3.3 illustrates group membership for these 1183 users.

To explore how far the number of tweets in the backchannel were representative of the different groups represented in the discussion, a chi-square goodness of fit test was conducted. Table 3.2 highlights the number of tweets provided by members of each group against the number of tweets that might have been expected given the number of tweeters in each group. The chi-square goodness of fit test indicated that the various user groups were not proportionally represented in the conversation[5]: some were over-represented while others were under-represented. Groups that were under-represented were the users whose possible connection to education and/or broadcasting were unknown; those who expressed an interest in education in their twitter bios; pre-service teachers; and media professionals. Groups whose tweets constituted a higher proportion of the backchannel than expected were university and school accounts; academics; education workers (other than teachers and academics); school leaders; teachers; and media organisations. Education organisations other than schools and universities and the very small number of school students in the sample tweeted approximately the number of times expected.

Network visualisation software Gephi was used to explore the 'shape' of the backchannel network, with particular emphasis on the connection formed between individuals in the conversation through 'retweets' and 'tagged' tweets. Figure 3.4 is a representation of the network, including as 'nodes' all individual twitter accounts that were mentioned five times or more in the backchannel, either via retweets, replied or tags. Nodes are sized according to eigenvector centrality, which utilises

TABLE 3.1 Categorisation of users

Category	Definition
Academic	Academics working in the field of education
Education as interest	People who indicated that education was a particular interest for them but not that they are an education professional
Education organisation	Education organisations other than schools or universities
Education worker	People working in the field of education but not in schools or universities, e.g. consultants, system employees
Media organisation	Media, production or communication organisations
Media professional	People working in the field of media, broadcasting, production, communications
Pre-service teacher	Student enrolled in an Initial Teacher Education program
School leader	School Principals, Deputy Principals, Assistant Principals
School student	Student enrolled in a K-12 school
Teacher	Teachers in K-12 and Early Childhood settings; retired teachers
University or school	Official accounts of schools and universities or organisational units within

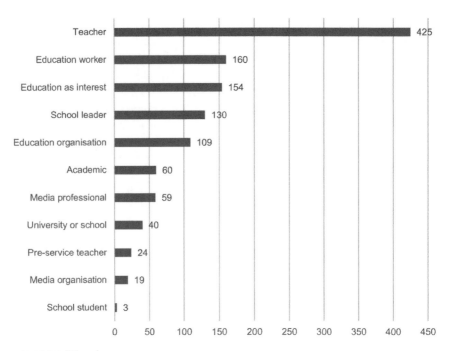

FIGURE 3.3 Users by group

TABLE 3.2 Observed vs expected tweets by user group

	Observed tweets	Expected tweets	% of expected
Unknown	2308	4175	55
Teacher	2183	1513	144
School leader	719	463	155
Academic	513	214	240
University or school	653	143	457
Media organisation	91	68	134
Pre-service teacher	63	86	73
Education organisation	393	388	101
Education worker	1004	570	176
Media professional	158	210	75
Education as interest	294	549	54
School student	9	11	82
Total	8388		

not only the number of connections within the conversation, but the relative 'importance' of those connections. Three primary hubs can be detected within the graph, one centred around @EduMelb, the official twitter account of the MGSE (also the account with the highest frequency of tweets, with its 488 tweets

Televising the revolution? 57

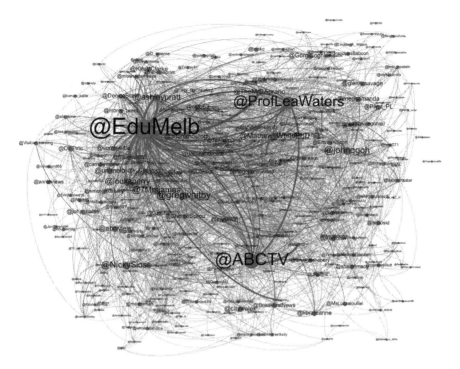

FIGURE 3.4 #revolutionschool network map

representing almost 300 more than those of the next most frequent tweeter, @ProfLeaWaters), another centred around @ABCTV, and a third around @ProfLeaWaters, who in addition to being the second most frequent tweeter into the backchannel, also appeared in *Revolution School* itself. These three twitter accounts provided recurring reference points in the backchannel conversation, as tweets from all three were repeatedly retweeted over the course of the six weeks, and as participants in the conversation engaged with these users. Interestingly, while 'Hattie' was the third most frequent lexical word in the backchannel (after 'school' and 'teachers', appearing in 1079 of the 8388 tweets), @john_hattie appears as a relatively small part of this network map, as this account – while it existed it had not issued any tweets at the time – did not participate in the conversation and was tagged in a total of only 28 tweets.

Had each of the 1079 tweets mentioning Hattie included the @john_hattie tag, the @john_hattie node in the graph would likely have been larger in size than that of @EduMelb (especially had this account been engaged in the backchannel also). This is a salient reminder that network maps such as this readily depict relationships between users in the conversation but are not effective in representing the nature of the conversation. For further exploration of the shape of the #revolutionschool backchannel, some basic, manual content analysis was conducted.

The 8388 tweets were read, re-read and coded in relation to their orientation to *Revolution School*. In this initial coding exercise, tweets were coded according only to whether their content represented affirmation/promotion of the documentary series, critique of the series, or were neutral in stance. Figure 3.5 represents the result of this initial round of coding.

Over 75% of the tweets in the backchannel were engaged in promotion or affirmation of the series (n=6322), while approximately 16% of the tweets (n=1312) took a critical stance on aspects of the series. A further 9% (n=754) were neutral in their stance.

Further content analysis was undertaken on the 7634 tweets identified as taking either a promoting/affirming or critiquing stance. Seven categories were identified for the promoting/affirming tweets, as represented in Figure 3.6.

Approximately one third of the promoting/affirming tweets (n=2067) were engaged in general promotion or affirmation of the series. These tweets included retweets of @ABCTV and @EduMelb tweets sharing information about the airing of *Revolution School*, along with tweets such as:

> Looking forward to #RevolutionSchool tomorrow night Struggling Melbourne School Opens Doors to TV Cameras.
>
> *(Phillips, 2016)*

There were 1327 tweets (21% of the 'promoting/affirming' tweets) that affirmed either teacher or school practices at Kambrya, while 2912 (46%) related specifically to the key ideas and individuals showcased in the series; 1534 specifically affirmed the 'clinical model' and John Hattie's approach to improvement, including the focus on impact; 875 related to the work of Lea Waters in relation to positive psychology and wellbeing; while 390 related to Diane Snowball's literacy work (and the associated reading program introduced at Kambrya), and finally, 113 to Bill Rogers' work around behaviour management.

Only 620 (26%) of users in the #revolutionschool backchannel issued one or more 'critiquing' or critical tweets. Five categories emerged from these tweets (n=1312), as represented in Figure 3.7.

There were 445 'critical' tweets engaged in critique of practices at Kambrya, including individual teacher practices and whole school practices (such as the

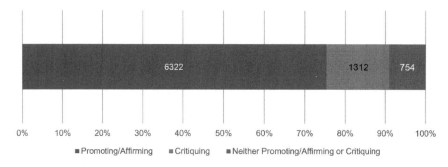

FIGURE 3.5 Initial content coding of #revolutionschool tweets

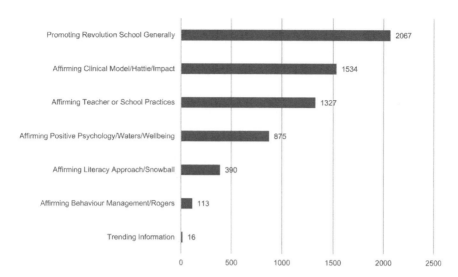

FIGURE 3.6 Promoting/affirming tweets

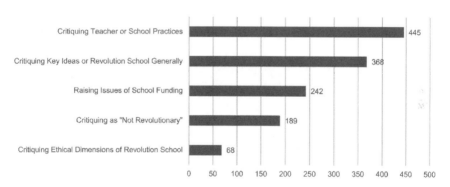

FIGURE 3.7 Critiquing tweets

debutante ball that featured in one episode). Meanwhile, 368 tweets critiqued the documentary series generally or the key ideas underpinning it, such as the focus on teacher quality or the premise of 'crisis'. Examples of this include:

> #RevolutionSchool we're letting down our children and the nation with our PISA test scores, apparently.
>
> *(Heffernan, 2016)*

> #RevolutionSchool When #hattie says it's not about smaller class sizes... Politicians smile and know that #education costs less . . .
>
> *(Connell, 2016)*

Check my school, ICSEA 998 average SES. #RevolutionSchool.

(Caro, 2016)

Of the critical tweets, 242 raised issues related to school funding, some of which noted the way in which Kambrya appeared to be particularly well resourced, or the difficulties of attending to school improvement in a resource-starved school community. There were 189 tweets that raised the issue of the documentary not demonstrating 'revolution', generally related to how such practices were commonplace within schools. Finally, 68 of the tweets critiqued ethical dimensions of the series, particularly with relation to the exposure of vulnerable young people on national television:

I have great respect for @EduMelb, but the airing of vulnerable children on #RevolutionSchool greatly concerns me. Who is this benefitting?

(Van Arkkels, 2016)

As an educator and a mother I am conscientiously objecting to #revolutionschool 'do no harm'.

(Jones, 2016)

Finally, a chi-square goodness of fit test was conducted to identify, based on the observed number of tweets overall, whether the critique was offered proportionally by the various groups of tweeters. Table 3.3 highlights the number of critical tweets provided by members of each group against the number of tweets that might have been expected given the number of tweets made overall by members

TABLE 3.3 Observed vs expected critiquing tweets by user group

	Observed tweets	*Expected tweets*	*% of expected*
Unknown	368	365	101
Teacher	371	345	108
School leader	146	114	128
Academic	132	81	163
University or school	23	103	22
Pre-service teacher	3	10	30
Education organisation	44	62	71
Education worker	126	159	79
Media professional	25	25	100
Education as interest	72	47	153
School student	2	1	200
Total	1312		

of each group. The chi-square goodness of fit test indicated that the various user groups were not proportionally represented in the conversation[6], and again, that various groups were over- and under-represented.

Education academics, people with education listed as an interest, and school leaders tweeted critically more than was expected[7], while university and school accounts, pre-service teachers, education workers and education organisations tweeted critically less than was expected based on the overall number of tweets from these groups. Teachers, people with affiliations unknown and media professionals tweeted critically approximately as much as expected. Media organisations did not tweet critically at all, and as such were removed from the analysis prior to conducting the test.

The disproportionately high number of critical tweets from academics (for whom it is arguably 'part of the job description' to problematise the unproblematised) and the disproportionately low number of critical tweets from university and school accounts (with @EduMelb as the most-frequent-by-far tweeter) might seem somewhat expected. The higher proportion of critical tweets from the 'education as interest' group and the school leaders is less expected.

Shaping the conversation: 'Top down' and 'bottom up' framing?

So, what does this mean about the framing of representations of education across the print media texts and social media discussion?

First, the frames in use in the print media texts resonate strongly with the framing of education in the series itself. The 'crisis' discourse that forms the premise upon which the series is predicated emerged as a key frame in these media texts, and the ongoing tension between complexity and simplicity, which I earlier argued characterises the documentary series, resonates with the frames of 'redemption' and school improvement that emerged strongly from the print media texts. The degree of consistency across these texts, particularly given that almost half of the print media texts were published prior to the airing of the first episode, suggests that what we see here is 'top down' framing (Nisbet, 2010). The representations of education in the print media texts accurately reflect those of the documentary itself.

These 'top down' frames were dominant but not entirely uninterrupted in the social media discussion. While, as I have shown, the dominant representations presented in *Revolution School* largely resonated with the 'ad hoc public' represented within the #revolutionschool, an undercurrent of critique was offered by both 'the usual suspects' and others. Bruns et al. (2016), in their work on 'hashtag publics', explore hashtag communities according to the prevalence of retweets and tweets containing URLs. Their research shows that hashtags attached to what they term 'acute events' (including natural disasters, political uprisings, etc.) tend to display relatively high proportions of both retweets and URL-tweets, pointing to 'gatewatching' (Bruns, 2005), a phenomenon whereby 'users actively seek out additional material and share it by posting new URLs into the hashtag, and where they help increase the visibility of already available material by frequently retweeting those tweets they deem to be important to others' (Bruns et al. 2016, p. 23).

Hashtags related to 'media events', ranging from reality television to coverage of events such as the Academy Awards and Eurovision Song Contest and television talk shows, tend to be characterised by 'communal audiencing' (Bruns et al., 2016, p. 23), with far lower proportions of information sharing via retweets and URL-tweets. Furthermore, they note that these categories easily become blurred where media events are related to more newsworthy stories (such as for hashtags related to current affairs talk shows) than to pure entertainment.

The #revolutionschool tweets occupy an interesting space according to this typology. Of the tweets into the backchannel, 5178 (61.7%, unusually high for a media event) were retweets, while only 431 (5.1%) were URL-tweets, mostly links to blog posts about the series, and resources related to the strategies in use. The proportions are not dissimilar to the #hottest100 hashtag in Bruns et al. (2016)'s research, which they account for by pointing to the large volume of tweets produced in real-time by media producers, in this case ABC radio station, Triple J. This seems to have been borne out in relation to the #revolutionschool hashtag: 14 of the 20 most retweeted tweets emanated from the accounts linked to either the Australian Broadcasting Corporation, the University of Melbourne, the Victorian Department of Education or individuals who appeared in the series. Indeed, over 30% of all tweets using the hashtag were either tweeted by or retweets of tweets by these users. Given that virtually all of these tweets fell into the 'promoting/affirming' category outlined earlier, they might be seen to have particular influence, whereby the messaging of the mainstream media is, through a critical mass of tweets issued by mainstream media-linked accounts, reinforced through the social media discussion. This raises questions about the generation of 'hashtag publics' such as this, and the potential for their manipulation or management at the hands of corporate or institutional interests.

This is to suggest that while some 'bottom up' framing was occurring on the #revolutionschool backchannel, the discussion was largely steered by those involved in the production of the documentary series. The reproduction and amplification of the representations of education that stand at the heart of *Revolution School*, whether through straight retweets, promotion of the series or affirmation of key ideas, was dominant in the Twitter conversation as it was in the print media texts. What is different about the social media texts is the existence of some alternative framing, wherein users problematised the key premise of the documentary or took issue with it on grounds of practice, policy or ethics. This contrasts with previous work on media framing of education (Mockler, 2014, 2016) which highlighted the robustness of 'top down' frames in the reporting of education policy issues, and raises the question of how far social media might provide a way for alternative conceptualisations and framing of education policy to be advanced within the public space.

Twitter has long been a space for robust conversations about education. This research indicates that the timbre of this conversation might be both similar to but different from that which takes place in the mainstream media. This chapter has taken on a very small part of a much broader discussion, and suggests that social media spaces such as the #revolutionschool backchannel might be useful in both scholarship and activism. They might provide scope to further develop our understanding of how education is regarded and discussed in the public space, and, potentially, open new space for educators to actively engage in shaping this public conversation.

Notes

1 A Twitter backchannel is a real-time conversation conducted by Twitter users, comprising a collection of tweets all employing the same hashtag (in this case #revolutionschool) to group the conversation and allow Twitter users who may not otherwise be connected to engage in discussion of a topic.
2 A note about print media ownership in Australia: four newspapers are owned by Fairfax media (*The Age, The Australian Financial Review, The Canberra Times* and *The Sydney Morning Herald*), while a further seven are owned by NewsCorp (*The Advertiser, The Australian, The Courier Mail, The Daily Telegraph, The Herald Sun, The Mercury* and *Northern Territory News*), and one (*The West Australian*) owned by Seven West Media. NewsCorp publications and *The West Australian* tend to be more conservative in their orientation than Fairfax-owned publications.
3 For a more fulsome discussion of this approach, see Mockler (2014)
4 This oft-quoted statistic relates to Victorian Certificate of Education results.
5 $\chi^2(11) = 3994.34$, $p<0.001$
6 $\chi^2(10) = 136.48$, $p<0.001$
7 Along with school students, although in this case the expected number of tweets was only one, due to the small size of the group and the small number of tweets they produced overall.

References

Back to classroom basics. (2016, 30 May). *The West Australian*, p. 5.
Baroutsis, A. (2016). Media accounts of school performance: Reinforcing dominant practices of accountability. *Journal of Education Policy*, 31(5), 567–582.
Blackmore, J., & Thorpe, S. (2003). Media/ting change: The print media's role in mediating education policy in a period of radical reform in Victoria, Australia. *Journal of Education Policy*, 18(6), 577–595.
Blundell, G. (2016, 21 June). Cue the musical as Kambrya graduates. *The Australian*, p. 17.
Bruns, A. (2005). *Gatewatching: Collaborative online news production*. New York: Peter Lang.
Bruns, A., & Burgess, J. (2011). #ausvotes: How twitter covered the 2010 Australian federal election. *Communication, Politics & Culture*, 44(2), 37–56.
Bruns, A., Moon, B., Paul, A., & Münch, F. (2016). Towards a typology of hashtag publics: A large-scale comparative study of user engagement across trending topics. *Communication Research and Practice*, 2(1), 20–46.
Caro, A. [@AnnCaro1]. (2016, 31 May). Check my school, ICSEA 998 average SES. #RevolutionSchool [Tweet]. Retrieved from: https://twitter.com/AnnCaro1/status/737599513129451520.
Cater, N. (2016, 7 June). Throwing cash at schools not the answer. *The Australian*, p. 12.
Connell, P. [@icameisawipad]. (2016, 31 May). #RevolutionSchool When #hattie says it's not about smaller class sizes… Politicians smile and know that #education costs less… [Tweet]. Retrieved from: https://twitter.com/icameisawipad/status/737594084294959105.

Cook, H. (2016, 22 June). Melburnians give local schools the thumbs down. *The Age*, p. 3.
Doherty, E. (2016a, 28 May). First lesson on schools. *Herald Sun*, p. 18.
Doherty, E. (2016b, 26 May). Homework pain. *Herald Sun*, p. 21.
Doherty, E. (2016c, 28 May). What a turn around. *Herald Sun*, p. 34.
Dunk, T. (2016, 29 May). Watch this. *Herald Sun*, p. 10.
Easy on the homework – it's just not worth it. (2016, 26 May). *The Courier Mail*, p. 5.
Fenech, M., & Wilkins, D. P. (2017). Representations of childcare in the Australian print media: An exploratory corpus-assisted discourse analysis. *The Australian Educational Researcher*, 44(2), 161–190.
Free-to-air highlights. (2016, 31 May). *The Advertiser*, p. 70.
Gamson, W., & Lasch, K. (1983). The political culture of social welfare policy. In S. Spiro & E. Yuchtman-Yaar (Eds.), *Evaluating the welfare state: Social and political perspectives* (pp. 397–415). New York: Academic.
Gamson, W., & Modigliani, A. (1989). Media discourse and public opinion on nuclear power: A constructionist approach. *American Journal of Sociology*, 1–37.
Goodyear, V. A., Casey, A., & Kirk, D. (2014). Tweet me, message me, like me: Using social media to facilitate pedagogical change within an emerging community of practice. *Sport, Education and Society*, 19(7), 927–943.
Heffernan, A. [@chalkhands]. (2016, May 31). #RevolutionSchool we're letting down our children and the nation with our PISA test scores, apparently [Tweet]. Retrieved from: https://twitter.com/chalkhands/status/737593418805739521.
Holmes, K., Preston, G., Shaw, K., & Buchanan, R. (2013). 'Follow me': Networked professional learning for teachers. *Australian Journal of Teacher Education*, 38(12), 55–65.
Jones, T. [@TJ0N3S]. (2016, June 7). As an educator and a mother I am conscientiously objecting to #revolutionschool 'do no harm' [Tweet]. Retrieved from: https://twitter.com/TJ0N3S/status/740152876991811584.
Miles, M. B., Huberman, A. M., & Saldana, J. (2013). *Qualitative data analysis: A methods sourcebook* (3rd ed.). Thousand Oaks, CA: Sage.
Mills, M., & Keddie, A. (2010). Cultural reductionism and the media: Polarising discourses around schools, violence and masculinity in an age of terror. *Oxford Review of Education*, 36(4), 427–444.
Mockler, N. (2014). Simple solutions to complex problems: Moral panic and the fluid shift from 'equity' to 'quality' in education. *Review of Education*, 2(2), 115–143.
Mockler, N. (2016). Naplan and the problem frame: Exploring representations of naplan in the print media, 2010–2013. In B. Lingard, G. Thompson, & S. Sellar (Eds.), *National testing in schools: An Australian assessment* (pp. 181–198). Abingdon: Routledge.
Molloy, S. (2016, 12 June). Watch this, p. 10.
Moreillon, J. (2015). # schoollibrarians tweet for professional development: A netnographic case study of # txlchat. *School Libraries Worldwide*, 21(2), 127.
Nisbet, M. C. (2010). Knowledge into action: Framing the debates over climate change and poverty. In P. D'Angelo & J. A. Kuypers (Eds.), *Doing news framing analysis: Empirical and theoretical perspectives*. New York: Routledge.
Phillips, M. [@esl_mel]. (2016, May 30). Looking forward to #RevolutionSchool tomorrow night Struggling Melbourne School Opens Doors to TV Cameras [Tweet]. Retrieved from: https://twitter.com/esl_mel/status/737270691624452100.
Powley, K. (2016, 11 June). Mind over matter. *Herald Sun*, p. 10.
Quinn, K. (2016, 26 May). Green guide: Our pick free to air. *The Age*, p. 14.
Rigden, C. (2016a, 25 May 2016). Out of the box. *The Courier Mail*, p. 40.
Rigden, C. (2016b, 31 May 2016). Switched on tv. *Herald Sun*, p. 38.

Toohey, B. (2016, 20 June). Clever schools help us to think beyond numbers in class. *Australian Financial Review*, p. 39.

Van Arkkels, A. [@AVanArkkels]. (2016, June 7). I have great respect for @EduMelb, but the airing of vulnerable children on #RevolutionSchool greatly concerns me. Who is this benefitting? [Tweet]. Retrieved from https://twitter.com/AVanArkkels/status/740144918455164932.

4

RE-MATTERING MEDIA AFFECTS: PEDAGOGICAL INTERFERENCE INTO PRE-EMPTIVE COUNTER-TERRORISM CULTURE

Shiva Zarabadi and Jessica Ringrose

Introduction

In this chapter, we explore how media events generate affect that resound across the contemporary climate of counter-terrorism in the UK (Sampson, 2012; Grusin, 2010, p. 76). In the first part of this chapter we show how viral media events create new forms of 'affective qualities' (Lupton, 2017, p. 13) and affective agential assemblages, constructing security thinking and pre-emptive risk adverse logics which then become a material means of regulating Muslim children. We explore the re-mediated coverage of three British girls who 'fled' to Syria to marry jihadi fighters in 2015 and their subsequent construction as 'jihadi brides'. Specifically, we argue these media events contribute to the construction (becoming) of Muslim girls in contemporary UK society as components of 'terrorist assemblages' (Puar, 2007). We show how the temporal and affective relations of these media events reach out to inform policy initiatives and shape school environmental educational systems through terrorism related policies such as UK Prevent Duty to prevent (religious) radicalisation. We draw upon Deleuze (1992) to think about this media event not as a story having a causal essence but rather a series of viral medialogical affective and relational intra-actions, with momentum and punctum piercing and travelling in the social terrain. We think about media events as rhizomatic, with connections that grow in-between the material forces and entanglements with bodies, matters, images, space and time. Indeed, this event itself as an affective assemblage opens up new assemblages emerging between the milieus of human body-subjectivity, educational environments and media images, forming a new collective that develops new potentialities and expressions.

In the second part of the chapter we move beyond a theoretical application to show how we can interfere into such logics of meaning and matter through pedagogical intra-actions with terror-thinking and terror-images that create uneasy openings for transformation. We explore the actual and virtual force that can affectively entangle us in relation to counter-terrorism culture and then demonstrate two experimental arts-based participatory pedagogical activities designed to interfere with and transform the affectivity of media events surrounding Muslim femininity, terrorjarring and quiltingveils. We argue such artistic, creative practices can subvert, reorganise and re-matter the pre-emptive logics of counter-terrorism through embodied entanglements.

The birth of the 'jihadi bride' – An always could be identity

The September 11, 2001 terrorist attacks on the New York Twin Towers are considered by many scholars to be a hallmark of the affective political turn in the world. The 'jihadi brides' in the UK have also emerged as a significant media event engendering new forces and capacities into the social, mental and environmental ecologies (Guattari, 2000) of our ordinary lives, schools, families, public and private. In February 2015 footage of three schoolgirls' 'flight' from London Gatwick Airport to Turkey and the Turkey–Syria border became a mass media spectacle in the UK.

The CCTV footage captured the three girls travelling through airport security but the story of their 'fleeing' to Syria to marry jihadi fighters captured the public imagination. Footage of the girls circulated in news and print assemblages alongside images of female jihadi fighters in veils holding guns, juxtaposed with the girls' earlier 'innocent' school photos. Coverage and interest in the girls continued after 2015 unabated, with news media tracking them and speculating on the possible death of one of them in a Syria air strike (*The Guardian*, August 12, 2016). This media coverage and repeated circulation of images through what Massumi (2015a) calls 'automatic image loops' led to the construction of a new figure 'jihadi brides' (*New Statesman*, October 10, 2016) and the condition of 'jihadibridism'. We developed this concept 'jihadibridism' (Zarabadi & Ringrose, 2018) to refer to what we consider as a paradigm shift in how the UK public conceives of Muslim girls. Public perception shifts from positioning Muslim girls largely ignorant/innocent to a schizoid (Renold & Ringrose, 2011) construction of potential threat which will contaminate their innocence.

Significantly, Muslim girls can be typecast and stereotyped as belonging to this category indiscriminately. In a climate of mass panic, the identity possibility spreads, to create a site of risk (grooming) potentially applicable to all Muslim girls who may be susceptible to desires to marry jihadi fighters. This figure and new identity category has become an important element of shifting public ideas about Muslim radicalisation but this is specifically sexualised around feminine subjectivity (Zarabadi & Ringrose, 2018). Jihadibridism as an immanent category that ripples through the reconstitution of counter-terrorism schemes and prevent policy in schools. A key way we have seen this actual material-discursive shift (Barad, 2007) is, for example, in late 2017 when the head of UK Ofsted (Office of Standards in Education) said 'creating an environment where primary school children are expected to wear the hijab could be interpreted as sexualisation of young girls' mandating a new principle for inspectors to question girls wearing the hijab (*The Guardian*, November 20, 2017). Here we see a discourse of sexualisation is repurposed around the hijab which becomes a key marker of religioned sexualisation tied to implication of radicalisation which is entangled with the wider terrorist assemblage. This then feeds *directly* into new surveillance practices sanctioned by government authorities.

Drawing upon Sampson's (2012) concept of virality as an ontology of relational encounter and affective contagion (Thrift, 2008; Grusin, 2010, p. 57) that is the exercising of many relational forces on the social field, we argue for the importance of sensory and relational approaches to explore such affective mediological contagious encounters that create jihadibridism. This helps us to better understand the affective tenors of the climate of counter-terrorism in educational environments in the UK.

The 'jihadi brides' event as an ongoing affective force is still looping and growing to other event-assemblages as it reappears in the media after each terrorist attack in the UK. The significance of this event propagated by news and social media in its affective mediality can lead to other bodily habits, registers of meaning, interactions and particular kinds of socio-political mediations in which everyday forms of affective terror-related mediation might engender new challenges and possibilities for educational school life. The 'jihadi brides' image loops re-mediate the event to vitalize and mobilize particular complex educational encounters in schools. The affective and material intensities of media events and images such as the three Muslim schoolgirls create 'sticky spaces' (Laketa, 2018) as performative embodied spaces saturated with affects that stay with and stick to us for a long time. Such affective sticky spaces provide a capacious space and time to assemble the particular negotiations between identity, affect, media and educational environment.

The otherisation of Muslim women emerges in the realm of a particular paradox and in-between a relational affective assemblage. Instead of forcing a particular *belief* in a political and/or ideological fact, the new affective turn which is the re-mediated counter-terrorism climate forces us to wander in a state of *hesitancy* by working at the micro level of perception, the paradox at the surface, the underside. Using the concepts of pre-emption and pre-mediation we discuss this proposition further.

Perception attack and pre-emptive, pre-mediated ontopower

The event and its otherisation are what Massumi (2017) calls the *perception attack*, reflecting the ways in which the battlefield shifts into the field of emergence and weaponising potentialities, leavening the threat and making it rise to be seen, recognised and stamped out before it solidifies into an objective present danger. The paradox in the ongoing event of 'jihadi brides' is about the pre-emptive logics (Massumi, 2015a) of counter-terrorism that operate in alliance with 'pre-mediation' that is 'the politics of information net-works' (Grusin, 2010, p. 47) as the novel medialogical turn since 9/11[1]. What is critical here is risk and the possibility of what may come to be.

Pre-mediation functions neither as a space of complete freedom, nor as a controlled, predetermined or pre-censored space, but as a space of virtuality to make us feel that the future has already been pre-mediated or that it could have been. Pre-mediation insists upon the 'liveness of futurity' (Grusin, 2010, p. 54) as a reality that will already have been pre-mediated through the 'continuous interactivity of the media' (Thrift, 2008, p. 35). This type of time-signatured paradox not only affectively and materially creates different politico-socio-cultural capacities in relation to global terrorism, immigration policies and global political economies but has also turned into a particular type of securitised culture in our everyday ordinary practices (Hall, 2015). Such lived paradox of pre-emptive culture has a conditional logic of 'could-have/would-have' (Massumi, 2015a, 2017) that operates to take pre-emptive actions, decisions and measurements for future not-yet-happened danger.

Massumi (2017) developed the notion of ontopower to refer to the pre-emptive would-have/could-have logic of pre-emption which he characterizes as the operative logic of our time. He argues that ontopower can make every decision from macro political measurements to micro interactions as right and true even if it was or is wrong. The doctrine of must-imperative to avert risk through pre-emptive logic has been explicitly articulated since George Bush's presidential era when, in justifying the invasion of Iraq, he pronounced that: 'Saddam Hussein did not have weapons of mass destruction but he *could have had them* ...; and ... *if he could have had them, he would have had them forthwith*, and he would have used them ...' (Massumi, 2017, p. 67 emphasis added).

Media coverage of capturing terrorists in the Boston Marathon bombing (2013), live and continuous developments of terrorist attacks on London Bridge (2017) and the Manchester Arena bombing (2017) serve to modulate people's moods and behaviours in public, evidenced by the increase in hate crimes in the UK from 29 to 80%[2], and work to legitimate future security risk action to prevent attack. Ontopower implies that media images and events operate independently of rational or ideological arguments working as a 'smooth-over-ability of the event' (Massumi, 2017, p. 63) to spread fear and anxiety. Grusin (2010) likewise claims that print, networked and particularly televised media are more concerned with an over-coded future risk than with the immediate present.

A similar logic has developed in UK schools since July 2015 which coincides with the 'jihadi brides' event. Prevent Policy (HM Government, 2015), which is an anti-radicalisation duty in schools, has forced school staff and teachers to monitor Muslim children and report them to school and counter-terrorism schemes on the basis of risk factors through which radicalisation is to be predicted (Best, 2008; Sian, 2015). The paradox is that teachers lack background knowledge or understanding of those targeted cultures and lack the time to learn about and really get to know students as a result of heavy workload, yet are being called upon to be vigilant about extremist ideas and views (HM Government, 2015) and to catalogue and call out predictive(pre-emptive) factors of extremism. This type of risk factor cataloguing as pre-emptive logics are what we call pre-event monitoring. The threat of Muslim pupils' radicalisation can be formulated in this way: Muslim students do not have extremist ideas and do not take extremist actions *but if they could have them, they would have them and, therefore, they would commit extremist actions*.

The doctrine of pre-emption for Massumi (2015a) is to act on 'the time of before' and to act upon the 'yet-to-happen' event. Despite the fact that '90% of referrals to authorities of Muslims under Prevent Policy end without action' (*The Guardian*, March 28, 2016), according to the viral 'must' security logic, it is pre-emptively right. 'Before' in the pre-emptive logic of the climate of paradox reveals a politics of time associated with politics-to-come (Manning, 2013), a politics that is intensive, divergent, incommensurable and conflictual and does not provide us with an easy answer (Springgay & Rotas, 2015). What is significant about pre-emptive logic in policy terms is that it can create a mandate to act which requires no scientific basis to legitimate itself nor to evaluate its effects. It is a new plateau in the risk society (Beck, 1992) but mediated risks work via media automatic images and news loops which intra-act with our bodies and minds. For instance, in Zarabadi's empirical research with young people the category of 'jihadi bride' emerged as a potential threat with a classmate telling a veiled Muslim girl 'its gonna be you next', referencing the media event and the sexual lure of 'jihadibridism' (Zarabadi, 2017).

Risk, threat, fear and danger pre-mediated and re-mediated by the media in this 'must'-security climate of paradox enable different but relational temporal capacities; future threat as yet-to-come and as future potential is present in the form of fear and danger so, in a sense, the fear we feel now is the futurity of threat. Pre-mediated and contagious threat vitalized by media including news media which blurs with social media in the age of Twitter (Jenkins et al., 2012) is not to be confused with prediction or getting the future right (Grusin 2010, p. 13). However, as Thrift (2008, p. 31) suggests, in the contemporary information capitalism the value increasingly arises 'from what is not yet but can potentially become' and the 'pull of the future' than from what is. Under a media regime of pre-mediation, the affective value of the automatic media loops repeating news and images increases rather than decreases as they morph into other affective assemblages. Ironically 'what has just gone into the past is still present' and what is about to go on in the future is also depicted as occurring in the present (Grusin, 2010, p. 53).

The shock event of the terror attack pre-mediated by media automatic loops transforms into a continuous contagious rumour and as an independent affective reliable source remains open as something that is just about to occur (Sampson, 2012). In this sense, the new affective encoding of feelings and perceptions into and out of our newer media may well produce new futures for educational environments and different challenges to education research.

Haptic-optic assemblages as media events

The 'jihadi brides' images are better understood as media events rather than representational forms and since they have material and affective capacity they are experienced as space-time matterings (Barad, 2007). They are posthuman circulating through affective atmospheres and feelings of threat and fear (Anderson in Ringrose & Renold, 2016). Media images rather than being considered as only regimes of signs are also haptic cyberspaces (Deleuze & Guattari, 1987) connected to other sensory capacities (Grosz, 2008). For Sontag (2003) the problem with the continuous thrust of mediated images of death and disaster which produce a confusing blurring of representation and reality is not that people remember through photographs, rather they remember *only* through photographs. In this sense the shock and fear of Muslim schoolgirls' radicalisation within the education environment function both as an 'affective trigger' and a 'hook' into 'more extended form[s] of engagement' (Bennett, 2005, p. 65). This contagious virality hooks into other mediated assemblages such as school interactions or establishment of educational policy (Prevent) operating as the 'processes of affective inhabitation' (Pedwell, 2017, p. 166) that are the re-mediation of forms of affective connection – acts of 'staying with' the image and the sensations through the media images' digital virality.

Bodies and images are entangled together as material assemblages (Deleuze, 2005; Coleman 2014) or as phenomena (Barad, 2007) beyond the understanding of images as representational texts consisting of a series of encoded signs that can be decoded to understand their meanings and messages (Coleman, 2014). Haptic images as phenomena enable haptic capacities. Any terror attacks or any terror-related media image loops create what Manning (2007) calls *sense-events*, whereby we experience terror feelings. Such haptic contagious resonances and reverberations among images; viewers and environment work to amplify affect (Rentschler & Thrift, 2015). Malinowska and Miller (2017) call this 'sensitive media' referring to the ways that media options of customised cases, personalised notifications and ringtones not only bind us emotionally but seek in them emotional relief and a showcase of private identities for public imaging.

The medialogical haptic entanglement to the pre-mediated images within the context of the security climate of paradox generates or propels a kind of response-ability that does not entail responding to a particular other but the enabling of responsiveness within particular relatings and to an extended phenomenon (Schrader, 2010). The particular mediality pre or re-mediated in the mediasphere mobilise particular affective responsiveness to potential threats. For instance, the medialogical significance of 'jihadi brides' media images working in concert with wider counter-terrorism initiatives create a new haptic-optic assemblage where, through sensory interrelationships between the eyes, ears, limbs, hands, memories, discourses, past, present and future, new forms of affective, embodied and embedded perception emerge incorporating us into the image space's textural quality, including temperature, mass, weight, density, pressure, humidity, presences and resonances (Karanika, 2009). This can be understood as the affective and sensorial 'unknown knowns' (Grusin, 2010) of the educational environments and practices mediated by new media that open up new challenges for education research.

The affective and haptic medialogical assemblages enabling the 'technological unconscious' (Thrift, 2004) can initiate, regulate and discipline the everyday habit in a sense that media images of 'jihadi brides' do not simply bring to our attention the criminal behaviour of some schoolgirls but our affective entanglement to a new loop of mediated terrorist assemblage and then of new realisation, action, thinking, feeling and even new forms of 'mediation' (Grusin, 2010).

The threat of terrorism and construction of risky Muslims as an affective device enables haptic thinking and haptic engagement. Prevent Policy and pre-emptive logic entangle with media events; they affectively attenuate and extend the haptic space around the Muslim-related incidents and terrorist attacks. The haptic is the tactile and more than looking machine (Ringrose & Coleman, 2013) which produces the capacity to 'must reach', 'must touch' and 'must see' at the same time and resolves the issues of farness to make proximity happen. Ingold (2011) suggests that the haptic engagement is hands-on, close range and bodied. We can say that the optic relation between mind and the world, for instance in the 'jihadi brides' event, is founded on distance and detachment (Kind, 2013), whereas in a haptic sense-experience, threat and fear sew us into the textures of the world along the pathways of sensory involvement (Pink, 2011). Our engagement with threat, must security thinking and automatic media image loops of terrorist attacks and Muslim-related incidents is haptic, its threat and fear vibrate us more than the visual, a felt-thought and touched-vison. These images 'jar' (Renold & Ringrose, 2017) us as a feeling-thinking-movement-sense event. In the following we explore affective entanglements to terror-related media images and offer some ideas on how to interfere with these as part of our social justice incentive as feminist pedagogues (see Ringrose, 2018).

Running interference, re-mattering terror with jarring and quilting haptic spaces

Here we introduce pedagogical strategies to begin to challenge and think critically with and through the capturing affects of media events that enact security thinking and pre-emptive futurity practices around Muslim girl subjects. Geerts and van der Tuin (2015) advocate that one way of grappling with intersectional identity and power hierarchies through a new materialist framework is to shift our attention from resisting secure identity contained through structural constraint (e.g. Muslim terrorist) to exploring patterns of interference that may be generated through political activism to enable micro practices of disruption and reformulation (Ringrose, 2015). These would include pedagogical provocations to directly disrupt fear and suspicion created through media events and the new identity of 'jihadi brides' that we have reviewed.

Following this aim to map interferences through social science cartographic methodologies (Ringrose, 2015), we created some pedagogical assemblages to re-matter and re-mediate the affective messages of these media events, stories tropes and identity categories surrounding Muslim terrorism and Muslim femininity. Our goal was to intervene into the pre-emptive futurity of threat in the image and to remake it and create a sticky space to engage the affect pedagogically (Hickey-Moody, 2013). We explore how terror jarring and quiltingveils of resistance are forms of pedagogical mangling practices (Jackson, 2013; Niccolini, 2016) capable of generating new 'uneasy openings' (Manning, 2013) and new forms of ethical 'response-ability' (Barad, 2007) around how we feel and act in relation to terror-time in our educational practices and research.

'Terror jarring' (Figure 4.1) has the aim of capturing what Massumi (2008, p. 3) calls 'the thinking-feeling of what happens'. In our teaching discussion activity, we showed students an advert for the Anti-Terrorist Hotline featuring the text 'IT'S PROBABALY NOTHING, BUT...', 'YOUR CALL COULD SAVE LIVES' (National Counter-terrorism Security Office, 2017). We asked students to write a word, draw a line, pictures, emojis or even make a sound of what jars, vibrates or shakes them on *seeing* the advert. They then folded, crumpled or made something with their response and put their messages/feelings into a jar (Renold, 2016). The advert written in white capital letters on a red background opened up new affective forces as we were becoming-with experiences of the thick presence of terrorism-thinking. The student's written messages revealed double conditional thinking and worlding as students took in and absorbed the embodied affective capacities of the advert.

Quiltingveil was another pedagogical exercise developed to respond to the sense of doom captured in terror jarring, this time by responding to an image of the burkini[3] ban in France. Students were given pieces of cloth, scissors and pins to create a 'quilted veil' of their feelings that emerged in their encounter with the image (see Figure 4.2). They quilted their haptic-optic feeling-thinking to the

FIGURE 4.1 Terror jarring assemblage
Photo credit: Shiva Zarabadi

FIGURE 4.2 Quiltingveil assemblage
Photo credit: Shiva Zarabadi

colourful patches of fabric, to the woman's burkini, to our pedagogical event and to our education research. We quilted not simply the fabric patches but a thicker ordinary event-time-image to our feeling, thinking and making enactment as 'a way to think-with a host of companions in sympoietic threading, felting, tangling, tracking, and sorting' (Haraway, 2016). With quilting, we safety-pinned the affective, material and temporal event-ness of the image to our embodied sense-event. Our quilt as a 'tangible output' (Hickey-Moody & Sayers, 2016) implied a thick and heavy theoretical, affective, material and pedagogical robe/veil.

What we see in the advert and the burkini ban news media image is a movement of seeing double, real and abstract; the material image is real and the movement that we cannot actually see but 'cannot not see either' is abstract (Massumi, 2008, p. 3). With and through the actual form of image and advert the threat and the double conditional climate of paradox become a launching pad for future threat, it 'takes off' (Massumi 2008) from the news media image, of state control over clothed Muslim women's bodies. In both practices we stayed with the *trouble* (threat of terrorism) through our pedagogical event to re-entangle, 're-lay and return' the 'game of response-ability' (Haraway, 2016, p. 11).

Terror jarring and quiltingveil of resistance can open up new and different possibilities and pedagogical imaginaries of relations, affects, bodies and materialities (Todd et al., 2016). They interact differently with these media images, times and objects in the classroom (Hohti, 2016), offering very different material and mediated entanglements than a simple verbal discussion. These pedagogies offer creative and arts-based ways to not only express oneself representationally but to materialise feelings through objects such as pens, pins and fabric (Bennett, 2010). The veils could intra-act with students' bodies and minds in the classroom which may form a different relationality to the veil and to the affectivity of counter-terrorism culture. In order to interrupt the climate of paradox and must security thinking we need to harness embodied practices of making and doing (Renold, 2017). The engagement of students' bodies and memories with materials was as if 'sewing itself on' to the textures of the world along the pathways of sensory involvement (Pink, 2011). With our terror jar and quiltveil that were the assemblages of humans and more-than-humans we were no longer just knots, parts and components of the assemblage but part of the movement that could intravene and materially disrupt terror-thinking (Ingold, 2015).

Conclusion

By focusing on the affective and material entanglements to media images we have suggested a way in which the collective threat and fear of counter-terrorism is generated via media events. Through the event of 'jihadi brides' we explained mediality as a haptic affective encounter beyond representationality (Grusin, 2010) that can function to modulate our affective entanglements to these media images solidifying fear around terrorism enabling new modes of connections, disconnections and public mobilizations. This can clearly extend into policy and practice as evidenced by UK Prevent Policy which offers unprecedented freedom to survey and monitor young people in schools. The notion of 'ontopower' (Massumi, 2015b) enables us to understand the power of mass media as less normative than affective (Massumi in Zournazi, 2003) and in legitimising political power of state through the contagious affective channels of social assemblages rather than through reason or the correct application of governmental judgment.

We suggest that the continuous remediation of media events particularly in relation to terrorism, radicalisation and threat of terrorism does not happen in isolation. For Latour (1993), also this remediation does not simply operate by neutrally reproducing meaning or information but by active transformation of conceptual and affective states; they affect educational bodies, matters, discourses, policies and research. The mediated images of 'jihadi brides' extend the public imaginaries beyond a representational demographic through 'the affective economies of speed, time, pace, circulation, transit, distribution, flows, and, of course, exchange' (Puar, 2007, p. 102). The minor affective tendencies of media images and particularly what they do rather than simply what they represent are what interest us, the ways in which these affective entanglements to the terrorist assemblages travel across the everyday, re-mediating and re-mattering existing educational environments and practices, activating new modes of connections and perceptions to experience and research the educational environments.

It is crucial to pay attention to the 'historically contingent blocs of affect' (Lesko & Niccolini, 2016, p. 11) operationalised within affective media events such as 'jihadi brides'. Such understanding of educational environments as ongoing non-linear processes that are not frozen into representation but rather folding and unfolding of memories, emotions and responses will help us to teach, educate and research 'against the obviousness' (Rotas, 2015, p. 91) of education practices, representational and binary thinking and linear time. By demonstrating the patterns of affective modulation, for instance automatic image loops, live coverage as pre-mediative logics and Prevent Policy as a pre-emptive strategy, we have argued that control is less visual than tactile, in a sense inviting us to hands-on participation (Shaviro, 2003). This requires hands-on tactile resistance, which is why we have presented modes and methods of interruption designed to intervene in media affective entanglements of fear to re-think, re-touch and re-matter counter-terrorism and must security culture. Our pedagogical experimental activities of terror jarring and quiltingveils were two attempts of re-mattering and remediating through digitally capturing the activities, the viral haptic and affective entanglements of media events surrounding Muslim femininity. These experiments show how artistic practices can create resistance that subverts and reorganises the pre-emptive logics of counter-terrorism. Our attempt here was to tap into what Deleuze (2011) suggests are the 'relentless movement, flow and transformation [of affect] in a universe where nothing ever truly repeats'. Our aim was to harness a new way of embodied understanding and feeling so that counter-terrorism could be rethought and remade and these media images of 'jihadi brides' and Muslim terrorism could be re-mattered at the visceral level of touch and feel through jarring with terror and quilting and wearing a resistant veil.

Notes

1 The September 11 attacks were a series of four coordinated terrorist attacks by the Islamic terrorist group al-Qaeda on the United States in 2001.
2 Hate crime surged in England and Wales after terrorist attacks: www.theguardian.com/uk-news/2017/oct/17/hate-soars-in-england-and-wales
3 A burkini is a type of swimsuit for women.

References

Barad, K. (2007). *Meeting the universe halfway: Quantum physics and the entanglement of matter and meaning*. Durham, NC: Duke University Press.
Beck, U. (1992). *Risk society: Towards a new modernity*. London: Sage.
Bennett, J. (2010). *Vibrant matter*. Durham, NC: Duke University Press.
Bennett, J. (2005). *Empathic vision: Affect, trauma and contemporary art*. Stanford: Stanford University Press.
Best, S. (2008). Terrorism and the role of the school in surveillance. *Education, Knowledge and Economy*, 2(2), 137–148.
Coleman, R. (2014). Inventive feminist theory: Representation, materiality and intensive time. *Women: A Cultural Review*, 25(1), 27–45.
Deleuze, G. (2005). *The logic of sensation*. Translated by D. W. Smith. New York, NY: Continuum.

Deleuze, G. (2011). *Difference and repetition*. London: Continuum.

Deleuze, G. (1992). *The fold: Leibniz and the baroque*. Minneapolis, MN: University of Minnesota Press.

Deleuze, G., & Guattari, F. (1987). *A thousand plateaus: Capitalism and schizophrenia*. Minneapolis, MN: University of Minnesota Press.

Geerts, E., & van der Tuin, I. (2015). From intersectionality to interference: Feminist ontoepistemological reflections on the politics of representation. *Women's Studies International Forum*, 41, 171–178.

Grosz, E. (2008). *Chaos, territory, art, Deleuze and the framing of the earth*. New York, NY: Columbia University Press.

Grusin, R. (2010). *Premediation: Affect and mediality after 9/11*. UK: Palgrave Macmillan.

Guattari, F. (2000). *The three ecologies*. London: The Athlone Press.

Hall, R. (2015). Terror and the female grotesque, introducing full-body scanners to U.S airports. In R. Dubrofsky & S. Magnet (Eds.), *Feminist surveillance studies*, pp. 127–150. Durham, NC: Duke University Press.

Haraway, D. (2016). *Staying with the trouble: Making kin in the chthulucene*. Durham, NC: Duke University Press.

Hickey-Moody, A. (2013). Affect as method: Feelings, aesthetics and affective pedagogy. In R. Coleman & J. Ringrose (Eds.), *Deleuze and research methodologies*, pp. 79–95. Edinburgh: Edinburgh University Press.

Hickey-Moody, A., & Sayers, E. (2016) Diffractive pedagogies: Dancing across new materialist imaginaries. *Gender and Education*, 28(2), 213–229.

HM Government. (2015). Revised Prevent Duty Guidance: for England and Wales. www.gov.uk/government/uploads/system/uploads/attachment_data/file/445977/3799_Revised_Prevent_Duty_Guidance__England_Wales_V2-Interactive.pdf

Hohti, R. (2016). Time, things, teacher, pupil: engaging with what matters. *International Journal of Qualitative Studies in Education*, 29(9), 1148–1160. doi:10.1080/09518398.2016.1201610

Ingold, T. (2015). *The life of lines*. New York, NY: Routledge.

Ingold, T. (2011). *Being alive: Essays on movement, knowledge, and descriptions*. New York, NY: Routledge.

Jackson, A. Y. (2013). Posthumanist data analysis of mangling practices. *International Journal of Qualitative Studies in Education*, 26(6), 741–748.

Jenkins, H., Ford, S., & Green, J. (2012). *Spreadable media*. New York, NY: New York University Press.

Karanika, M. (2009). *Haptic space and bodily expressions: A bi-directional relation of affect*. Paper presented at AISB 2009 Convention, Edinburgh, April 6–9. Retrieved from: www.aisb.org.uk/convention/aisb09/Proceedings/MENTALSTATES/FILES/KaranikaM.pdf

Kind, S. (2013). Lively entanglements: The doings, movements and enactments of photography. *Global Studies of Childhood*, 3(4), 427–441.

Laketa, S. (2018). Between 'this' side and 'that' side: On performativity, youth identities and 'sticky' spaces. *Environment and Planning D: Society and Space*, 36(1), 178–196.

Latour, B. (1993). *We have never been modern*. Translated by C. Porter. Cambridge, MA: Harvard University Press.

Lesko, N., & Niccolini, A. (2016). Historicising affect in education. *Knowledge Cultures*, 4(2), 2327–2573.

Lupton, D. (2017). Feeling your data: Touch and making sense of personal digital data. *New Media & Society*, 19(10), 1599–1614.

Malinowska, A., & Miller, T. (2017). Sensitive media. *Open Cultural Studies*, 1, 660–665. doi:10.1515/culture-2017-0060

Manning, E. (2013). *Always more than one: Individuation's dance*. Durham, NC: Duke University Press.
Manning, E. (2007). *Politics of touch: Sense, movement, sovereignty*. Minneapolis, MN: University of Minnesota Press.
Massumi, B. (2017). *The principle of unrest, activist philosophy in the expanded field*. London: Open Humanities Press.
Massumi, B. (2015a). *Politics of affect*. New York, NY: Polity Press.
Massumi, B. (2015b). *Ontopower*. Durham, NC: Duke University Press.
Massumi, B. (2008). The thinking-feeling of what happens; a semblance of a conversation. *INFleXions*, 1. doi:1_massumihtml.html
National Counter-terrorism Security Office (2017). Surrey Police. www.surrey.police.uk/advice/protect-yourself-and-others/counter-terrorism/
Niccolini, A. (2016). Animate affects: Censorship, reckless pedagogies, and beautiful feelings. *Gender and Education*, 28(2), 230–249.
Pedwell, C. (2017). Mediated habits: Images, networked affect and social change. *Subjectivity*, 10, 147–169.
Puar, J. K. (2007). *Terrorist assemblage, homonationalism in queer times*. Durham, NC: Duke University Press.
Pink, S. (2011). Sensory digital photography: Re-thinking 'moving' and the image. *Visual Studies*, 26, 4–13.
Renold, E. (2016). *Agenda: A Young People's Guide to Making Positive Relationships Matter*. Cardiff University, Children's Commissioner for Wales, NSPCC Cymru, Welsh Women's Aid and Welsh Government. Retrieved from www.agenda.wales
Renold, E. (2017). 'Feel what I feel': Making da(r)ta with teen girls for creative activisms on how sexual violence matters. *Journal of Gender Studies*. doi:10.1080/09589236.2017.1296352
Renold, E., & Ringrose, J. (2011). 'Schizoid subjectivities?: Re-theorising teen-girls' sexual cultures in an era of 'sexualisation'. Journal of Sociology, 47(4), 389–409.
Renold, E., & Ringrose, J. (2017). Pin-balling and boners: The posthuman phallus and intra-activist sexuality assemblages in secondary school. In L. Allen and M. L. Rasmussen (Eds.), *The Palgrave Handbook of Sexuality Education*, pp. 631–655. London: Palgrave Macmillan.
Rentschler, C., & Thrift, S. (2015). Doing feminism in the network: Networked laughter and the "binders full of women" meme. *Feminist Theory*, 16(3), 329–359.
Ringrose, J. (2015). Schizo-feminist educational research cartographies. *Deleuze Studies*, 9(3), 393–409. doi:10.3366/dls.2015.0194
Ringrose, J. (2018). Digital feminist pedagogy and post-truth misogyny. *Teaching in Higher Education*, 23(5), 647–656. doi:10.1080/13562517.2018.1467162
Ringrose, J., & Coleman, B. (2013). Looking and desiring machines: A feminist Deleuzian mapping of affect and bodies. In B. Coleman and J. Ringrose (Eds.), *Deleuze and research methodologies*, pp. 125–145. Edinburgh: Edinburgh University Press.
Ringrose, J., & Renold, E. (2016). Cows, cabins and tweets: Posthuman intra-acting affect and feminist fires in secondary school. In C. Taylor and C. Hughes (Eds.), *Posthuman research practices in education*, pp. 220–241. Basingstoke: Palgrave Macmillan.
Rotas, N. (2015). Ecologies of praxis: Teaching and learning against the obvious. In N. Snaza and J. Weaver (Eds.), *Posthumanism and educational research*, pp. 91–104. London: Routledge.
Sampson, T. (2012). *Virality, contagion theory in the age of networks*. London: University of Minnesota Press.

Schrader, A. (2010). Responding to Pfiesteria Piscicida (the fish killer): Phantomatic ontologies, indeterminacy, and responsibility in toxic microbiology. *Social Studies of Science*, 40.

Shaviro, S. (2003). *Connected, or what it means to live in the network society*. Minneapolis, MN: University of Minnesota Press.

Sian, K. (2015). Spies, surveillance and stakeouts: Monitoring Muslim moves in British state schools. *Race Ethnicity and Education*, 18(2), 183–201. doi:10.1080/13613324.2013.830099

Sontag, S. (2003). *Regarding the pain of others*. London: Penguin.

Springgay, S., & Rotas, N. (2015). How do you make a classroom operate like a work of art? Deleuzeguattarian methodologies of research-creation. *International Journal of Qualitative Studies in Education*, 28(5), 552–572.

Thrift, N. (2004). Remembering the technological unconscious by foregrounding knowledges of position. *Environment and Planning D: Society and Space*, 22(1), 175–190.

Thrift, N. (2008). *Non-representational theory: Space, politics, affect*. London: Routledge.

Todd, S., Jones, R., & O'Donnell, A. (2016). Shifting education's philosophical imaginaries: Relations, affects, bodies, materialities. *Gender and Education*, 28(2), 187–194.

Zarabadi, S. (2017). Seeing fingers and touching eyes: The haptic-optic media materialization of Muslim girls in an age of counter-terrorism. Paper presented at Gender and Education Conference (2017). London: Middlesex University.

Zarabadi, S., & Ringrose, J. (2018). The affective birth of 'Jihadi Bride' as new risky sexualized 'other': Muslim schoolgirls and media panic in an age of counter-terrorism. In S. Talburt (Ed.), *Youth sexualities: Public feelings and contemporary cultural politics*. New York, NY: Praeger.

Zournazi, M. (2003). *Navigating movements: An interview with Brian Massumi*. Open University Research Projects: Collaboratory in Critical Security Methods, www.open.ac.uk/researchprojects/iccm/library/117.html

5

EXAMINING MEDIA DISCOURSES OF DIVERSITY AND 'INDOCTRINATION': PUBLIC PERCEPTIONS OF THE INTENDED SCREENING OF *GAYBY BABY* IN SCHOOLS

Michelle Jeffries

Introduction

The emergence of new technologies over the last two decades has seen the birth of a new political subject labelled the 'digital citizen' (Isin & Ruppert, 2015, p. 19). These digital citizens use the internet to engage politically and economically in society (Mossberger, Tolbert, & McNeal, 2008). In contrast to constraints imposed on journalistic reporters, digital citizens experience greater freedom and anonymity in making public commentary on social issues and, as such, provide access to a broader range of discourses than traditional media alone (Bruns, 2003; McCluskey & Hmielowski, 2012). These discourses circulate within institutions, and often constrain methodological possibilities for those who research diverse genders and sexualities in schools, as research in this field has been discursively constructed as controversial, risky, and problematic (Allen et al., 2014). In the current political climate, conservative discourses are often privileged in political decision-making about representing gender and sexual diversity in education, and this has resulted in negative regressions to educational policy (Ferfolja & Ullman, 2017).

This chapter draws upon social media and online news platforms to explore discourses (re)produced when digital citizens engaged in online commentary in response to a frenzy of traditional media about the intended whole-school showing of *Gayby Baby* (Mars & Newell, 2015), a documentary following the journey of four children growing up with same-sex parents, and subsequent ministerial decision to prevent the event from going ahead. Drawing on the four orientations framework developed by Jones (2009; 2011a; 2011b; 2013), public commentary from online newspaper articles and Facebook were examined using the following lenses: (i) Conservative (maintains the status quo); (ii) Liberal (draws on notions of individualism and competition; includes neo-liberalism); (iii)

Critical (social justice lens); and (iv) Postmodern (problematises knowledge, deconstructs cultural 'truths'). Examining online commentary using this framework provides an opportunity to consider multiple, often competing discourses relating to the representation of sexual diversity, particularly same-sex parented families, in schools.

The two themes extrapolated from these data centre on discourses of diversity and indoctrination. I argue that both conservative and liberal perspectives were utilised in related commentary to oppose the proposed whole-school screening and associated event, and a critical lens was drawn upon to advocate support. Across the dataset, comments reflecting a postmodern orientation were extremely rare and I reflect that, given queer methodologies draw on postmodern perspectives, this rarity provides insight into the landscape in which queer education research is undertaken. For education researchers, using the four orientations framework to examine social media and online news commentary allows an understanding of how arguments were employed to oppose and support inclusion and representation of sexual diversity in schools. As such, the methodology employed in this chapter offers education researchers an approach for making sense of the broad range of discourses circulating in a context of increasing online public commentary in order to talk back to resistances to their research and opposition to inclusion of diverse sexualities in education.

Contextualising the media event

In August, 2015, a media frenzy unfolded in response to news that Burwood Girls High School (BGHS) in New South Wales (NSW), Australia, intended to screen *Gayby Baby*, a documentary following the journey of four children growing up with same-sex parents. The school was one of 20 in NSW planning to show the documentary in celebration of *Wear It Purple Day* (Bagshaw, 2015a), a nationally recognised annual event aiming to 'foster supportive, safe and accepting environments' for young lesbian, gay, bisexual, transgender, intersex, and queer (LGBTIQ) people (Wear It Purple, n.d.).

A media furore began on 26 August with a large, attention grabbing headline on the front page of *The Daily Telegraph* which read 'Gay class uproar' (2015). The lead paragraph stated, 'Parents and community leaders are angry after Burwood Girls High School said all of its 1200 students would be skipping classes in order to dress in purple and watch a documentary on gay parenting'.

The newspaper included several related pieces (Akerman, 2015a; McDougall, 2015; Schools learn their PC before the ABC, 2015a), each opposing the showing of *Gayby Baby* in schools. In his opinion piece, the journalist Piers Akerman (2015a) labelled the film 'an overtly political documentary on homosexual parenting' and asserted that both the screening of the film and the 'purple dress code' breached departmental guidelines (p. 4). He argued his case of a breach by claiming that the film and Wear It Purple event aimed at furthering a political cause, lacked relevance to curricular goals, and did not consider the ages of all students. Similarly, an editorial in the same edition of *The Daily Telegraph* avowed that the intended showing of *Gayby Baby* meant that 'children in their most impressionable years' would be 'brainwashed with propaganda', 'taught opinion as fact', and 'thrust into adult concepts they might not be ready for' (Schools learn their PC before the ABC, 2015a, p 24). It is useful to recognise here that editorial pieces set the agenda for news items, otherwise known as the 'editorial line', and reflect the opinion of editors and newspaper owners (Baroutsis, 2017).

In addition to fears raised about political agendas, age-appropriateness, and assertions about lack of curricula relevance, *The Daily Telegraph* journalists spoke of the views of school parents and community leaders. McDougall (2015) reported 'outrage', 'concern', and 'criticism' from these groups in relation to several aspects of the event, including the content of the film, dressing in purple to support gender and sexual diversity, promotion of a 'gay lifestyle', and beliefs that children who did not participate would be subject to bullying (p. 4). The newspaper reported there were numerous complaints by parents to the school; however, it was revealed later by *The Guardian* that the NSW Department of Education confirmed the school received no complaints directly from parents (Safi, 2015a).

The initial news was picked up quickly by conservative talkback radio on 2GB. In his introduction to the topic, the host of *The Alan Jones Breakfast Show* on the day, Chris Smith (2015), expressed concern that schools were teaching about sexuality and morality, stating that this is the domain of the family. Smith (2015) and his listeners echoed cries by *The Daily Telegraph* writers that the film should not be shown in schools. There was also pressure that the Education Minister should address the situation immediately, including one caller who insisted the Minister announce within half an hour that 'this indoctrination of susceptible and vulnerable high school students will end'. At approximately 8:50 am, just hours after the initial media were published, Smith announced that the NSW Education Minister, Adrian Piccoli, had just provided a directive that the film should not be shown during school hours in any NSW public school. In an interview soon after with Smith, Piccoli justified his decision saying that, in school hours, students are expected to be 'doing maths and English and curriculum matters' Smith (2015). When Smith then suggested that the Minister had essentially 'green lighted gay movies being played in public schools', Piccoli responded with: 'During school hours parents rightly expect that students will be doing curriculum subjects and that's what I expect too. Not movies. Not movies like this. I know it's a very sensitive issue' (Piccoli in Smith, 2015).

The decision by the Minister to prevent a whole-school screening had been made without the Minister viewing the film and despite the NSW Personal Development, Health and Physical Education (PDHPE) Years 7–10 Syllabus providing scope for exploring diverse family structures, including same-sex parented families (Board of Studies, NSW, 2003) and the NSW Education Standards Authority (n.d.) listing 'Diversity and Difference' as an important learning area across all NSW K-10 syllabi. Although at the time, *The Daily Telegraph* journalists expressed a belief that the NSW 'Controversial Issues in School' policy had been breached, the Education Minister and NSW Premier later clarified that their objections were to the suspension of classes rather the content of the documentary, and that sections of the film could still be shown during PDHPE classes where relevant to the syllabus (Gerathy, 2015).

The government intervention and prevention of the whole-school screening of the documentary during school hours, labelled a 'ban' by many, sent a message about the appropriateness of representing sexuality diverse families in schools. This was especially true given that regular classes had previously been cancelled for religious programs, films, and visits by politicians, without the government stepping in (Jeong, 2015). In this instance, given that the government singled out this one event and prevented it from being shown in schools brings to the fore Ferfolja's (2013) assertion that sexual diversity is rarely represented or acknowledged in schools as it is often positioned as 'sensitive or too controversial for schooling communities' (p. 162). The Minister's decision provides an example of how political debates are influenced by the popular media and raises questions about the power of conservative media to influence our social services and the day to day workings of public institutions such as schools.

The furore unfolded during a period when the Prime Minister announced the Federal Government's intention to hold a national plebiscite in which all Australians would vote on whether to allow same-sex couples to marry (Hudson, 2015). In many ways, this announcement launched a lengthy period in which the Australian public were invited to comment and pass judgement on same-sex relationships and families. It also created a context that led to some commentators viewing the planned BGHS screening of *Gayby Baby* as a political act. In deep contrast to this view, Shannon and Smith (2017) argue that the Education Minister's decision to prevent the planned screening politicised the inclusion and representation of same-sex parented families and sexual diversity in schools, by locating such content as sensitive and controversial. Such politicisation creates barriers for those advocating for representation of diverse sexualities in schools (Shannon & Smith, 2017).

Methodology

This chapter analyses data drawn from public commentary made in response to the proposed screening of *Gayby Baby* in schools. The dataset is comprised of 15 online news articles and opinion pieces collected from four mainstream Australian newspapers (*The Daily Telegraph* – metropolitan, Sydney based, owned by News Corp Australia; *The Sydney Morning Herald* – metropolitan, Sydney based, owned by Fairfax; *The Courier Mail* – metropolitan, Brisbane based, owned by News Corp Australia; *The Guardian* – national reach, owned by the Scott Trust) and one alternative online news platform (*ABC The Drum*), as well as comments in response to 11 Facebook posts (news, political, and group pages engaging in significant discussion about these media events). Data were collected for a period of ten days from the day the first article was written until the issue quietened on these online platforms. Data excluded commentary unrelated to the topic, replies in conversational threads that could not stand alone, and sarcasm as the meaning is lost when taken out of the context of conversation.

Examining online public comments about the showing of *Gayby Baby* and the subsequent ministerial directive that prevented the screening provides an opportunity to consider a wider range of discourses than would be available when analysing journalistic reporting within news articles alone (McCluskey & Hmielowski, 2012). Journalists traditionally hold a gatekeeping role, choosing the content and positioning of news delivered to the public (Friend & Singer, 2015) although as previously noted, editorial pieces often set the agenda (Baroutsis, 2017). Additionally, constraints are imposed on journalists potentially limiting the discourses evident within news items. For instance, in Australia, enforced standards on journalists include 'avoidance of harm', 'fairness and balance', and 'accuracy' (Australian Press Council, 2014). Digital citizens who participate in online news commentary are able to step outside these constraints and the typical gatekeeping processes (Bruns, 2003). This freedom conjoins with an anonymity that leads people to share their thoughts and feelings online more openly with 'less pressure to conform to societal norms' (McKenna & Green, 2002, p. 119; Santana, 2014). By accessing both online newspaper and social media commentary, there is potential to access perspectives from different demographics. For example, a recent study published by the USA Pew Research Centre (Mitchell, Gottfried, Shearer, & Lu, 2017) found that the majority of men and those aged over 50 tend to consume online news via news organisation websites and apps, whereas women and those in younger demographics tend to do this through social media. The extensive public commentary analysed within this chapter comprises multiple and often competing educational discourses and underlying values, some of which have the potential to cause harm.

This chapter draws on the concept of discourse as a 'way of speaking' (Foucault, 2002 [1969], p. 135), understanding that 'discourse does ideological work, constitutes society and culture, is situated and historical, and relates to/mediates power' (Jones, 2013, p. 11). Thus, the discourses within the public commentary are both influenced by culture and society, while also having a generative effect. Initially, a deductive analysis was used to designate comments to a discursive orientation in accordance with Jones' four orientations framework (Jones, 2009, 2011a, 2011b, 2013), that is, as (i) Conservative (maintains the status quo); (ii) Liberal (draws on notions of individualism and competition; includes neo-liberalism); (iii) Critical (social justice lens); or (iv) Postmodern (problematises knowledge, deconstructs cultural 'truths') (see Table 5.1). Important to note here is that the framework is a construct and there are not always 'clean lines' (Jones, 2013, p. 26); however, by examining each orientation in isolation the key aspects can be identified. Following the designation of the dataset to the four orientations, a thematic analysis was undertaken to identify key ideas within each orientation. While numerous themes emerged, this chapter draws specifically on two themes that were relevant across orientations: discourses of diversity and 'indoctrination'.

TABLE 5.1 Conceptions of education and sexuality by orientation

Orientation	Conceptions of education (Jones, 2013)	Conceptions of sexuality (Jones, 2011a)	
Conservative	• education should 'transmit' conventional beliefs, practices, and values in order to maintain social stability	• Sexuality and gender viewed as fixed and binary	• sex as procreative and occurs within heterosexual marriage • sexual diversity deemed as invalid or wrong
Liberal	• encourages individual excellence, competition, and inquiry • government focus on improving educational trends • neo-liberal discourses are included in this orientation	• Sexuality and gender viewed as fixed and binary	• sexual diversity acknowledged as a matter of informed personal choice, however is not normalised
Critical	• encourages students to interrogate mainstream ideologies and take action on unsustainable and unjust values, assumptions, and practices in society • inclusion of non-dominant knowledges and voice to redress marginalisation	• Sexuality and gender viewed as fixed and binary	• actively supports sexual diversity • promotes equity for those who identify as sexuality diverse
Postmodern	• problematises knowledge • draws on de-constructive principles to interrogate 'reality,' cultural 'truths,' hegemony, and one's own partiality/bias	• Acknowledges fluidity and deconstructs binaries	• acknowledges fluidity • deconstructs binaries to demonstrate inherent power relations, thereby exposing hegemony in relation to constructions of sex, gender, sexuality, desire, and the body

Discourses of diversity

Representing sexual diversity and sexuality diverse families in schools were prevalent in social media and online news public commentary. As a conservative orientation is underpinned by a procreative view of sex and beliefs that education should reinforce dominant societal conventions, representation of sexual diversity was considered inappropriate content for students and schooling contexts. Indicative excerpts from social media and online newspaper commentary include:

> What they are trying to do? Convince children that it [being gay] is normal? It's not . . . Gay people are not normal and should not be allowed to have children if they can't produce them together . . . kids are fu★★★d up enough already without this crap.
> *('Mario' in Starts at 60, 2015) [dots and asterisks in original; parentheses added]*

> The job of the Government is to protect, promote, and support marriage for life between a man and a woman, because they – and their children – constitute the foundation of a stable, just and healthy society.
> *('GM' in Devine, 2015)*

Comments such as these stem from a narrow and heteronormative perspective of sexuality and family. Heteronormativity is a regulatory practice that draws on binaries to position heterosexuality as normal and natural, while constructing homosexuality as the unnatural and abnormal Other (Warner, 1993). Traditional constructions of family that idealise a two-parent male-female headed household are grounded in heteronormativity (Davies & Robinson, 2013). Normative narratives of family fail to recognise that the nuclear family is not natural, but a constructed, politicised social unit reflecting Western, white, patriarchal, capitalist ideologies and histories (Carrington, 2002). For instance, conservative perspectives often correlate children's wellbeing to living within a family unit headed by a mother and father. These notions of complementarity emerged, in part, from the 20th century psychological turn which positioned male-female couple parents as necessary for children's stability and wellbeing (Carrington, 2002). Here, gender expressions were viewed as innate; women were positioned as nurturer and father as provider and disciplinarian (Carrington, 2002). An absence of this complementarity was viewed as leading to individual deficits and antisocial behaviours (Carrington, 2002). Another example of the constructedness of normalising discourses of family relates to capitalism, with the smaller, nuclear family being a better functional match for the changes created by industrialisation, such as children transforming from labour force to an expense (Barrett & McIntosh, 1991). Comments within this theme draw on normalising nuclear representations of family to position same-sex parents as abnormal and a threat to children and society. Within conservative commentary, such constructions were used to argue that sexual diversity and sexuality diverse families should not be represented in schools through films such as *Gayby Baby*. "Family" was therefore reflected as nuclear and there was a lack of acknowledgement and acceptance of family diversity in society. Rather than ensuring family diversity is represented in its many forms, conservative discourses privilege and elevate Western, nuclear, two-parent, heterosexual-headed households, while marginalising other forms of family, in this case same-sex parented families.

A liberal orientation, while recognising to some degree the authority and influence of institutions on the individual, places emphasis on individual choice (Jones, 2013). As such, viewing a film about sexuality diverse families is positioned as a choice for individual children or parents. There were very few examples within liberal data about the rights of children to select whether they would attend the screening, with significant liberal choice-related commentary advocating for parental agency. For instance, 'Allow one film like this and open the door. Parents should have a say as to what their children are shown in school' ('metoo' in Bagshaw, 2015b).

Such commentary suggests that a liberal orientation supports consultation with parents and community about policies (Jones, 2013). Consultation forms part of parent engagement, which is increasingly acknowledged as an important factor in children's success both in school and beyond. However, the competing orientations evident within this analysis raise questions as to which knowledges, perspectives, and discourses would be valued over others, if consultation were to occur on this matter. Vincent (2000) warns that dominant knowledges can be privileged in schools and power can therefore function in such a way that the voices of parents belonging to minority groups are marginalised. *The Daily Telegraph* reporting and the subsequent decision by the Minister to cancel the screening of *Gayby Baby*, for instance, privileged particular voices and marginalised the voices of same-sex parents and their families.

Notions of parent choice were also evident within these data suggesting topics of sexual diversity related to morals and values and as such were not within the scope of school responsibility. Jones' (2009) framework suggests a liberal orientation places responsibility for morals/values development with individual students or parents, not with schools. Liberal data within the commentary about values and morals predominantly positioned topics of diverse sexualities as parental domain. This does not necessarily equate to commentators viewing diverse sexualities as invalid or wrong as within a conservative orientation, rather, through a liberal lens, sexual orientation is considered to be the choice of individuals (Jones, 2011a). It certainly indicates that diverse sexualities are not normalised in this frame; however, this is demonstrative of blurry lines that can exist between orientations, as conservative discourses of sexuality tend to underpin perspectives of diverse sexualities as a morals/values issue. An example of such commentary that positions sexuality as a values/morals issue for parents to address, not schools, includes:

> Morality and ideology should be taught by parents and family .... It's my opinion that educational institutions (talking public ones here anyway) are funded by the taxpayer and therefore... should be neutral. At the end of the day, public schools are there to teach kids how to add up and spell correctly, not to sell them ideology.
>
> ('John' in *ABC News*, 2015)

The correlation of sexual diversity with morals and values raises questions and concerns. Schooling includes exposure to many educational resources that represent heterosexual-headed households without claims of this being a morals and values issue. Consequently, that sexual diversity is considered a morals/values issue reflects the invisibility of heteronormativity and the silence of normalising discourses that actively and passively maintain heterosexuality as the norm (DePalma & Atkinson, 2009). Nancy Fraser (2008) associates *representation* with 'social belonging, and thus determining who counts as a member' of a community (p. 278). If education settings only includes heteronormative representations of family, invisibility and exclusion may give children the understanding that same-sex parented families are less valid or do not belong in society.

In contrast to a liberal orientation which promotes individualism, a critical orientation reflects social justice ideologies and is underpinned by an overarching goal to create a world that is more sustainable, just, and peaceful (Jones, 2013). As such, a critical orientation advocates inclusion and representation of sexual diversity in schools. Online public commentary reflecting this idea positions education, and therefore the showing of *Gayby Baby*, as part of a broader focus to improve society by teaching children respect for diversity. For example,

> The whole point of education should be to make society a better place for all, to shape future generations… Teaching students to be open minded and respectful to different backgrounds, to understand diversity, should undoubtedly be intertwined into their school life.
>
> ('Maggie' in The Project, 2015)

> Learning about LGBTIQ is something everyone should be exposed to so that we are creating a progressive and supportive world for all.
>
> ('Burwood' in Schools learn their PC before the ABC, 2015b)

Comments such as these acknowledge the powerful position schools hold in challenging heteronormative bias and discrimination. Decisions about 'programming, resource selection and policies send messages to children and their parents about the meaning of family' in educational settings (Cloughessy & Waniganayake, 2014, p. 1267). Consequently, curriculum choices have the power to legitimise, privilege, and include particular family representations, and marginalise, silence, and render others invisible. Family is a fundamental aspect of children's lives and, as such, acknowledgement, respect, and visibility of diverse family structures is essential in challenging bias and ensuring a sense of belonging for children of diverse families (Derman-Sparks & Olsen Edwards, 2010). By taking the unprecedented step of cancelling the *Gayby Baby* event, the NSW Education Minister (re)produced systemic bias, heteronormativity, and invisibility of diverse sexualities, including same-sex parented families.

Discourses of indoctrination

Discourses of 'indoctrination' were found to align with discourses of diversity and were evident in media commentary data. A variety of language was used within commentary to talk about indoctrination which was understood as 'social engineering', 'brainwashing', 'recruiting', or 'propaganda'. Discourses of indoctrination were used within both conservative and liberal commentary to oppose the planned whole-school showing of *Gayby Baby* on the basis that it would push a particular social agenda. Blame for indoctrination was attributed to various groups/people including those with Leftist political views, same-sex marriage advocates, the 'gay lobby', teachers, principals, and the teachers' union. Despite these similarities, discourses of indoctrination were framed quite differently within conservative and liberal lenses.

Within a conservative orientation, as has been discussed, diverse sexualities are positioned as abnormal and invalid and there is an expectation that there should be no education on this topic as schools are considered responsible for maintaining the status quo (Jones, 2013). Furthermore, children are constructed as 'wide-eyed' innocents and as empty vessels that passively receive knowledge (Jones, 2013, 2011b). Within these data, these concepts were brought together to position the BGHS *Gayby Baby* event as indoctrination of vulnerable, innocent children. For example, indicative social media and online news comments included:

> This is indoctrination, this is grooming, this is brainwashing. This is negative… 'Gays' only have sexual 'intercourse' with their own gender. They can't be 'parents.' This is devious social engineering at its worst.
>
> ('Scott' in ABC News, 2015)

> Why can't you just let kids be kids and stop trying to indoctrinate them… Leave our children in their innocence.
>
> ('Mariane' in Gayby Baby, 2015)

> All children have an innate goodness and know that family means a mum and dad. To try and perverse this truth by using children in Gayby baby is abhorrent and shows how far some will go to corrupt innocent minds.
>
> ('Wendy' in ABC News, 2015)

Through this lens, exposure to representations of sexuality diverse families in school is positioned as indoctrination and a threat to children's innocence. Robinson (2013) contends that discourses of childhood innocence position knowledge about sexuality as being solely the domain of adults, ultimately locating adults as controllers of information. She argues that positioning children as too innocent for sexual knowledge is 'detrimental to children's wellbeing and their development as competent, responsible, resilient, critical-thinking subjects with agency in their lives' (Robinson, 2013, p 18). Constructing children as vulnerable and innocent positions them as needing adult protection, and social and moral conservatives use this as a platform to create moral panic[1] about topics of diverse sexualities entering educational contexts (Robinson, 2008).

In contrast to a conservative orientation, a liberal lens positions students as active learners who, although influenced by culture and institutions, choose their own values and beliefs (Jones, 2013). It was noted earlier that significant commentary about choice related to 'parents'; however, these data provide some commentary about student choice. Commentary reflecting concerns about indoctrination within a liberal orientation expressed the importance of students choosing their own views but considered the showing of *Gayby Baby* as a standalone, with no alternatives alongside, as propaganda. In other words, commentary suggested that if children are not given the opportunity to view a film advocating mainstream parenting or one denigrating same-sex parenting alongside *Gayby Baby*, they would be unable to develop an informed, individual view. By being shown just one 'side' it was considered that children were being indoctrinated into a particular social agenda. For instance,

> Was a film shown giving other views on this subject or just the one point of view shown. If not then this isn't education but one sided propaganda and indoctrination.
>
> *('Ertimus' in Safi, 2015a)*

> Gay parenting? Have they watched a documentary on mainstream parenting first??
>
> *('Leah' in Daily Telegraph, 2015)*

These comments do not recognise that children are continually exposed to representations of mainstream parenting in curricular materials, culture, and media, with limited representations of diverse sexualities. That this is not recognised again demonstrates the invisible pervasiveness of heteronormativity. Additionally, when commentary spoke of children choosing their own informed views on particular topics, there appeared to be no concern or understanding about inherent and unchallenged individual and systemic biases that may impact on the values and beliefs that students 'choose'.

A critical orientation challenges indoctrination discourses evident within conservative and liberal framings. Students are actively engaged in social issues within this orientation, and participate in questioning and critical thinking about unjust societal values and practices (Jones, 2013). Therefore, within critical commentary, rather than positioning the intended showing of *Gayby Baby* as indoctrination, it was considered important for the development of children as critical, socially aware, and active citizens. This approach is supported by the *Melbourne Declaration* which sets a goal that 'all young Australians become… active and informed citizens' (Ministerial Council on Education, Employment, Training and Youth Affairs, 2008). Commentary reflecting such views include:

> Piccoli and Baird are happy to have values taught when those values are mainstream and free from controversy. They should stop to consider that

making this sort of material part of the curriculum content is necessary if our students are to develop as thinking, critical, socially aware citizens.

('Sunsetclause' in *Safi*, 2015b)

Commentary within this orientation challenges conservative perceptions of children as passive vessels and liberal notions that the curriculum can be neutral purely by providing alternate perspectives. As such, perceptions of indoctrination are called into doubt, with the idea that exposure to diversity helps students to become socially aware and critical thinkers. This particular orientation advocates for including voices of non-dominant groups to redress broader marginalisation (Jones, 2013). As such, a critical approach to education aligns with McNaughton's view of a transformative curriculum, as it provides a platform to transform society by equipping children to 'recognise and confront injustice and to resist oppressive ways of becoming' (McNaughton, 2003, p 183). Furthermore, a transformative curriculum empowers young people 'to develop the knowledge, skills, and values needed to become social critics who can make reflective decisions and implement their decisions in effective personal, social, political, and economic action' (Banks, 1991, p. 131). There were a few comments within these data from self-identified BGHS parents reflecting this position in response to the initial media furore and subsequent 'ban' on showing the film during school time. For example, a parent asserted:

> This beat up has resulted in a massive increase in the amount of positive discussion at school about the issues in this film. As well as discussing the film's issues, it has also generated an ethics discussion about intolerance and exclusivity, political and religious interference and hypocrisy, and how social inclusiveness is what we need.
>
> ('Alan' in Bagshaw, 2015a)

In contrast to conservative and liberal perspectives, this commentary demonstrates transformative perspectives of education. They are also offered in contrast to conservative and liberal lenses privileged in the initial *The Daily Telegraph* reporting that led to the NSW government preventing this and similar events from being run across the state.

Finally, a postmodern orientation to education, which was not evident in diversity discourses discussed earlier, allows a space where the concepts of reality, truth, and authority can be analysed and deconstructed, and multiple theoretical perspectives considered (Jones, 2011a, 2013). This orientation was evident in the following response to others' claims that showing the film represented indoctrination and attempts at social engineering:

> What? you think that school is not a place for social engineering?... School is compulsory as a piece of social engineering. Every time a student gets disciplined it's social engineering. So why should social engineering not extend to showing a film about people who don't live the way you do?
>
> ('Richard' in Jensen, 2015)

Here, the commentator interrogates the perspective that showing the film in school hours represents social engineering by suggesting that this is no different to many other aspects of schooling which are also not neutral. The writer of this commentary notes that all schooling is social engineering and calls out the original commentator, suggesting that the objection was based on something that is seen as fundamentally different to their own life, and their preferences for how such debates are represented. As such, this comment brings notions of diversity and indoctrination together to raise the question – if schooling is a tool of social engineering, what kind of world do we wish to 'engineer', one that pretends diversity does not exist or one that acknowledges diversity and challenges heteronormative practices in education?

Conclusions

Digital citizenship and the rise of a participatory media culture has provided a platform for individuals to step outside the usual gatekeeping processes of traditional media and engage politically online. This participatory media culture provides education researchers with access to a broad range of circulating public discourse. The methodology employed in this chapter draws on Jones' four orientations framework to consider online commentary about *Gayby Baby* within four discursive orientations: Conservative; Liberal; Critical; and Postmodern. By analysing online social commentary using this framework, educational researchers can explore more deeply the discourses drawn upon to reject or support the inclusion of particular knowledges in schools, as well as circulating discourses which may constrain methodological possibilities for their research. In the case of *Gayby Baby*, the analysis showed that conservative, liberal, and critical orientations were regularly employed in this digital debate, with very few comments that represented a postmodern orientation being evident.

The analysis showed that both liberal and conservative discourses of diversity and indoctrination were employed to oppose the planned *Gayby Baby* event. However, each orientation drew on differing logics. For instance, within a conservative framing, constructions of childhood innocence and deficit perspectives of diverse sexualities combined to position the event as an attempt to corrupt the minds of innocent, vulnerable children. In contrast, indoctrination discourses within a liberal orientation problematised the showing of the film as a standalone, viewing this approach as lacking the 'neutrality' necessary for children to draw their own individual conclusions. While outside the scope of this chapter, it is worth noting that other discursive themes similarly provided access to such nuances between conservative and liberal lenses. For instance, while commentary within both orientations positioned watching the film as a waste of valuable learning time, such claims were underpinned by differing assumptions about education. Arguments reflecting a conservative framing demonstrated a perspective of education as preparation for work (Jones, 2013) whereas liberal commentary often drew on competitive global testing regimes such as PISA to argue the point.

Teasing out the nuances between conservative and liberal commentary is helpful in understanding how each orientation might function differently with similar purpose. Pinpointing these nuances may assist education researchers in speaking back to individual and institutional resistances to their research, as well as opposition to the inclusion of diverse sexualities in education. While for the most part, liberal perspectives were used to oppose *Gayby Baby*, sometimes they were supportive, for instance, with regard to individual student beliefs and choices about attending the film.

Given that conservative and liberal orientations were privileged in both media and the Education Minister's 'ban', it is worth noting that considerable online commentary demonstrated support for the planned event. Commentary within a critical orientation argued for the showing of *Gayby Baby* on the basis of including marginalised voices, encouraging respect for diversity, developing students as active, socially aware citizens, and preventing bullying and suicide. Such commentary provides researchers with evidence of public support for inclusion and representation of diverse sexualities in schools and provides a counter-narrative to oppositional discourses that might constrain methodological possibilities in such research. Comments reflecting a postmodern lens were extremely rare, but also demonstrated support for the showing of the film. Research about diverse genders and sexualities in education is often underpinned by theories that draw on postmodernism. As such, the lack of postmodern commentary is notable and provides insight into the landscape in which such work is undertaken. Several months after the *Gayby Baby* furore, another media panic unfolded, this time in relation to the Safe Schools Coalition (see Law, 2017). Media debates about Safe Schools introduced postmodern discourses into the mediascape. Consequently, further research exploring online commentary in response to Safe Schools media would provide an opportunity to examine whether postmodern concepts are now more evident in public discourse.

The methodology outlined in this chapter offers education researchers a useful approach in making sense of the broad range of discourses employed by digital citizens in a context of increasing online public commentary. Such an analysis provides scope for talking back to some of the resistances to research that has been positioned as controversial and dangerous. In this instance, the analysis showed that discourses supporting and rejecting representation of diverse sexualities and sexuality diverse families were evident in these data. This suggests that no matter what decisions government, policy makers, schools, universities, and educators make about including and representing diversity, there will be those who vehemently agree or disagree. Understanding the complexity of this space has the potential to empower decision-makers to consciously, rather than reactively, create policy and curricula that promotes inclusion and representation of diverse genders and sexualities, including same-sex parented families. Such moves help to challenge heteronormative discourses that silence diverse identities and family structures and create spaces of belonging for sexuality diverse families.

Note

1 Moral panic refers to when 'a condition, episode, person or group of persons emerges to become defined as a threat to societal values and interests' (Cohen, 2011 [1972], p. 1).

References

ABC News. (2015, August 27). 'If this was a film about disabilities or perhaps cultural diversity or ethnicity, I wonder whether or not we would see a similar kind of response', a child sexual development expert says [Facebook status update]. Retrieved from www.facebook.com/abcnews.au/posts/10154349836724988

Akerman, P. (2015a, August 26). Gay push should be kept out of schools. *The Daily Telegraph*, p. 4.

Allen, L., Rasmussen, M., Quinlivan, K., Aspin, C., Sanjakdar, F., & Brömdal, A. (2014). Who's afraid of sex at school? The politics of researching culture, religion and sexuality at school. *International Journal of Research and Method in Education*, 37(1), 34–43.

Australian Press Council. (2014). Statement of general principles. Retrieved 28 October, 2017, from www.presscouncil.org.au/statements-of-principles/

Bagshaw, E. (2015a, August 27). NSW Education Minister bans schools from screening gay film. *The Sydney Morning Herald*. Retrieved from www.smh.com.au

Bagshaw, E. (2015b, August 28). Gayby Baby: Education Minister Adrian Piccoli and Premier Mike Baird ban film without seeing it. *The Sydney Morning Herald*. Retrieved from www.smh.com.au

Banks, J. (1991). A curriculum for empowerment, action, and change. In C. E. Sleeter (Ed.), *Empowerment through multicultural education* (pp. 125–142). Chicago: The University of Chicago Press.

Baroutsis, A. (2017). Understanding media mentalities and logics: Institutional and journalistic practices, and the reporting of teachers' work. *Discourse: Studies in the Cultural Politics of Education*. doi:10.1080/01596306.2017.1399861

Barrett, M., & McIntosh, M. (1991). *The anti-social family* (2nd Ed.). London: Verso.

Board of Studies, NSW. (2003). Personal development health and physical education (PDHPE) 7–10 syllabus. Sydney: Board of Studies, NSW. Retrieved from NSW Education Standards Authority website http://educationstandards.nsw.edu.au/wps/portal/nesa/k-10/learning-areas/pdhpe/pdhpe-7-10

Bruns, A. (2003). Gatewatching, not gatekeeping: Collaborative online news. *Media International Australia, Incorporating Culture & Policy*, (107), 31–44. Retrieved from https://search.informit.com.au

Carrington, V. (2002). *New times: New families*. Dordrecht, The Netherlands: Kluwer Academic Publishers.

Cloughessy, K., & Waniganayake, M. (2014). Early childhood educators working with children who have lesbian, gay, bisexual and transgender parents: What does the literature tell us? *Early Child Development and Care*, 184(8), 1267–1280.

Cohen, S. (2011) [1972]. *Folk devils and moral panics*. London: Routledge.

Daily Telegraph. (2015, August 26). Parents are angry that a high school is making 1200 students watch a documentary on gay parenting instead of normal classes [Facebook status update]. Retrieved from www.facebook.com/dailytelegraph/posts/10152950839406105

Davies, C., & Robinson, K. H. (2013). Reconceptualising family: Negotiating sexuality in a governmental climate of neoliberalism. *Contemporary Issues in Early Childhood*, 14(1), 39–53.

DePalma, R., & Atkinson, E. (2009). 'No outsiders': Moving beyond a discourse of tolerance to challenge heteronormativity in primary schools. *British Educational Research Journal*, 35(6). 837–855.

Derman-Sparks, L., & Olsen Edwards, J. (2010). *Anti-bias education for young children and ourselves*. Washington DC: National Association for the Education of Young Children.

Devine, M. (2015, August 28). Gayby Baby imbroglio – Denials, fear and a lack of tolerance. *The Daily Telegraph*. Retrieved from www.dailytelegraph.com.au

Ferfolja, T. (2013). Sexual diversity, discrimination and 'homosexuality policy' in new south wales' government schools. *Sex Education*, 13(2), 159–171.

Ferfolja, T., & Ullman, J. (2017). Gender and sexuality in education and health: Voices advocating for equity and social justice. *Sex Education*, 17(3), 235–241.

Foucault, M. (2002) [1969]. *The archaeology of knowledge*. Tr. A. M. Sheridan Smith. Abingdon, Oxon: Routledge Classics.

Fraser, N. (2008). Reframing justice in a globalising world. In K. Olson (Ed.), *Adding insult to injury: Nancy Fraser debates her critics* (pp. 273–291). London: Verso.

Friend, C., & Singer, J. B. (2015). *Online journalism ethics: Traditions and transitions* [EBL version]. Abingdon, Oxon: Routledge. Retrieved from www.tandfebooks.com

Gay Class Uproar. (2015, August 26). *The Daily Telegraph*, p. 1.

Gayby Baby. (2015, August 26). Many of you will have seen the media coverage today over the screening of our films in schools. We firmly believe our film has positive benefits for all students and we're committed to supporting the schools who are celebrating Wear [Facebook status update]. Retrieved from www.facebook.com/GaybyBaby/posts/865235726864530

Gerathy, S. (2015, September 3). Gayby Baby: NSW Premier Mike Baird 'very distressed' over way documentary intervention played out. *ABC News*. Retrieved from www.abc.net.au/news/

Hudson, P. (2015, August 12). Coalition nails colours to traditional marriage. *The Australian*, p. 4.

Isin, E., & Ruppert, E. (2015). *Being digital citizens*. New York: Rowman & Littlefield.

Jensen, M. (2015, August 31). Whatever your thoughts on Gayby Baby, this wasn't about education. *ABC The Drum*. Retrieved from www.abc.net.au/news

Jeong, S. (2015, August 26). Gayby Baby film: Burwood Girls High School students find hypocrisy in debate. *Brisbane Times*. Retrieved from www.brisbanetimes.com.au.

Jones, T. M. (2009). Framing the framework: Discourses in Australia's National Values Education policy. *Educational Research for Policy and Practice*, 8(1), 35–57.

Jones, T. (2011a). A sexuality education discourses framework: Conservative, liberal, critical, and postmodern. *American Journal of Sexuality Education*, 6(2), 133–175.

Jones, T. M. (2011b). Saving rhetorical children: Sexuality education discourses from conservative to post-modern. *Sex Education*, 11(4), 369–387.

Jones, T. (2013). *Understanding education policy: The 'four education orientations' framework*. Dordrecht: Springer.

Law, B. (2017). Moral panic 101: Equality, acceptance and the Safe Schools Scandal. *Quarterly Essay, 67* (pp. 1–80). Australia: Schwartz Publishing Pty Ltd

Mars, C. (Producer), & Newell, M. (Director). (2015). *Gayby Baby*. Australia: Marla House.

McCluskey, M., & Hmielowski, J. (2012). Opinion expression during social conflict: Comparing online reader comments and letters to the editor. *Journalism*, 13(3), 303–319.

McDougall, B. (2015, August 26). Anger over school's gay parenting doco. *The Daily Telegraph*, p. 4.

McKenna, K. Y. A., & Green, A. S. (2002). Virtual group dynamics. *Group Dynamics*, 6(1), 116–127. doi:10.1037//1089-2699.6.1.116

McNaughton, G. (2003). *Shaping early childhood*. Maidenhead, Berkshire: Open University Press.

Ministerial Council on Education, Employment, Training and Youth Affairs. (2008). Melbourne declaration on educational goals for young Australians. Retrieved from www.curriculum.edu.au/verve/_resources/National_Declaration_on_the_Educational_Goals_for_Young_Australians.pdf

Mitchell, A., Gottfried, J., Shearer, E., & Lu, K. (2017). How Americans encounter, recall and act upon digital news. Retrieved from Pew Research Center, Journalism and Media website www.journalism.org/2017/02/09/part-i-an-analysis-of-individuals-online-news-habits-over-the-course-of-one-week/

Mossberger, K., Tolbert, C. J., & McNeal, R. S. (2008). *Digital citizenship: The internet, society, and participation* [EBL version]. Cambridge, Mass: MIT Press. Retrieved from https://ebookcentral.proquest.com

NSW Education Standards Authority. (n.d.). *NSW English K-10 Syllabus: Learning across the curriculum*. Retrieved from http://syllabus.nesa.nsw.edu.au/english/english-k10/learning-across-the-curriculum/

Robinson, K. (2008). In the name of 'Childhood innocence': A discursive exploration of the moral panic associated with childhood and sexuality. *Cultural Studies Review*, 14(2), 113.

Robinson, K. (2013). *Innocence, knowledge, and the construction of childhood: The contradictory nature of sexuality and censorship in children's contemporary lives*. Abingdon, Oxon: Routledge.

Safi, M. (2015a, August 26). Sydney school received no complaints from parents about Gayby Baby film. *The Guardian*. Retrieved from www.theguardian.com

Safi, M. (2015b, August 27). Daniel Andrews attacks NSW government over Gayby Baby 'rubbish'. *The Guardian*. Retrieved from www.theguardian.com

Santana, A. D. (2014). Virtuous or vitriolic: The effect of anonymity on civility in online newspaper reader comment boards. *Journalism Practice*, 8(1), 18–33.

Schools learn their PC before the ABC [Editorial]. (2015a, August 26). *The Daily Telegraph*, p. 24.

Schools learn their PC before the ABC [Editorial] [Electronic version]. (2015b, August 26). *The Daily Telegraph*. Retrieved from www.dailytelegraph.com.au

Shannon, B., & Smith, S. J. (2017). Dogma before diversity: The contradictory rhetoric of controversy and diversity in the politicisation of Australian queer-affirming learning materials. *Sex Education*, 17(3), 242–255. Smith, C. (Host). (2015, August 26). *The Alan Jones Breakfast Show* [Radio Program]. Sydney: 2GB. Retrieved 29 April, 2016, from www.2gb.com/audioplayer/124411

Smith, C. (Host). (2015, August 26). *The Alan Jones Breakfast Show* [Radio Program]. Sydney: 2GB. Retrieved 29 April, 2016, from http://www.2gb.com/audioplayer/124411

Starts at 60. (2015, August 26). This video has been banned by the Education Minister, after parents' complaints. See the film everyone's been talking about and tell us, would you care if this were shown in your grandchildren's school? [Facebook status update]. Retrieved from www.facebook.com/startsat60/posts/1046684302032258

The Project. (2015, August 26). We discuss the outrage over the proposed 'Gayby Baby' screening at a Sydney high school #TheProjectTV [Video file]. Retrieved from www.facebook.com/TheProjectTV/videos/10153102555843441/

Vincent, C. (2000). *Including parents? Education, citizenship and parental agency*. Buckingham: Open University Press.

Warner, M. (1993). *Fear of a queer planet: Queer politics and social theory*. Minneapolis: University of Minnesota Press.

Wear It Purple. (n.d.) About wear it purple. Retrieved 8 October, 2017, from http://wearitpurple.org/about-wear-it-purple/

PART II
Communicating education research using traditional and social media

6

ENTERING THE POLITICAL FRAY: THE ROLE OF PUBLIC EDUCATION SCHOLARS IN MEDIA DEBATES

Cynthia Gerstl-Pepin and Cynthia Reyes

Introduction

Information in democracies across the globe has become more dispersed with the demise of print media and the proliferation of web 2.0 and web-based media sources (Mitchell & Holcomb, 2016; Newman, 2009; Varney, 2011). Media coverage of political issues has undergone disruption as the field of journalism has declined in the United States (Mitchell & Holcomb, 2016). Coverage of educational policy issues and school reform has been particularly affected; education reporters were often the first news jobs to be eliminated with print media downsizing due to the loss of advertising revenue (Mitchell & Holcomb, 2016; Tucker, 2016). High quality journalism with its emphasis on nonpartisanship and factual accuracy has been greatly reduced and with it the news media's historic role in supporting a free and self-governing democracy (McChesney, 2015). News sources have also greatly diminished in favour of value-laden citizen journalism. One only has to look at news coverage of the aftermath of the 2016 presidential election in the United States (US) to see a salient example of how social media can be used for political campaigning and controlling policy narratives (Allcott & Gentzkow, 2017; Bertoni, 2016; Dewey, 2016; Milbank, 2016; Silverman, 2016) and the use of 'alternative facts' as a media strategy (Bradner, 2017; Newman, 2017; Sinderbrand, 2017). An equally concerning trend is the decentralisation of news 'coverage' in online sources and social media outlets which has both the promise of engaging a broader public, and simultaneously the potential to weaken democracy by serving only as an 'echo chamber' or 'filter bubble' where truth is self-generated with only like-minded citizens (Allcott & Gentzkow, 2017; McGuinn & Supovitz, 2016). The demise of traditional media spaces and social media tribalism creates both an opportunity and a need for public scholars to fill the gap in terms of supporting well informed educational policy decisionmaking.

The role that social media plays in educational policy debates is an emerging field, given that media communication and social media venues are increasingly serving news sources for citizens in a democracy (Gerstl-Pepin, 2002; 2015). With the demise of print newspapers, digital media communication via web 2.0 such as blogs, Facebook and Twitter provide new outlets for public dialogue and advocacy, yet scant research exists about their potential role in education policy debates (Supovitz, Daly, & del Fresno, 2015) or the role that scholars themselves play in these debates (Gerstl-Pepin & Reyes, 2015). As Halpern and Gibbs (2012) noted, 'although social media may not provide a forum for intensive or in-depth policy debate, it nevertheless provides a deliberative space to discuss and encourage political participation, both directly and indirectly' (pp. 115–116).

In the midst of this shift, educational research outlets have also undergone transformation. We now have online journals, some of which are open source, making their published research free and available to all, but we know very little about the role this plays in educational research (Veletsianos & Kimmons, 2012). These shifts have highlighted how social media has gained in popularity as a source through which the public understands educational problems and the policy needed to remedy them. Within this shifting context, education scholars have ventured into social media as an outlet for their scholarship via such outlets as Twitter and Facebook by sharing and promoting their research through these venues (Gerstl-Pepin & Reyes, 2015).

On the one hand this proliferation can be seen as democratizing the media, as now everyone potentially has a voice in one of these venues. Unfortunately, this also means that the usual controls over media reporting, such as fact checking, do not exist in most social media realms. The 2016 presidential election in the US highlighted this shift in dramatic ways. Immediately following the inauguration, President Trump's campaign spokesperson, Kelly Ann Conway, disputed factual information by talking about 'alternative facts' to describe when President Trump presents an unsubstantiated viewpoint via Twitter; a reference that many harkened back to George Orwell's book *1984* (Bradner, 2017; Newman, 2017; Sinderbrand, 2017). President Trump's overestimation of the size of the crowd that attended his inauguration was the first of many alternative facts that Trump and his administration would assert via Twitter. Other research by Barbera et al. (2015) suggested that 'communication structures are dynamic and flexible and that citizens do come into contact with information from diverse ideological perspectives' (p. 10). Therefore, social media does have the potential to serve as a venue through which to cross party lines and value systems. In media arenas anyone can claim to know the truth these days even if what they say is unsubstantiated or ungrounded in high quality, rigorous research.

In her 2016 Presidential Address to the American Educational Research Association conference (one of the more eminent educational research conferences in the U.S.), Jeannie Oakes (2017) utilised Nichols' (2018) *The Death of Expertise* to argue that the purpose of scholarship should be to counter the idea that everything is knowable and that every idea is as good as any other. Oakes (2017) suggests that educational researchers have a responsibility to counter unsubstantiated claims and faulty research. 'Going public' then requires that public scholarship is rigorous and trustworthy and... 'deepens scholars' knowledge production because when it is done well, it is inclusive and empowering – both for education professionals and the publics who are facing immediate problems' (Oakes, 2017, p. 92). Additionally, Rogoff (2018) described how researchers have an ethical responsibility to act as 'stewards' and should translate their research so that it can serve the needs of schools, families, teachers, and students. Stewardship becomes central to the idea of safe-guarding the ethical nature of doing educational research. Entering the political fray as an education scholar can be seen as an ethical obligation and responsibility if one wants their scholarship to have an impact on political decisionmaking.

A few brave individuals have sought to enter the political fray to serve as public scholars via direct sharing through social media such as Twitter and blogging and/or engaging in traditional media routes by serving as experts in traditional media articles or broadcast news. Given the new terrain of serving as an engaged scholar, it is important to understand how this work is conducted and the role researchers are playing as public scholars in this emerging discourse space (Gerstl-Pepin & Reyes, 2015).

In this chapter, we explore the multiple ways US educational researchers have engaged in national and global media debates as they seek to make their work more accessible to policymakers, the general public, and those most affected by educational policies such as teachers, parents, students, and community members. We define education researchers who seek to challenge misconceptions of educational policy issues in news media reporting and public arenas as public scholars. These media dialogues they seek to inform are conceptualised as being embedded with inequitable power relations that can often operate invisibly and limit participation. We used the term public scholar as opposed to the more traditional terms of public intellectual to refer to educational researchers who seek to challenge misconceptions of educational issues in news media reports and public arenas (Gerstl-Pepin & Reyes, 2015). In particular, the paper reports on a media content analysis (Altheide & Schneider, 2012) conducted on the work of public scholars who are engaged in public dialogues in both electronic and print media. How do educational scholars enter public policy dialogues on education? What strategies do they use to inform the public and enter contested public dialogues?

Conceptual framework

The role of media related to educational policy can be conceptualised through the concept of the public sphere. Habermas (1962/1989) theorised the public sphere as the arena through which dialogue in a democracy occurs and differences can be mediated. The public sphere arbitrates the relationship between the state, citizens, and the economy. Thus, it can be seen as 'a theater in modern societies in which political participation is enacted through the medium of talk' (Fraser, 2008, p. 57). Traditional media sources operate as a type of 'thin' public where major outlets control the flow of information about issues such as education reform; and education topics are treated superficially, not informed by research but rather values (Gerstl-Pepin, 2002; 2007). Power relations in media representation can often operate invisibly and limit participation (Williams & Carpini, 2008), therefore, one purpose of this chapter is to understand the strategies educational researchers use to participate in this limited space.

In the new age of social media there is an assumption that social media serve as a form of direct democracy. In terms of Habermas' theory, they could be perceived as a new, more equitable form of the public sphere. We will suggest in this chapter that it too serves as a 'thin' public where power and information can be controlled and manipulated. Under the right circumstances collective action can be fomented (Bennet, 2012) as with the wave of state-wide public teacher strikes in West Virginia, Oklahoma, and other American states in 2018 (Fernández Campbell, 2018). Power within this space, though, is still limited and social inequities often operate invisibly.

Methodology

Given the exploratory nature of the study, the research utilises media content analysis (Altheide & Schneider, 2012) as a means for examining media documents created by public education scholars. Media content analysis is a methodological approach aimed at analysing media documents:

> by studying documents as representations of social meanings and institutional relations. Documents are studied to understand culture—or the process and the array of objects, symbols, and meanings that make up the social reality shared by members of a society.
>
> *(p. 5)*

Content analysis does not seek literal interpretation but rather it seeks to identify motifs or trends that are not immediately observable. This process is methodical and it 'involves discerning meaning about attitudes, symbols, cultures, and institutions from which inferences are immediately drawn' (Saraisky, 2015, p. 27). Often compared to discourse analysis with relation to epistemology, content analysis is still seen as different because while both engage in textual analysis, content analysis relies on the idea that meaning can be coded and totaled while discourse analysis is more subjective and interpretivist (Saraisky, 2015). Content analysis generally uses *a priori* codes that can assist the researcher with discerning patterns. A notable form of content analysis is media analysis because media are generally regarded as playing a significant role in interpreting and circulating public policy. As such, media documents such as digital media forms are data to be analysed within a specific cultural context similar to observational and interview data in ethnography. This approach provided a way to interpret media artifacts, specifically public media biographies and public writings, of a diverse set of public scholars.

The scholars were selected using a combination of criterion-based and maximum variation sampling (Patton, 2014). Criterion-based sampling was used to identify four scholars that had successfully entered national debates and were cited and/or contributed to media reports on education and who in 2016 (when we started our research) were listed in at least the top 20 of *Education Week*'s annual Edu-Scholar Public Influence Rankings (Hess, 2016a, 2016b, 2017a, 2017b, 2018a, 2018b). These high-profile scholars actively engaged in educational policy dialogues via multiple strategies including social media platforms (e.g. Twitter), blogs, newspaper letters to the editor, critiques of research, published scholarly work, newspaper and magazine articles, and expert testimony/media interviews to inform educational policy dialogues concerning such topics related to school reform and educational policy. They were relatively diverse in terms of their gender (two are female and two are male; we are unsure of whether they are non gender conforming), race/ethnicity (two are persons of colour and one immigrated to the US), geography (representing East coast, West coast and the Mid-west), and they vary in terms of how they engage in public arenas of political discourse, but are less diverse in terms of the intersection of race and gender. We intentionally searched for scholars of colour and found that the field of public scholars is relatively homogeneous. We tried to balance the diversity of the scholars we examined with the types of strategies they used and sought scholars whose narratives would represent different approaches to public scholarship both in terms of their research agenda and media strategies.

The writings and biographies of these four public education scholars were collected through internet searches (such as Google scholar, Firefox, and Safari) and through the LexisNexis database over the past five years. These scholars were actively engaged in public media dialogues addressing public misconceptions that were unsubstantiated by quality research. Data analysis on these data sources involved extensive reading, focused coding, sorting, and then writing summaries of themes that emerged. The focused coding frames we used sought to understand who the scholars were in terms of their training, work experience, and scholarly agenda. We also examined the venues in which they published their research and the strategies they used to communicate their work through media venues.

We decided to identify the scholars we studied. We only used publically accessible data and while media content analysis does not technically qualify as human subjects research we acknowledge that in identifying our scholars there is a potential for harm (Zimmer, 2010). We only used publically accessible data and did not examine Facebook data which requires one to become a 'friend' in order to access data. Instead we focused on publically accessible data and data where the scholars were publically attempting to share their research and expert knowledge. Additionally, we focused on the strengths of their work as public scholars. We felt the risks of naming the scholars were worth the value of the reader being able to assess the work of the scholars themselves and to aid in the credibility of our research and to aid in transparency (Patton, 2014). Given the scholars are openly entering the political fray, this type of transparency and public focus seemed appropriate to the research.

Education scholars as public influencers

The voices of those who commit to being public scholars in the world of education are varied and diverse. Three of the scholars, Pedro Noguera, Sara Goldrick-Rab, and Yong Zhao, took a more traditional path in academia starting out as assistant professors and working their way up to the rank of full professor, while the fourth, Diane Ravitch, worked primarily in Washington, D.C. directly on educational policy issues for the government and for a think tank. When we first began our search for academics who were carrying on with their teaching, research, and service while also engaging in social media platforms such as blogging, we perceived the blogosphere to be more generally inhabited by white male scholars. We wondered, even, about the limitations of ontological public scholarship and the ethical and moral dilemmas that people of colour (e.g., see writings from Leigh Patel) and indigenous faculty (e.g., see writings on settler colonisation from Linda Tuhiwai Smith and Eve Tuck) continue to face when questioning how knowledge is claimed in the academy. Nevertheless, given these larger fundamental questions we wanted to establish a starting point, and as we strived to search for more female and faculty of colour public scholars we eventually settled on the previously mentioned scholars for their prominence on the internet. As we chose these names, we also understood that the fluidity and growth of public scholarship would continue even as we focused on just these four. The one unifying element that ties the work of these scholars together is their credibility and participation in national media outlets. Their public work is very intentional in terms of how they frame educational issues through the news media, public discussions about education, social media, and alternative internet outlets such as blogging. Rather than let public figures without much training in research or background in education alone influence how educational issues are portrayed and represented in these public arenas, they choose to enter the political fray. Nichols (2018) argued that today's populism has particular contempt for scholars be they in the field of education, politics, and even science undermining institutions, rational debate, and even the way we lead our lives. According to Nichols (2018), there is a rising tide of public anger toward the rule of experts and it is this quagmire that we argue our public scholars have chosen to enter in order to maintain stewardship over the most pressing issues related to the educational field and to strive to maintain national attention to the more vulnerable voices at stake such as our children and teachers.

As noted in the methodology section, each of the four scholars selected for examination are considered to be media influencers according to the *Education Week*'s Edu-Scholar Public Influence Rankings compiled by Rick Hess (2010b, 2012b, 2013b, 2014b, 2015b, 2016b, 2017b, 2018b). Although we use this list to identify some of the most prominent public scholars of education, an examination of the ranking system itself serves as an object lesson in how power dynamics subtly and often invisibly shape public discourse. The rankings officially started in 2010, and purport to identify the top 200 'university-based scholars in the US who are doing the most to shape educational practice and policy' (Hess, 2018a). The ranking scores encompass several categories including Google Scholar citations, books, Amazon rankings, education press mentions, web mentions, newspaper mentions, Congressional Record mentions, and Klout points. Klout points are determined by a website that measures online public influence and branding on a scale from one to 100 on social networks such as Twitter, LinkedIn, and Facebook (Updyke, 2013). The compiler of these rankings, Rich Hess, openly acknowledges their limitations each year, 'I'm not sure that I've got the measures right or even how much these results can or should tell us' (Hess, 2017b, p. 1). Despite this disclaimer, the rankings tend to be valued by U.S. universities and are promoted in public relations strategies. Higher education institutions such as New York University (2018), the University of Pennsylvania (2018), and Stanford University (2018) promote them as an honour similar to how the US News & World Report rankings as used by universities in the US as marketing tools to show quality and competitiveness (Gnolek, Falciano, & Kuncl, 2014). Moreover, the rankings can also enable journalists from traditional media to identity experts who they can approach for help or comment, and thus have the potential to serve as a gatekeeper that determines which voices get heard more frequently.

These rankings are as problematic as the US News & World Report rankings on universities and colleges, in that they are not fully transparent and represent a certain perspective on what constitutes public influence in education. For example, one fourth of the list is nominated by a select group of the top 150 scholars who are selected by Rick Hess (between 27–31 members of the list). It is unclear how this group is chosen or what the process is by which the additional 50 are selected to be added to the list. The top 150 Edu-Scholars from the previous year are automatically included in the rankings for the next year and a subset of the automatic qualifiers (somewhere between 26 and 31) nominate the bottom 50 who are referred to 'at-large' nominees. This serves as a type of safety net for the previously ranked scholars. The top 150 are assured to be on the list the following year. It also limits who can join the list. The only way on the list at this point is to be nominated by one of the scholars that Hess selects from the previous year. The exclusionary feature of how new individuals are selected for the list is not openly touted as limiting by Hess even though it essentially creates an exclusive membership where you have to know one of the elite members of the club in order to gain entrance. One also can't help but wonder as the metrics are tweaked each year, whether the measurement tweaks might benefit certain members.

A review of the rankings from 2010 to 2018 suggest that the four scholars we examined have been highly successful on the indicators used in the Edu-Scholar rankings (see Table 6.1) and have either held steady or gained in prominence over time. While Zhao was not ranked for the first two years of the rankings, presumably someone nominated him to the list and he quickly rose to the eighth spot on the rankings in 2013 and has remained in the top 20 since then. Goldrick-Rab has climbed steadily in the rankings since the beginning entering the top 10 in the past two years. Noguera has also maintained top 20 status and Ravitch has been ranked first or second with the exception of 2018 when she moved to fifth place.

TABLE 6.1 Edu-Scholar rankings from 2010–2018

Year	Ravitch	Noguera	Goldrick-Rab	Zhao
2018 Rank	5	12	7	18
2017 Rank	2	7	10	16
2016 Rank	2	7	13	8
2015 Rank	1	11	29	9
2014 Rank	2	20	62	9
2013 Rank*	1	15	60	8
2012 Rank	2	8	31	–
2010/11 Rank	1	8	68	–

*Klout score added in 2013

Over the years since the ranking's inception, Hess has tweaked with the way the rankings are measured which has led to some volatility in how scholars are ranked. Table 6.1 shows the rankings since 2010 for the four scholars we studied (Hess, 2010a, 2012a, 2013a, 2014a, 2015a, 2016a, 2017a, 2018a). It makes one wonder who else might be neglected from the list.

A Google search on April 29, 2018 on each of the four scholars' studied (Ravitch, Noguera, Zhao, and Goldrick-Rab) limited to the news stories tab and limited to the name of the scholar and the word education drew interesting results (non-relevant entries of incorrect persons were deleted). A search for Yong Zhao yielded 380 Google news results, compared to a search for Pedro A. Noguera which yielded 730 news results, a Sara Goldrick-Rab search yielded 1,150 Google news results, and a search for Diane Ravitch yielded 3,290 Google news results. While only one measure, this search suggests that Diane Ravitch's reach to national news media is significant in comparison to the other three scholars examined. Edu-Scholar disaggregates via newspaper mentions, education press mentions, and web mentions. While these rankings have gained prominence in academic circles they should be looked at with a great deal of skepticism as indicators of a scholar's public influence particularly as it relates to the discourse on education policy. These are all indirect measures and do not assert a causal relationship between their activities and policy influence. The one category that is more direct in terms of policy influence is the Congressional Record mentions. This is a category where very few scholars on the list score any points. In 2018, Diane Ravitch scored five points in this category and was the only member of the list to score any points (Hess, 2018b). The rankings should not be assumed to be a clear indicator of media influence, as the list is slanted toward scholars who know other scholars on the list. How scholars judge influence is not necessarily reflective of how policymakers of the general public view influence.

While establishing credibility and prowess as a scholar is a prerequisite for being on the Edu-Scholar Public Influencer list, the type of research that one does is also critical. Bruer (2016) conducted an analysis of the Edu-Scholar rankings and concluded that certain research communities were over represented in the rankings while others were under represented. As Bruer (2016) noted in his analysis, 'the work of some research communities is perceived to have broader policy implications or having more general interest than others' (p. 4). Based on his bibliometric analysis the three largest research communities are instructional design, motivation, and science education. He found that these areas were under represented in the rankings while the fields of School Organisation and Management and Politics and Education were over represented (Bruer, 2016). However, despite its limitations, it remains one of the very few tools at our disposal to make an initial screen for public impact, particularly when applied to the highest ranked names on the list, where the sheer volume of public participation creates some separation from others lower down.

The next four sections outline the scholarship and the main media strategies the four scholars studied used to enter public discussions on educational policy and school reform.

Overview: Diane Ravitch

Unlike the other three scholars who hold traditional faculty positions, Diane Ravitch is currently a Research Professor at New York University. She describes herself as 'a historian of education' and the founder and President of the Network for Public Education (Ravitch, 2018). Ravitch co-founded the Network for Public Education (NPE) in 2013 – 'an advocacy group whose mission is to preserve, promote, improve and strengthen public schools for both current and future generation of students' (Network for Public Education, 2018). Compared to most scholars on the Edu-Scholar Public Influence Rankings, Diane Ravitch has an unusual background. According to her website (Ravitch, 2018), from 1991 to 1993 she was Assistant Secretary of Education and Counselor to Secretary of Education Lamar Alexander when George H.W. Bush was President. As Assistant Secretary, 'she led the federal effort to promote the creation of voluntary state and national academic standards' (Ravitch, 2018).

Later in her career, from 1997 to 2004, Secretary of Education Richard Riley (under the Bill Clinton Presidency) appointed her to the National Assessment Governing Board, the group that is responsible for the federal testing program: the National Assessment of Educational Progress. Ravitch also held the Brown Chair in Education Studies at the Brookings Institution and edited *Brookings Papers on Education Policy*. If we look at the Google Scholar citation metric, an indicator of scholarly prowess, as of May 6, 2018, Ravitch leads the four scholars with 16,155 citations and a total h-index 41 (author-level metric measures the impact of a scholar in terms of number of citations across their work). Unencumbered with the trappings of a traditional academic position, Ravitch appears to devote significant time to her online presence. She is a frequent commentator and writer for *The New York Times, Huffington Post, The New York Review of Books*, and has a personal blog with over 16,000 posts and 149,000 Twitter followers. Her public presence appears to be significant. One of her significant strategies for influence is her own writing in newspapers both electronic and print.

Overview: Pedro Noguera

Dr. Noguera was trained as a sociologist. He is currently a Distinguished Professor of Education at the University of California at Los Angeles. As Noguera notes in his bio, his scholarship 'focuses on the ways in which schools are influenced by social and economic conditions as well as by demographic trends in local, regional and global contexts' (Noguera, 2018). He started out as a classroom teacher K-12 in 1981 and was an executive assistant to the mayor of Berkeley, California and later was President of the School Board for the Berkeley Unified School District. Noguera's public scholarship includes serving on the boards of numerous national and local organizations. As of early May, 2018, he did not have an open Google Scholar profile. Noguera is represented by an agent for his speaking engagements and receives $12,500 to $17,500 for lecture appearances (Cassidy and Fishman, Inc., 2018). He also appears as a regular commentator on educational issues on CNN, MSNBC, National Public Radio, and other national news outlets. Noguera is also a prolific writer for the *The Nation* and *Huffington Post* (with over 70 articles in popular press and practitioner outlets), and he also has 30,600 Twitter followers.

Overview: Sara Goldrick-Rab

Sara Goldrick-Rab received a Ph.D. in Sociology in 2004 from the University of Pennsylvania. She is Professor of Higher Education Policy and Sociology at Temple University. Goldrick-Rab is a self-described 'scholar-activist with a singular mission to identify novel approaches to making higher education the accessible and affordable place that families want and need it to be' (Goldrick-Rab, 2018a). She founded the Wisconsin HOPE laboratory aimed at supporting ways that college can be affordable, and also the Faculty and Students Together (FAST) Fund for struggling college students (Goldrick-Rab, 2018c). Her commitment to scholar-activism is evident in her broad profile of research and writing that explores 'the intended and unintended consequences of the college-for-all movement in the United States' (Goldrick-Rab, 2018b). Goldrick-Rab examines transfer practices, welfare reform, and financial aid policies as they relate to college students. She has 2,690 citations on Google Scholar and an h-index of 26 which is relatively modest compared to Ravitch and Zhao. Goldrick-Rab is a frequent commentator for *The Nation, Time Magazine, The New York Times, Inside Higher Ed, Washington Post, American RadioWorks*, has appeared on the Daily Show with Trevor Noah (Goldrick-Rab, 2018a), and has 26,200 Twitter followers.

Overview: Yong Zhao

Yong Zhao received his Ph.D. in Educational Psychology in 1996 from the University of Illinois at Urbana-Champlain. He is currently a Foundation Distinguished Professor in the School of Education at the University of Kansas. Zhao is also a Global Chair at the University of Bath in the United Kingdom and a fellow at the Mitchell Institute for Health and Education Policy at Victoria University in Australia. According to his website his scholarship focuses 'on the implications of globalization and technology on education' (Zhao, 2018). He started his career as a middle school English teacher and Lecturer of English and Methodology in Sichuan, China and then immigrated to the US. Zhao has amassed 11,905 citations according to Google Scholar and an h-index of 48. Zhao has written in Chinese for a Chinese Information Technology and Education Magazine called *Educational Technology Information*, has developed several software and web projects, is a personal blogger and frequent writer for *Education Week*, has given 121 invited presentations around the world, and has 28,000 Twitter followers.

Themes across public scholars

In conducting the content analysis, we focused on four broad themes: 1) How are the scholars credible in terms of their training, their experience, and their career? 2) What public engagement strategies do they use? 3) How do they use their research to inform policy? 4) What are the dangers and benefits of this type of work? We wrote case studies for each of the scholars beginning with a biography describing their trajectory in higher education including where they worked and the language they used to describe their own scholarship and areas of expertise. The case studies also included their publications in the traditional venues including peer-reviewed journals and books to book chapters. Then we examined the social tools they used to communicate their work, focusing on topics of interest that they highlighted as well as aligned with the more traditional academic journals. After we coded the scholars' data, we shared our case study findings on a google doc that we shared with each other, again returning to our criteria and discussing what we discovered from our content analyses.

Several themes emerged in the analysis in terms of the strategies used by each of the four scholars we reviewed. First, each scholar had established credibility through a solid body of research. Second, their research had direct implications for policy. Third, they are what might be referred to as a multitool player, in other words, they use a wide variety of strategies to share their expertise with the public and to inform public dialogues on educational policy. Finally, Goldrick-Rab's brush with controversy also generated a theme related to the potential dangers of doing this type of public engagement. In the next sections, we will lay out the four themes.

Establishing credibility

When we examined the careers of the four scholars, it was clear that the first criterion for establishing credibility is high quality, refereed research. All four have highly regarded and credible bodies of established research that are well cited per Google Scholar's h-index, a measure of a scholar's research impact, both in terms of the number of publications and the number of citations for each publication

(Hirsch, 2005). While what constitutes an excellent h-index varies from discipline to discipline, Hirsch (2005) suggested that an h-index of 20 or more indicated that a scholar was successful. Each of the scholars studied have won awards for their scholarship and they have all written successful books. As noted in their biographical overviews, Noguera, Zhao, and Goldrick-Rab are full professors, and Ravitch is a Research Professor with significant credibility from her work in Washington for the Department of Education under Presidents George H. W. Bush and William J. Clinton. Their *curriculum vitae* indicate publishing prowess, presenting and speaking effectiveness, and numerous awards for their research.

An array of public engagement strategies

Ravitch, Noguera, Zhao, and Goldrick-Rab transcend the traditional venues for scholarly research communication (journal publications, books, and speaking engagements). Added to activity in these traditional forms of communication, they are all active on Twitter with a significant community of followers, they have engaged in writing for popular press venues, they offer their expert commentary for news media outlets, they speak to policy implications in public forums, they own and maintain personal websites, and are active in public speaking engagements (Goldrick-Rab, 2018b; Noguera, 2018; Ravitch, 2018; Zhao, 2018). Noguera has his own website for booking speaking engagements (www.pedronoguera.com/). Godrick-Rab featured her book *Paying the Price* on Comedy Central when she interviewed with Noah Trevor, a South African comedian, writer, and producer reaching an audience of mostly young viewers (Daily Show, 2016).

Adding to their repertoire, Ravitch and Zhao are also active bloggers (Ravitch, 2018; Zhao, 2018). Ravitch is especially voluminous in her writing for popular press and practitioner venues with over 120 pieces (Ravitch, 2018). Noguera (2018) has also written over 60 of these types of pieces. Each is not only a prolific writer but are also an excellent communicator via multiple news media and social media venues.

Engaging in scholarship that informs policy dialogue

Ravitch's research directly critiques the Common Core, standardised testing, and charter schools which are all hot button policy issues. This also forms the primary theme for her writing in elite news media outlets. For example, since President Trump's selection of Betsy DeVos to run the federal Department of Education, Ravitch's commentary in media outlets such as the *The New York Times Review of Books* has been very critical of DeVos (Ravitch, 2017). She has also used a media platform of her nonprofit, Network for Public Education, to openly criticise DeVos' stand on charter schools and vouchers. This has been echoed through reports in news media sources such as *HuffPost* (Singer, 2017).

Goldrick-Rab's public engagement is very focused on the economic struggles of students in college. Her research on college affordability, financial aid, and food insecurity among college students has particular resonance as families and students in the US struggle to pay the increasing costs of postsecondary education. Goldrick-Rab, in the 2016 publication of her book *Paying the Price: College Costs, Financial Aid, and the Betrayal of the American Dream*, led to opportunities to give expert commentary on how college students are struggling with food insecurity and insufficient financial aid. For example, she appeared on C-SPAN and the Daily Show to discuss the contents of the book (C-SPAN, 2016; Daily Show, 2016).

Pedro Noguera's research speaks directly to the achievement gap for African American and Latinx students and a number of topics related to social inequity. Recently he has focused some of his public commentary on the planned closing of the DACA (Deferred Action for Childhood Arrivals) program, which protects immigrants who were brought to the US illegally while they were very young children. For example, in 2017 Noguera wrote a short commentary for *HuffPost* featuring a personal story about a young Dreamer named Miguel, to critique the attempt to rescind DACA. As Noguera noted,

> Vilifying immigrants in order to justify attacks against them is an old tactic first used by nativists to justify discrimination against the Irish, and later to rationalize that exclusion acts that targeted immigrants from Asia in the late 19th century.
>
> (Noguera, 2017)

This is also a good example of how public scholars can adjust their rhetorical styles when seeking to reach a wider audience. Rather than using statistical tables or dense critical theory, Noguera shaped his argument around a single individual to humanise the program and to give his research evidence an added emotional resonance.

Yong Zhao's scholarship on creativity and innovation in the US and China speaks directly to concerns about testing, failing schools, and international competition with China. He has been sought out by news outlets such as the *The New York Times* and *CNN* to provide commentary and compare the Chinese and US education systems often stressing there are problems with the Chinese education system, such as its high-pressure testing system that should not be emulated (Strauss, 2017; Zhao, 2018). As he noted in a CNN opinion piece where he argued that, while there are benefits to the Chinese education system, there are also downsides: 'Stress, anxiety, poor physical health and a lack of social and practical life skills are well-known characteristics of Chinese students' (Zhao, 2014). Zhao's scholarship speaks directly to US fears concerning economic competition with China, a controversial topic which he is well suited to inform.

Each of the four scholars studied provide expert commentary in numerous media outlets related to their areas of research knowledge. In each case they use research and evidence to make their points as well as well reasoned arguments. They use multiple avenues (high quality scholarship including books, a social media presence, media commentary, expert commentary, news interviews, and public speaking engagements) to share their research. Through these multiple communication avenues, they inform the public about their research and the available evidence we have about how to improve education and support vulnerable populations.

To be effective in these multiple public arenas, these scholars often shift their rhetorical style to fit the audience. The language used to gain publication in a highly competitive refereed journal is significantly more education jargon prone compared to how one might talk on the *Daily Show* or CNN where stories of personal struggle may carry more emotional weight and pull for an audience. These scholars are versatile in shifting their discourse to suit a particular audience.

Outweighing the dangers of public scholarship

While this chapter explores how scholars promote their work in the public sphere, it is important to note that this type of engagement also has its dangers. Putting oneself in the public eye also can open oneself up to criticisms. Goldrick-Rab is one scholar who has personally experienced this type of controversy while she was still at the University of Wisconsin (she subsequently moved to Temple University). Frustrated over Governor Scott Walker's removal of tenure protections, she communicated via Twitter that she had a discussion with her grandfather about the similarities between Governor Walker and Hitler and in a later tweet called Governor Walker and other legislators fascists (Jaschik, 2015). These comments set off a social media backlash and she received negative comments including anti-Semitic comments and calls for her firing via email, snail mail, and social media (Jaschik, 2015; Supiano, 2016). Things further escalated when she questioned the decision of students to attend Wisconsin after tenure was abolished, arguing that the quality of the education would be diminished without tenure.

Goldrick-Rab continued to focus on her research and did not slow down her media presence despite the fact that faculty and administrators at Wisconsin were also angered by her criticisms of the University (Jaschik, 2015; Supiano, 2016). She subsequently moved to Temple University which has a faculty union, tenure, and a diverse student body. This example shows the potential dangers of being a public scholar. At the time Goldrick-Rab was a highly successful scholar. Calls for her firing were ignored and she was able to find a new job with tenure. An assistant professor may not have been so fortunate. A less savvy professor may have also suffered professionally from the threats she received.

According to Oakes (2017), the challenges with the advocacy work that Goldrick-Rab experienced and others like her in higher education is not surprising given the slower pace of communicating education research for public consumption. Using a critical lens, Oakes (2017) claims that educational research has made little impact on policy or practice in the history of US education and there has been little support in higher education for building an infrastructure for supporting this type of work much less incentivising it within a tenure-track system. Too few academics spend time introducing their work in public venues in a language that can be understood. Nevertheless, we don't suggest that all academics should become advocates in the same way. According to the American Association of University Professors (AAUP), academic freedom defends one's right to express one's ideas and the pursuit of knowledge wherever that may lead. Perna (2018) suggests that some faculty choose never to engage publicly, preferring to keep their research within closed doors and are only interested in the production of knowledge, but this behaviour results in lack of change to our educational systems. In order to contribute to a fundamental tenet such as educational equity we argue that scholars must enter into the fray by using their privilege as researchers and investing in projects that promote social change. Several edited US books (Darling-Hammond, 2010; Gerstl-Pepin & Reyes, 2015; Ladson-Billings & Tate, 2006; Perna, 2018) explore through the diverse array of scholarly work in higher education rigorous research that potentially impacts society.

Through these scholars' work, they consider their constituencies – who benefits from this research – the ways in which they communicate their results, and the communities of knowledge that build upon their work. They speak of the benefits of using research to solve social issues, but also of the disadvantages such as using external funding that is premised on a political bias. While there may be dangers such as these to pursuing public scholarship the dangers to not doing so prove a greater risk. Perna (2018) explores three areas that may be helpful to unpack when engaging in public scholarship such as examining the kind of relationships that researchers have with their stakeholders, being diligent about translating and disseminating one's data, and understanding the privileged roles and responsibilities that come with one's academic position when making the decision to 'engage in advocacy as proclamation and persuasion' (p. 13). Evoking Rogoff's idea of stewardship of good research, we argue that entering into the fray recognises the dangers of public scholarship but nonetheless forges ahead due to one's civic commitment to the educational field.

Limitations

Our focused data collection was limited to the four scholars studied. Analysis of the other 196 scholars may yield different assertions. Additionally, given that we only analysed media documents, our analysis is limited to public representations of these scholars. We did not ask them questions that may shed more light on their beliefs about their public engagement in policy dialogues. For example, were they provided with institutional supports to support their work such as reduced teaching loads or media professionals that supported their work? How did they find the time to both be prolific scholars and prolific social media users? Is there a connection between their scholarship, their public presence, and policy change? Further research is needed to examine these possible connections to determine which strategies might be most effective in influencing policy.

Concluding thoughts

The outcome of the 2016 presidential election in the US highlighted the inherent dangers of the social media outlets that do not contain the standards of fact-checking and investigative journalism that guide reputable news outlets like *The New York Times* and the *Washington Post*. We know that power operates invisibly in these arenas. Social media venues that serve as alternative or counter-publics and function as echo chambers run the risk of weakening democracy. Education, critical thinking, and deliberation are the key to strengthening our democracy (McChesney, 2015). The need to search out multiple perspectives and viewpoints and to move beyond one's perspective is important for a thriving democracy and exposing inequitable power relations.

Effective education scholars who venture into the public arenas to raise issues about inequities and to support students, teachers, and schools are sorely needed. It is important to ponder Rogoff's (2018) suggestion that we think of educational researchers as stewards who have an ethical responsibility to share their work with the public. Becoming a public scholar is not for everyone as it can be dangerous. Established education scholars with strong communication skills, however, doing work that relates directly to educational policy and/or that can support the life experiences of children, teachers, educators, communities, and schools should consider entering the fray. Without their voices and focus on reasoned argument and research evidence, public discourse on educational policy is more likely to succumb to 'alternative facts' perpetuated by policy advocates with little care for public education.

References

Altheide, D. L. & Schneider, C. J. (2012). *Qualitative media analysis*, 2nd Edition. SAGE Publications.

Allcott, H. & Gentzkow, M. (2017). Social media and fake news in the 2016 election. *Journal of Economic Perspectives*, 31(2), 211–236.

Barbera, P., Jost J. T., Nagler, J., Tucker, J. A., & Bonneau, R. (2015). Tweeting from left to right: Is online political communication more than an echo chamber? *Psychological Science*, 1–12. doi:10.1177/0956797615594620

Bennett, L. W. (2012). The personalization of politics: Political identity, social media, and changing patterns of participation. *The ANNALS of the American Academy of Political and Social Science*, 644(1), 20–39.

Bertoni, S. (2016, November 22). Exclusive interview: How Jared Kushner won Trump the White House. *Forbes*. Retrieved from www.forbes.com/sites/stevenbertoni/2016/11/22/exclusive-interview-how-jared-kushner-won-trump-the-white-house/#6950714d2f50

Bradner, E. (2017, January 23). Conway: Trump White House offered 'alternative facts' on crowd size. *CNN*. Retrieved from www.cnn.com/2017/01/22/politics/kellyanne-conway-alternative-facts/

Bruer, J. T. (2016, May 20). Mapping education research and judging influence. *Evidence Speaks Reports*, 1(17), Retrieved from www.brookings.edu/research/mapping-education-research-and-judging-influence/

C-SPAN. (2016, September 27). *After words with Sara Goldrick-Rab*. Retrieved from www.c-span.org/video/?415168-1/after-words-sara-goldrick-rab

Cassidy and Fishman, Inc. (2018, May 4, 2018). *Pedro Noguera*. Retrieved from www.cassidyandfishman.com/speakers/pedro-noguera/

Daily Show. (2016, September 27). *Interview with Sara Goldrick-Rab*. Retrieved at: www.cc.com/video-clips/uurxys/the-daily-show-with-trevor-noah-exclusive—sara-goldrick-rab-extended-interview

Darling-Hammond, L. (2010). *The flat world and education: How America's commitment to equity will determine our future*. New York, NY: Teacher's College Press.

Dewey, C. (2016, November 17). Facebook fake-news writer: 'I think Donald Trump is in the White House because of me.' *The Washington Post*. Retrieved from www.washingtonpost.com/news/the-intersect/wp/2016/11/17/facebook-fake-news-writer-i-think-donald-trump-is-in-the-white-house-because-of-me/?utm_term=.770af6466d4f

Fernández Campbell, A. (2018). Facebook is in crisis mode. The teacher strikes show it can still serve a civic purpose. *Vox.com*. April 12, 2018. Retrieved from www.vox.com/policy-and-politics/2018/4/12/17198404/facebook-zuckerberg-testimony-teacher-strikes

Fraser, N. (2008). *Scales of justice: Reimagining political space in a globalizing world*. Hoboken, NJ: Wiley-Blackwell.

Gerstl-Pepin, C. I. (2002). Media (mis)representations of education in the 2000 presidential election. *Educational Policy*, 16(1), 37–55.

Gerstl-Pepin, C. I. (2007). Introduction on the special issue on the media, democracy, and the politics of education. *Peabody Journal of Education*, 82(1), 1–9.

Gerstl-Pepin, C. (2015). Popular media portrayals of inequity and school reform in The Wire and Waiting for 'Superman' . *Peabody Journal of Education*, 90(5), 691–710.

Gerstl-Pepin, C., & Reyes, C. (Eds.). (2015). *Reimagining the public intellectual in education: Making scholarship matter* New York, NY: Peter Lang Publishing, Inc.

Gnolek, S. K., Falciano, V. T., Kuncl, R. W. (2014). Modeling change and variation in U. S. News & World Report college rankings: What would it really take to be in the top 20? *Research in Higher Education*, 55(8), 761–779.

Goldrick-Rab, S. (2016) *Paying the price: College costs, financial aid, and the betrayal of the American dream*. Chicago, IL: University of Chicago Press.

Goldrick-Rab, S. (2018a, May 3). *Sara Goldrick-Rab*. Retrieved from http://saragoldrickrab.com/

Goldrick-Rab, S. (2018b, May 3). *Sara Goldrick-Rab: Professor of Higher Education Policy and Sociology*. Retrieved from https://education.temple.edu/faculty/sara-goldrick-rab-phd

Goldrick-Rab, S. (2018c, May 3). *Sara Goldrick-Rab: The Fast Fund*. Retrieved from http://saragoldrickrab.com/fastfund/

Habermas, J. (1962/1989). *The structural transformation of the public sphere: An inquiry into a category of bourgeois society*. Translated by Thomas Burger. Cambridge, MA: The MIT Press.

Halpern, D., & Gibbs, J. (2013). Social media as a catalyst for online deliberation? Exploring the affordances of Facebook and YouTube for political expression. *Computers in Human Behavior*, 29, 1159–1168.

Hess, R. (2010a, December 27). RHSU Exclusive: The Five-Tool Policy Scholar. *Education Week*. Retrieved from http://blogs.edweek.org/edweek/rick_hess_straight_up/2010/12/rhsu_exclusive_the_five-tool_policy_scholar.html

Hess, R. (2010b, December 28). RHSU Exclusive: RHSU's 2010 Edu-Scholar Public Presence Rankings. *Education Week*. Retrieved from http://blogs.edweek.org/edweek/rick_hess_straight_up/2010/12/rhsu_exclusive_rhsus_2010_edu-scholar_public_presence_rankings.html

Hess, R. (2012a, January 3). RHSU Exclusive: The Five-Tool Policy Scholar. *Education Week*. Retrieved from http://blogs.edweek.org/edweek/rick_hess_straight_up/2012/01/rhsu_exclusive_the_five-tool_policy_scholar_1.html

Hess, R. (2012b, December 28). The 2012 RHSU Edu-Scholar Public Presence Rankings. *Education Week*. Retrieved from http://blogs.edweek.org/edweek/rick_hess_straight_up/2012/01/the_2012_rhsu_edu-scholar_public_presence_rankings.html

Hess, R. (2013a, January 8). The 2013 RHSU Edu-Scholar Public Presence Scoring Rubric. *Education Week*. Retrieved from http://blogs.edweek.org/edweek/rick_hess_straight_up/2013/01/the_2013_rhsu_edu-scholar_public_presence_scoring_rubric.html

Hess, R. (2013b, January 9). The 2013 RHSU Edu-Scholar Public Presence Rankings. *Education Week*. Retrieved from http://blogs.edweek.org/edweek/rick_hess_straight_up/2013/01/the_2013_rhsu_edu-scholar_public_presence_rankings.html

Hess, R. (2014a, January 7). The RHSU Edu-Scholar Public Influence Scoring Rubric. *Education Week*. Retrieved from http://blogs.edweek.org/edweek/rick_hess_straight_up/2014/01/the_rhsu_edu-scholar_public_influence_scoring_rubric.html

Hess, R. (2014b, January 8). The 2014 RHSU Edu-Scholar Public Influence Rankings. *Education Week*. Retrieved from http://blogs.edweek.org/edweek/rick_hess_straight_up/2014/01/the_2014_rhsu_edu-scholar_public_influence_rankings.html

Hess, R. (2015a, January 6). The RHSU Edu-Scholar Public Influence Scoring Rubric. *Education Week*. Retrieved from http://blogs.edweek.org/edweek/rick_hess_straight_up/2015/01/rhsu_edu-scholar_public_influence_scoring_rubric.html

Hess, R. (2015b, January 7). The 2015 RHSU Edu-Scholar Public Influence Rankings. *Education Week*. Retrieved from http://blogs.edweek.org/edweek/rick_hess_straight_up/2015/01/2015_rhsu_edu-scholar_public_influence_rankings.html

Hess, R. (2016a, January 5). The 2016 RHSU Edu-Scholar Public Influence Scoring Rubric. *Education Week*. Retrieved from http://blogs.edweek.org/edweek/rick_hess_straight_up/2016/01/the_rhsu_edu-scholar_public_influence_scoring_rubric_1.html

Hess, R. (2016b, January 6). The 2016 RHSU Edu-Scholar Public Presence Rankings. *Education Week*. Retrieved from http://blogs.edweek.org/edweek/rick_hess_straight_up/2016/01/the_2016_rhsu_edu-scholar_public_influence_rankings.html

Hess, R. (2017a, January 10). The 2017 RHSU Edu-Scholar Public Influence Scoring Rubric. *Education Week*. Retrieved from http://blogs.edweek.org/edweek/rick_hess_straight_up/2017/01/the_2017_rhsu_edu-scholar_public_influence_scoring_rubric.html

Hess, R. (2017b, January 11). The 2017 Edu-Scholar Public Influence Rankings. *Education Week*. Retrieved from http://blogs.edweek.org/edweek/rick_hess_straight_up/2017/01/the_2017_rhsu_edu-scholar_public_influence_rankings.html

Hess, R. (2018a, January 6). The 2018 RHSU Edu-Scholar Public Influence Scoring Rubric. *Education Week*. Retrieved from http://blogs.edweek.org/edweek/rick_hess_straight_up/2018/01/the_2018_rhsu_edu-scholar_public_influence_scoring_rubric.html

Hess, R. (2018b, January 10). The 2018 Edu-Scholar Public Influence Rankings. *Education Week*. Retrieved from http://blogs.edweek.org/edweek/rick_hess_straight_up/2018/01/the_2018_rhsu_edu-scholar_public_influence_rankings.html

Hirsch, J. E. (2005). An index to quantify an individual's scientific research output. *Proceedings of the National Academy of Sciences of the United States of America*, 102(46), 16569–16572. doi:10.1073/pnas.0507655102

Jaschik, S. (2015, July 17). Debate escalates over Twitter remarks by Sara Goldrick-Rab, professor at Wisconsin-Madison. *Inside Higher Ed*. Retrieved from www.insidehighered.com/news/2015/07/17/debate-escalates-over-twitter-remarks-sara-goldrick-rab-professor-wisconsin-madison

Ladson-Billings, G. & Tate, W. (2006). *Education research in the public interest: Social justice, action, and policy*. New York, NY: Teachers College Press.

Milbank, D. (2016, November 18). Opinions, Trump's fake-new presidency. *The Washington Post*. Retrieved from www.washingtonpost.com/opinions/trumps-fake-news-presidency/2016/11/18/72cc7b14-ad96-11e6-977a-1030f822fc35_story.html?utm_term=.836463678db7

McChesney, R. W. (2015). *Rich media, poor democracy*. New York, NY: The New Press.

McGuinn, P. & Supovitz, J. A. (2016). Parallel play in the education sandbox: The Common Core and the politics of transpartisan coalitions. *New America*. Retrieved from https://static.newamerica.org/attachments/12298-parallel-play-in-the-education-sandbox/common_core_1.13.e146c9a3e44b4dcea030bf4ac1efda59.pdf

Mitchell, A. & Holcomb, J. (2016, June 15). State of the new media 2016. *Pew Research Center*. Retrieved from www.journalism.org/2016/06/15/state-of-the-news-media-2016/

Network for Public Education. (2018). Network for Public Education. Retrieved from https://networkforpubliceducation.org/

New York University. (2018, May 5). About New York Steinhardt: How We Rank: Latest Honors. Retrieved from https://steinhardt.nyu.edu/about/rank

Newman, N. (2009). The rise of social media and its impact on mainstream journalism: A study of how newspapers and broadcasters in the UK and US are responding to a wave of participatory social media, and a historic shift in control towards individual consumers. *The Reuters Institute for the Study of Journalism*. Retrieved from http://reutersinstitute.politics.ox.ac.uk/fileadmin/documents/Publications/The_rise_of_social_media_and_its_impact_on_mainstream_journalism.pdf

Newman, T. (2017, February 28). Jeff Sessions adds to Trump administration's 'alternative facts' on marijuana and legalization. *The Huffington Post*. Retrieved from www.huffingtonpost.com/entry/jeff-sessions-marijuana_us_58b6061ac4b0a8a9b786ff86

Nichols, T. (2018). *The death of expertise*. New York, NY: Oxford University Press.

Noguera, P. A. (2014, June 18). In defense of teacher tenure: A few ineffective teachers are not the primary reason why schools are struggling. *The Wall Street Journal*. Retrieved from www.wsj.com/articles/pedro-noguera-in-defense-of-teacher-tenure-1403134951

Noguera, P. (2017, September 9). DACA and the American dream. *HuffPost*. Retrieved from www.huffingtonpost.com/entry/daca-and-the-american-dream_us_59b4108fe4b0bef3378ce092

Noguera, P. A. (2018, April 30). Dr. Pedro A. Noguera. Retrieved from www.pedronoguera.com/bio/

Oakes, J. (2017). Public scholarship: Education research for a diverse democracy. *Educational Researcher*, 47(2), 91–104.

Patton, M. Q. (2014). *Qualitative research & evaluation methods: Integrating theory and practice*, 4th Edition. Thousand Oaks, CA: SAGE Publications, Inc.

Perna, L. (2018). *Taking it to the streets: The role of scholarship in advocacy and advocacy in scholarship*. Baltimore, MD: John Hopkins University Press.

Ravitch, D. (2017, June 5). The demolition of American education. *The New York Times Review of Books*. Retrieved from www.nybooks.com/daily/2017/06/05/trump-devos-demolition-of-american-education/

Ravitch, D. (2018, April 20). Bio. Retrieved from http://dianeravitch.com/about-diane/

Rogoff, B. (2018, April 14). Communicating research and engaging public and policy audiences – The story of doing so. Panel presentation at the American Educational Research Association, New York City, New York.

Saraisky, G. (2015). Analyzing public discourse: Using media content analysis to understand the policy process. *Current Issues in Comparative Education*, 18(1), 26–41.

Silverman, C. (2016, November 16). This analysis shows how fake election news stories outperformed real news on facebook. *Buzz Feed News*. Retrieved from www.buzzfeed.com/craigsilverman/viral-fake-election-news-outperformed-real-news-on-facebook?utm_term=.evg4BbpwRb#.hprJG65ZW6

Sinderbrand, R. (2017, January 22). How Kellyanne Conway ushered in the era of 'alternative facts.' *The Washington Post*. Retrieved from www.washingtonpost.com/news/the-fix/wp/2017/01/22/how-kellyanne-conway-ushered-in-the-era-of-alternative-facts/?utm_term=.4e6c1749bcea#annotations:11213462

Singer, A. (2017, September 18). Ravitch responds to Devos and school privitazation. *HuffPost*. Retrieved from www.huffingtonpost.com/entry/ravitch-responds-to-devos-and-school-privatization_us_59bf99b6e4b02c642e4a186f

Stanford University. (2018, January 10). Stanford Center for Education Policy Analysis: Informing and advancing effective policy. Retrieved from http://cepa.stanford.edu/news/cepa-faculty-and-alumni-score-high-marks-2018-rhsu-edu-scholar-public-influence-rankings

Strauss, V. (2017, September 19). There's a new call for Americans to embrace Chinese-style education. That's a huge mistake. *The Washington Post*. Retrieved from www.washingtonpost.com/news/answer-sheet/wp/2017/09/19/theres-a-new-call-for-americans-to-embrace-chinese-style-education-why-thats-a-huge-mistake/?utm_term=.b4bd570ad180

Supiano, B. (2016). The many battles of Sara Goldrick-Rab. *The Chronicle of Higher Education*. Retrieved from www.chronicle.com/article/The-Many-Battles-of-Sara/235666

Supovitz, J. A., Daly, A. J., & del Fresno, M. (2015). #CommonCore: How social media is changing the politics of education. Retrieved from http://repository.upenn.edu/cgi/viewcontent.cgi?article=1000&context=hashtagcommoncore&seiredir=1&referer=https%3A%2F%2Fscholar.google.com%2Fscholar%3Fstart%3D20%26q%3D%2522badass%2Bteachers%2Bassociation%2522%26hl%3Den%26as_sdt%3D0%2C46#search=%22badass%20teachers%20association%22

Tucker, M. (2016, September 22). On the death and transfiguration of the education press. [Blog post]. Retrieved from http://ncee.org/2016/09/on-the-death-and-transfiguration-of-the-education-press/

University of Pennsylvania. (2018, February). Angela Duckworth and Marybeth Gasman: Scholar Public Influence Rankings, Pennsylvania Almanac, 64(24). Retrieved from https://almanac.upenn.edu/articles/angela-duckworth-and-marybeth-gasman-rhsu-edu-scholar-public-influence-rankings

Updyke, A. (2013). *Klout for dummies*. Hoboken, NJ: John Wiley & Sons.

Varney, C. (2011). *Dynamic competition in the newspaper industry*. Washington, DC: Department of Justice.

Veletsianos, G. & Kimmons, R. (2012). Networked participatory scholarship: Emergent techno-cultural pressures toward open and digital scholarship in online networks. *Computers & Education*, 58, 766–774.

Williams, B. A. & Carpini, M. X. D. (2008). The eroding boundaries between news and entertainment and what they mean for democratic politics. In L. Wilkins and C.G. Christians (Eds.), *The handbook of mass media politics* (pp. 177–188). Routledge.

Zhao, Y. (2014, December 10). Common Core, don't copy China's test-prep culture. *CNN*. Retrieved from www.cnn.com/2014/11/17/opinion/zhao-common-core-testing/index.html

Zhao, Y. (2018, April 30). Yong Zhao: Creative, Entrepreneurial, and Global: 21st Century Education. Retrieved from http://zhaolearning.com/

Zimmer, M. (2010). But the data is already public: On ethics of research in Facebook. *Ethics and Information Technology*, 12(4), 313–325.

7

WHO SPEAKS FOR TEACHERS? SOCIAL MEDIA AND TEACHER VOICE

Pat Thomson and Stewart Riddle

Introduction

The notion of teachers having a 'voice' in education policy, practice and public discourse is not new (see Connell, 1985; Goodson, 1991). Teacher voice is often understood to be silenced or rejected by policymakers and therefore something to be struggled for. However, in England and Australia, where teachers are engaging in public debate via social media platforms such as Twitter and blogging, it may seem that the struggle for teacher voice is over. Yet this voice is far from united. Edu-Twitter, for example, has become a site for fractious conversation. Debates rage over everything from neo-traditionalist v progressivist teaching methods through to strict 'no excuses' behavioural and school uniform policies, as well as inclusionary and exclusionary school cultures. Social media appears to be a Hobbesian space enacting the radical sovereignty of the individual within the State apparatus; teachers, education researchers, policymakers and other interested 'educationalists' virtually assemble in disagreement on almost every conceivable education-related topic. At the centre of this cacophony lie deepening social and political divides, which are amplified by the tendency for social media to encourage echo chambers, homophily and social exclusion (Hodkinson, 2016).

It could be argued that social media is an ideal public space, a place where argument happens. Yet education debates on social media often do not accord with Habermas' (1987) notions of respect and reciprocity, as there is no a priori agreement on the terms of engagement. Nor is there a binding commitment to relationality and reciprocity of productive discourse. Arguing for a greater rationality of disagreement, Rancière (1999) contends that,

> before any confrontation of interests and values, before any assertions are submitted to demands for validation between established partners, there is the

dispute over the object of the dispute, the dispute over the existence of the dispute and the parties confronting each other in it.

(p. 55)

From this perspective, it can be argued that although the struggle for the voice of the teacher is being activated through the landscape of social media, the implications for public discourse, policy and practice are not well-examined. We suggest that it is important to develop both a conceptual and practical understanding of how the mediatised nature of teacher voice is affecting broader education debates, and public debate more generally.

We are particularly concerned here with the question of who counts as a teacher and who is permitted to speak on behalf of teachers. Our focus is on England and Australia, where we are based, and where considerable North-South social media chatter occurs. In this chapter, we activate two distinct theorisations of the social mediatisation of teacher voice, using a sociological framing of the ecology of teacher voice, followed by a Deleuzean reading of the de- and re-territorialising effects of social mediatisation on voice as an abstract social machine. The chapter proceeds in three sections: (1) a brief examination of the notion of teacher voice and its history, (2) a survey of a teacher voice 'ecology', including social and print media as well as other forms of publication and (3) some potential theoretical explanations.

Teacher voice

The notion of voice is vexed but also popular. For instance, voice can be used to mean:

- a democratic value and right – the right to have a say in things which concern you;
- an assertion of identity – the right to speak in a mother tongue or in an accent and/or vernacular, using particular situated knowledges and cultural references;
- a relational practice – practitioners, including researchers, find ways of recognising, valuing and taking account of participants' perspectives;
- an organisational practice – there are structured processes which allow various voices to be incorporated into decision-making;
- an authorial move in which a writer develops a distinctive style through the use of syntax, lexicon, metaphor and so on;
- resistance to the exercise of power – the collective action of marginalised people asserting their voice in public arenas, refusing to be silenced. (Britzman, 1989; Czerniawski & Kidd, 2011; Smyth & Hattam, 2001).

None of these versions of voice are entirely separate: they overlap and find meaning in a specific context and in use. To add to the possible confusion, there are also multiple critiques of the notion of voice. For example, the category voice is often said to homogenise difference: the plural 'voices' is preferable as it points to the heterogeneity of 'difference' and the potential for disagreements, debates and struggles over meaning (St John, Griffith & Allen-Haynes, 1997). A voice also implies a unified self: perhaps individuals also speak in many voices – and silences (Jackson & Mazzei, 2009). In organisations, voice can be a meaningless good idea if nobody listens, understands and takes action (Fielding, 2004). For instance, in school improvement literatures and practice, students are rarely asked to exercise their voice in relation to pedagogy, despite their considerable classroom experience (Arnot & Reay, 2007). In wider society, democratic voice requires those in power to be prepared to, or be made to, listen; this can be stymied by party politics or require actions in addition to words (Young, 1997).

Given this definitional uncertainty, is there any mileage in using the term and the concept of voice? We suggest that there is, understanding that there is no pure unadulterated lexicon; everything, as Foucault (1991) famously pointed out, is discursive and therefore dangerous. Provided that the complexities of the idea of voice are visible, the notion of voice as we will use it refers both to a collective teacher voice – an activist professional (Sachs, 2000) perhaps – and the multiple voices that exist within the teaching workforce. In this chapter, we aim to use both the general meanings attributed to the idea of voice, as well as the critiques.

Struggling for/with teacher voice

Teacher voice has long been of concern to educational researchers (e.g. Stenhouse, 1975). Here we briefly signal some key historical and contemporary issues in the struggle for/with teacher voice in England and Australia. In doing so, we signpost some of the main issues that are germane to the current social-mediatisation of teacher voice and consider potential implications.

When schools moved away from highly centralised and prescribed text-based courses to school-based curriculum development, progressive and critical educational academics were not far behind. They focused on what teachers needed to know and do in order to design learning programmes that would meet the needs of their students. Like teachers in schools, academics were particularly concerned with working class young people whose families often had limited access to and experience of a full secondary education. They produced material that supported teachers to advocate for particular kinds of pedagogical and curricular changes (Boomer, 1982; MacDonald & Walker, 1976). Education academics encouraged teachers to take charge of their own learning (Schon, 1983; Tripp, 1993; Warren Little, 1994), and to approach reforming schools through action research (Elliott & Ebbutt, 1985; Kemmis & McTaggart, 1988). At the time, teacher voice was understood as pedagogical/professional and as a lens for examining teachers' lives and development (Goodson, 1991).

The ideas of teacher voice guiding school change, and speaking with academic colleagues in an idealised mutually respectful and beneficial public space (Carr & Kemmis, 1986), spread widely and were put into practice. In Australia, the 70s and

80s saw nationally funded reform programmes such as the *Disadvantaged Schools Programme* and the *Participation and Equity Programme*; these brought academics and teachers together in ongoing conversations and partnerships (Thomson, 2007). The same kind of practice was promoted in England through the activities of *Local Education Authorities*. However, such programmes did not address the ongoing hierarchies of knowledge and power, which placed academic knowledge ahead of the professional and 'folk' knowledge held by teachers. School–university partnerships often floundered because of the different needs and interests eloquently expressed by teacher and academic voices (Sachs, 1997; Somekh, 1994).

Once schools had opened up to teacher voice – through their participation in curriculum design and school decision-making more generally – there seemed little chance they might be silenced. But this was not the case. When educational policymakers moved away from school-based to nationally framed curricula, and steered equity programmes towards literacy rather than more loosely defined educational improvements, the scope for teachers to design new curricula within their schools was constrained. Only some teachers got to say what they thought. While silencing increasingly happened at school level, the national level did not open up a new arena where all teachers could speak. Some professional participation was necessary for national political party legitimation, but teacher unions were not seen as the way to achieve this. Subject associations were consulted instead. It was hardly surprising that, at the time, there were concerns that teachers had been largely side-lined or silenced in the shift to a national curriculum (Lingard, 1997; McCollow & Graham, 1997; McConaghy, 1997). The search for a way to consult teachers through some kind of national representative body – a professional rather than industrial organisation – began; there have since been subsequent and ongoing versions of teaching councils and boards in both England and Australia. The political struggle at a national level has been, and continues to be, not whether teachers have a voice, but rather who speaks for them, about what, and to what ends (Bascia & Hargreaves, 2000).

Legitimacy and power were also at issue in the academy. Progressive educators who had eagerly taken up the challenge of working with teachers to promote various educational reforms began to question their easy positional assumptions (Goodson, 1997). The power knowledge hierarchies at work in university-school partnerships were discomforting (Gore, 1993). But at the same time, conservative policy attacks on teacher education and on 'political correctness' (Dunant, 1994) forced many to renew a focus on themselves, to defend academic status, freedom and scholarship. At the same time, many educational researchers continued to work with teachers for some kind of collegiate resistance to the beginnings of what we often call 'neoliberal' agendas – the imposition of globally oriented audit and market architectures into all areas of public services, including education (Ball, 2018; Rizvi & Lingard, 2009).

These voiced trajectories of silencing and selectivity have continued in both Australia and England. Teacher education has been increasingly given over to schools, as teacher educators are seen to be remote, bookish and out of date, if not dangerously progressive (Lowe, 2007). Teacher voice in local curriculum making is now a patchy affair. At one end of the spectrum are schools that opt for commercially published texts as the way of ensuring a national curriculum is 'delivered'. At the other end are schools where bespoke design curricula for the students who attend is the norm. In the middle are the majority of schools which combine some elements of teacher curriculum development, and offer limited opportunities for some to participate in decision-making. In England, as in Australia, there is now significant attention paid to working with the results of particular kinds of 'what works' research in which teachers' expertise is limited to implementation rather than design. England has arguably deskilled its teachers more, to the point where the national school inspection agency, Ofsted, has recently expressed concern about the lack of teachers' basic curriculum knowledge – a situation where teachers can no longer speak with any degree of expertise about pedagogical, assessment and curriculum questions[1].

Regardless of who is in power, national governments now speak selectively with some teachers. They signal the voices that they deem most important through the distribution of prizes and rewards, and demonise those that they do not wish to hear (Blackmore & Thomson, 2004). As one example, when in charge of education in England, Michael Gove took up the rhetoric of political correctness to dub education academics with contrary opinions to his own as 'The Blob'. While Australian politicians have not been quite so crass, the same highly selective choice of teachers who can speak and be highly dismissive of others is evident in various panel selections, tenders and membership of research and review committees, as well as government-endorsed policy documents.

This is the contemporary landscape – teacher voice strongly steered and framed within schools, and selective teacher voice carefully solicited at the national level – in which social media, particularly the social mediatisation of teacher voice, now plays a significant role.

Social mediatisation of teacher voice

The concept of mediatisation is used to 'understand and theorise the transformation of everyday life, culture and society in the context of the ongoing transformation of media' (Krotz, 2017, p. 103). In a review of the history of mediatisation scholarship, Krotz suggests that in the twentieth century media were largely independent mass media which offered 'symbolically based experiences' (p. 104) – information in specific aesthetic forms, which people interpreted in and through their own contexts. According to Krotz (2017), mediatisation changes everything, because it creates new conditions for communication, and must take account of wider social, political, cultural and economic changes.

Educational sociologists who study media have taken up the term 'mediatisation' to describe the ways in which media education policy is made in and through print, radio and television media (e.g. Koh, 2006; Lingard & Rawolle, 2013; Thomas, 2006). Education policy actors use media as a means of exercising influence on governments, who carefully monitor and manage their image, responding to variations in polls in order to ensure their continued popularity, thus electability, and legitimacy. Politicians use media to pave the way for new education policy, to garner support for policy agendas and to announce new policies.

The advent of digitalisation has brought three new forms of media: content-driven media (e.g. blogs, vlogs and podcasts); interactive media, which support human to computer interactions (e.g. games); and social media, which organise human activities through the collection and analysis of data (e.g. Facebook, YouTube, Twitter). However, there is little in the way of education policy sociology which examines social media in the ways in which Krotz suggests. The convergence of social media and the breakdown of the boundaries between the public/private, direct/mediated experiences of teachers has resulted in what we are calling the social mediatisation of teacher voice. Yet there is a rapidly growing body of social media research in other disciplines, some of which examines higher education pedagogies, academic writing and research and academic lives (Carrigan, 2016; Lupton, Mewburn, & Thomson, 2017; Veletsianos, 2016; Weller, 2011). These texts offer potential theoretical resources to bring to our analysis of teacher voice.

Teachers and social media

The advent of content-driven and social media, and the changes in independent mass media, which must now work online and cater for niche as well as mass readerships, has opened up new opportunities for teachers to have a public 'voice'. The Echo Chamber[2], an anonymised UK teacher blog, aims to collect and share blogposts about education – defined as:

1. Written by *classroom* teachers. The more junior they are in the hierarchy, the better.
2. Expressing opinions you cannot easily find anywhere else.
3. From writers who do not have easy access to national media, although I am willing to make exceptions if their access to the media was earned through writing about being a teacher.
4. Containing views that are of interest to ordinary classroom teachers.
5. Written by people who have done their time supporting and promoting teacher bloggers.
6. Provoking debate. Sometimes something will be worth re-blogging just to get people going.
7. Coming from new bloggers. We will try to encourage people to blog by giving particular consideration to somebody's first post, or first contribution after a hiatus from blogging.

The Echo Chamber constructs teacher voice as individual, not collective. Teachers whose blogs will be promoted have no elected status, they do not speak for teachers, but are solo professionals giving their own views. Their voices have perhaps been silenced by school hierarchies. But they may have views less frequently expressed, and may need support in order to keep blogging. The 'grass roots' approach taken by The Echo Chamber opposes those who would speak for teachers, or about teachers. It takes a libertarian approach grounded in the authoritarian realities of English schooling, in the historical individualised liberalism of English politics and in the contrarianism of contemporary UK realpolitik.

Not surprisingly a few individual education bloggers are selectively promoted and quoted by UK politicians as representative of teachers[3]. Their 'voice' is used to support government policy. This is not the same as teachers 'having a say' in policy formation and enactment at national and school level; this can be better seen in the ways in which teacher unions and teacher social movements work with and through social media, as we will show in section (2) later.

The Echo Chamber regularly compiles a list of UK education blogs. Our analysis of the 3,741 blogs listed suggests that, in addition to the online work they do for their schools, some teachers now routinely publish independently on blogging platforms; use social media to exercise a collective professional voice; and communicate and network through social media.

(1) Publish independently on blogging platforms[4]

Two 'successful' examples of teacher blogs are helpful in understanding independent blogging. According to a list compiled by The Echo Chamber, @teachertoolkit appears to be the most popular teacher blog in the UK. Now a limited liability company led by Ross Morrison McGill, it began as a Twitter account and grew. Its website strapline claims 7.5 million readers in 210 countries. @teachertoolkit's aim is 'to give teachers a professional platform from which to be heard' as well as to provide resources, support teachers and 'promote the community by challenging policy, guidance and publications'.[5] The website lists 14 staff, not all of whom are currently teachers, as well as an extended team of 24 bloggers, all of whom are practising teachers. @teachertoolkit has also moved into book and resource publication.

The organisation behind @teachertoolkit can be contrasted with the solo effort by Australian vlogger, Eddie Woo, a teacher who has been filming his own Maths lessons for the last five years. Woo has his own YouTube channel, misterwootube, which in February 2018 had over eight million views. Most of his videos are made for students, although there are vlogs for teachers and his website offers downloadable worksheets. In February 2018, Eddie was a finalist in the 'Global Teacher Prize' from the UK-based Varkey Foundation, an international charity which aims to improve education for underprivileged children around the world, particularly through support for the development of teachers.

Both @teachertoolkit and misterwootube share a focus on classroom teaching, and present themselves as a pedagogic/professional voice of and for teachers. Of the two, the online presence of @teachertoolkit is much more 'business-like'; publications, consultancy and professional development are offered together with an online bookshop, which links through to Amazon. Woo is the 'dedicated amateur': his YouTube channel proffers a representation of a teacher driven by his passions for Mathematics to share his enthusiasm.

Despite their apparent differences, both blogs illustrate an entrepreneurial sensibility, and show the potential for monetisation and celebrity status that is afforded to some voices and not others. Both show the 'market' desire for ready-made curriculum and pedagogical materials beyond what is offered in the local school. While these independent blogs can be seen as sharing pedagogical knowledge, it is clear that versions of self-promotion and profit are also implicated.

(2) Use social media to exercise a collective professional voice

Social media were initially much vaunted for their potential to expand democratic dialogue and support a range of self-organised groups and even social movements (Loader & Mercea, 2011). For example, in the UK, two groups serve to illustrate how this potential has been realised:

- Headteachers' Roundtable is both a blog and Twitter account. Operating outside of headteacher and teacher unions, it is a non-party policy think-tank, which aims to 'influence national education policymakers so that education policy is centred upon what is best for the learning of all children'[6]. The group was formed at a meeting held at *The Guardian* newspaper office in 2012, and has published policy papers for two national elections and an alternative green paper. Its Twitter account had 30k followers in February 2018. The group has an overt political agenda, and operates through a conference, elected spokespeople structure. Because of the numbers of followers, the government is likely to take notice of its views.
- As women and leadership slipped off the policy agenda, #WomenEd was born. #WomenEd is a self-proclaimed 'grassroots movement' which connects existing and aspiring women school leaders. Started in 2015, it now has five national leaders, 14 regional networks, holds regional events and an annual conference, maintains an active blog and yammer list, and has 17k Twitter followers (February 2018).

Both organisations are supported through voluntary labour of members and exist to provide a 'voice' for educators who feel that they are not heard in the current political climate. Social media provides them with a platform from which they can speak to each other and to policymakers about issues that are of concern. However, their political intent is different. The headteacher organisation is a more 'classic' instance of voice as it intends to influence policy; it is also an instance of political voice bypassing unions or quasi-official platforms. On the other hand, #WomenEd does not aim to speak primarily to policymakers. Its social media and face to face activities are designed for those whose voices are undervalued in education. But it has a limited emancipatory intent, as it is largely oriented to promotion and career advancement of employed women as opposed to, say, educational and employment issues for girls and women more generally.

(3) Communicate and network through social media

Social media also provides ways in which individual teachers can communicate with each other. Twitter chats around hashtags such as #edchat, #charactereducation, #learnEnglish #ukedchat #scied #stemeducation offer focused fora and sometimes dedicated moderated times where teachers can chat. It is probably the case that a minority of teachers are active on social media. The US edu-business, Front Row (it sells online modules of work with built in assessments), surveyed 1,000 teachers and reported that social media is not widely used to communicate with students or parents; teachers prefer Facebook for personal use and Pinterest for professional; but age and location affected both use and choice of platform[7]. However, as the lists of followers and hits in the previous examples suggest, even if this is true, a minority of teachers online is still a substantial number. While many who follow on Twitter do not actually take part in conversations, there are still many others who do. Our interest in this chapter is particularly in this latter area, communication and networking and on conversations between practising school teachers and educational researchers.

Critical incidents: When voices clash and quarrel

There are certainly many social media sites and events where educational researchers and teachers come together. #WomenEd is a prime example of collaborative and mutually beneficial relationships that have developed around a common cause. Similar cooperative and collegial conversations occur around other curriculum areas of common interest and around campaigning issues related to academisation, school funding and the arts in education.

But we have been particularly concerned by one thread of conversation online. It is not, as we have already indicated, the bulk of conversation – the majority of which is offered in a spirit of sharing or advising. As shown in The Echo Chamber notes, there can be a rather tetchy side to some of the conversations that occur via asynchronous blogging and more synchronous Twitter. We are particularly concerned with those conversations where educational researchers come into direct conflict with teachers. This is perhaps something unique to education.

Most academics are focused on the benefits and affordances of social media for teaching and generating research impact; however, they express concern about lack of time, volume of email, unreliable information, commercialisation and privacy/security (Jordan & Weller, 2018). Some are concerned about plagiarism and trolling – when what they say is vilified by partisan, largely non-academic networks, which do not engage in debate, but simply abuse.

Our concern here is around conflict arising between educational researchers who support the 'voice' of teachers and teachers themselves, where issues of difference quickly escalate into ad hominem remarks and entrenched statements of position. While this can be understood as trolling, we suggest that it is a kind of 'insider' conversation that (re)produces existing policy-supported debates and demarcations. For ethical reasons, we have decided not to reference the details of hard line, online conversations back to particular individuals, Twitter or blog accounts. While we could offer screen shots of Twitter exchanges and cite specific blogs, we have decided to follow the advice offered by ESRC-funded research into digital practices. Townsend and Wallace (2016) suggest that the:

> risk of harm is most likely where a social media user's privacy and anonymity have been breached, and is also greater when dealing with more sensitive data which when revealed to new audiences might expose a social media user to the risk of embarrassment, reputational damage, or prosecution.
>
> (p. 7)

In our view, the risk of harm to individual teachers and academics outweighs the need to provide unanonymised evidence in this chapter. Here, therefore, we speak in more abstract terms, where we utilise the conceptual and theoretical resources at our disposal. The description in Figure 7.1 is of the phenomenon of socially mediatised insider division. It is drawn from a critical discourse analysis (see Fairclough, 2003) of a corpus of blogs and Twitter exchanges (2015–2018). We have constructed it as an avatar representing these exchanges in the general, rather than specific, sense.

Positional exchanges are usually focused on more contentious educational practices – particular behaviour management routines, special education diagnoses, particular approaches to teaching. Much of this comes under a binary discussion around 'traditional versus progressive' (trad v prog) education, a distinctly English debate (although it is also infiltrating Australian eduTwitter discourses) which pits a teacher-directed, 'knowledge-based curriculum' and 'traditional teaching' against creativity, student-centred learning, group work, 'learning styles' and 'hands on' approaches. Educational researchers, referred to pejoratively as 'educationalists', are said to be ideologically motivated defenders of discredited 1970s approaches to teaching and curriculum, and opponents of any teaching of knowledge (as per Gove's The Blob). Many educational researchers are flummoxed by the lack of teacher recognition of their critiques of empty-headed and vacuous use of learning styles, activity for its own sake, and lack of debate about which knowledge is important. Australian educational researchers not familiar with the English context find the trad v prog binary difficult to comprehend, and express bewilderment at the vitriol of online accusations that they are not teachers and therefore cannot comment on schooling and are simply out of touch ivory tower dwellers. Researcher refusals of the binary are seen as teachers not being listened to and as a re-assertion of a power knowledge hierarchy in which their expertise is discounted. Teachers seeking to assert their will and voice online see teacher educators, university education departments, and educational research as an obstacle to realising their full potential.

FIGURE 7.1 Antagonism in, through and with social media

Given our description in Figure 7.1, we are hard-pressed to think of educational researchers who advocate purely process-driven approaches to teaching (see for example the critique of learning styles by Coffield, Mosely, Hall, & Ecclestone, 2004) and argue for a return to the 1970s. The sociologist Michael Young (2010), for instance, has written of his move from advocacy of 'working class pedagogies' (Young, 1971) to a position which takes knowledge into account. He makes a clear distinction between canonical and sociological approaches to disciplinary teaching:

> The traditional model treats knowledge as given and as something that students have to comply with. In contrast, although the model I am arguing for also treats knowledge as external to learners, it recognises that this externality is not given, but has a social and historical basis. I also distinguish the knowledge-based curriculum I am arguing for, from the traditional model by their different relationships with learners and, therefore, their different implications for pedagogy and what teachers and pupils do. The former I shall refer to as a 'curriculum based on compliance' and the latter as a 'curriculum based on engagement'.
>
> (p. 22)

However, the socially mediatised discourse of 'trad v prog' does not brook variation with the category of knowledge-based curriculum, nor that work is required in both curriculum and pedagogy as Young advocates. The homogenising binary is familiar Michael Gove territory, and the advocacy of strict discipline, phonics and a return to a canon is clearly at the centre of Tory education policy. Yet many of the most vocal teachers espousing these views are self-proclaimed Labour supporters.

So how then are we to make sense of these clashes, and what implications might this have for the practical engagement of educational researchers and teachers? We suggest that theorising the impacts of social mediatisation of teacher voice might offer some potential for moving beyond counterproductive social media encounters.

Theorising social mediatisation of teacher voice

Having been engaged in some fruitless socially mediated arguments ourselves, we suggest that it is imperative that educational researchers do more than simply describe the phenomenon and its effects/affects. In order to support teachers who use social media to exercise voice, and to engage with them in reasoned debate rather than sound-byte positioning, some deeper theoretical engagement with the phenomena at hand might be helpful.

Looking at the ways in which social theory has been brought to social media in other fields of study, we can see a range of possibilities. Foucault, for instance, might give some purchase on the discursive formations in which social media conversation takes place and how power flows within and across the relative positions of teachers, educational researchers and others, within social media discourses. Additionally, a Bourdieusian perspective could afford an analysis of the changing field position of teacher and teacher educator, and the struggle over which field position has the most valued capitals. Goffman – and the notion of a post Goffman life world – allows a view of social media as a time/space in which 'backstage' behaviour becomes 'front' to create a deeply divided virtual staff room. Celebrity cultural studies could throw light on the ways in which particular and contrarian edu-bloggers and tweeters become 'the ones to follow'. Here, however, we offer a more Deleuzean-framed analysis, as an example of what might be gained through bringing theory to the ecology of socially mediatised educational debate.

Teachers' voice and social mediatisation as an abstract machine

Deleuze and Guattari (1987) contend that the concept of abstract machines provides a map or diagram of relations between forces and elements of assemblages. The abstract machine functions like a series of organising principles, where, for example, the celebrity edu-blogger is understood not as simple expression of teacher voice, but rather as a series of relations between sedimentary strata (education discourses, teacher v educationalist, trad v prog, and so on) and flows of power, subjectivity and representation. These various relations are held on what Deleuze and Guattari describe as a plane of consistency, that is importantly always in a state of fluidity and flux. While there is potential for difference in the abstract machine, it is also able to function as an apparatus of homogenisation, determining what teachers are permitted to be, and what they are permitted to say. Additionally, Deleuze and Guattari (1987) argue that mass media is itself a powerful machine of reproduction and *fuzzification*, whereby its subject (in this case, teachers and their voice in public debates about education) is rendered as a series of mediated signifiers.

Rather than taking a simplistic causal view of the mediatisation of teacher voice and its growing influence in Australian and UK educational debates on social media and in other spaces of public discourse, Deleuze and Guattari's (1987) focus on the formation of abstract machines allows us to question how different things are able to come into relationship with each other and how these relationships are dynamic and fluid. Rather than making claims of effect, where one thing causes another to be, within an abstract machine the emphasis is on how relationality produces particular concepts, percepts and affects. As such, in this theorisation, the edu-blogger is not a distinct individual subject, but rather a series of flows and affective relations that have political, social and ethical consequences.

Savat (2013) picks up on the fluidity of social politics of networked actors in digital assemblages, in this case, teachers and their social media exchanges, blog posts and so on, as being simultaneously a modulatory mode of power and in a perpetual flow-state. In other words, there is a precarity to socially mediated teacher voice, which is open to dissolution, saturation, absorption and other fluid exchanges. Nothing is permanent. The next blog post or tweet might bring it all undone. In this way, there is both a sedimentary effect of overcoding, where teachers become binarised as traditional or progressive, while also performing a deterritorialising of teacher voice, coming together in new and different formations. The teacher voice is thus always temporary and exhibits a simultaneous fragility and agility.

There are several implications for teacher educators/researchers who remain committed to supporting teacher voice and engaged in productive socially mediatised conversation with teachers. One is to recognise the de- and re-territorialising effects of mediatised and digital assemblages on teachers and their relationship to others, including researchers, policymakers and various publics. These include: the atomisation of teachers and their voices, while presenting them as being 'heard' in public debates; the deprofessionalisation of teachers and their work, while simultaneously providing platforms for particular versions of celebrity teachers who are venerated in both social and mainstream media; and the simultaneous opening up and closing down of particular ways of thinking and being afforded to teachers. Additionally, the series of binaries becomes problematic and nonsensical – teacher/non-teacher (educationalist); progressive/traditionalist, and so on – which potentially reshapes the struggle for the voice of the teacher.

We are not suggesting here that a Deleuzean reading of the ethics and politics of online engagement between teachers and teacher educators/researchers would somehow magically remove the fractious and divisive nature of some Twitter and blog exchanges. It seems to us that there is a small, yet vocal, group of users who actively support and encourage the binaries and polarised debate for their own particular self-promotion and positional purposes. However, we do suggest that the wider politics of educational debate requires us to make a careful examination of the effect of social mediatisation on teacher voice, as well as the role of academics in supporting teacher voice. We have only gestured in this chapter to some possible theorisations and conceptual tools that might be put to work on the problem. There is much work to be done if we are to collectively move beyond the unproductive online debates that do little beyond ensuring further division and enmity.

Notes

1 See Amanda Spielman's comments on www.gov.uk/government/speeches/hmcis-commentary-october-2017
2 https://educationechochamber.wordpress.com
3 See https://teachingbattleground.wordpress.com/2018/04/04/educationalists-welcome-my-contribution-to-the-debate-on-setting/

4 There is no accurate index of blogs, let alone teacher blogs. Blogarama, which claims to be the oldest directory and refers to some 136,830 blogs, categorises by content, not the occupation of the writer(s). Our Google search of 'teacher blogs' returned some 87,000,000 responses, the first few pages of which were mainly UK/US compilations of the 10 best, 13 best, top, most influential blogs, blogs 'you should follow'. More usefully, in February 2017, the blog The Echo Chamber (maintained by a voluntary teacher collective) listed 3,741 active 'blogs about education' (https://educationechochamber.wordpress.com/2017/02/21/list-of-uk-education-blogs-version-17/). The list covers higher, further and school education and blogs which were written by people in or from the UK, have been updated in the last two years and have a working feed. The indexer notes that 'I have tried to be inclusive and not removed anything on grounds of low quality or objectionable opinions including bloggers who largely "debate" through insults.'
5 www.teachertoolkit.co.uk/about/.
6 https://headteachersroundtable.wordpress.com/about/
7 http://blog.frontrowed.com/2016/07/27/social-media-use-amongst-teachers

References

Arnot, M., & Reay, D. (2007). A sociology of pedagogic voice. *Discourse*, 28(3), 327–342.

Ball, S. (2018). *The education debate* (3rd ed.). Bristol: The Policy Press.

Bascia, N., & Hargreaves, A. (Eds.). (2000). *The sharp edge of educational reform. Teaching, leading and the realities of reform*. London: Falmer.

Blackmore, J., & Thomson, P. (2004). Just 'good and bad news'? Disciplinary imaginaries of head teachers in Australian and English print media. *Journal of Education Policy*, 19(3), 301–320.

Boomer, G. (1982). *Negotiating the curriculum*. Sydney: Ashton Scholastic.

Britzman, D. (1989). Who has the floor? Curriculum teaching and the English student teacher's struggle for voice. *Curriculum Inquiry*, 19(2), 143–162.

Carr, W., & Kemmis, S. (1986). *Becoming critical. Education, knowledge and action research*. London: Psychology Press.

Carrigan, M. (2016). *Social media for academics*. London: Sage.

Coffield, F., Mosely, D., Hall, E., & Ecclestone, K. (2004). *Learning styles and pedagogy in post-16 learning: A systematic and critical review*. London: Learning and Skills Research Centre.

Connell, R. W. (1985). *Teachers' work*. Crows Nest: Allen & Unwin.

Czerniawski, G., & Kidd, W. (Eds.). (2011). *The student voice handbook: Bridging the academic/practitioner divide*. London: Emerald.

Deleuze, G., & Guattari, F. (1987). *A thousand plateaus: Capitalism and schizophrenia* (B. Massumi, Trans.). Minneapolis: University of Minnesota Press.

Dunant, S. (1994). *The war of the words. The political correctness debate*. London: Virago.

Elliott, J., & Ebbutt, E. (1985). *Facilitating action research in schools*. York: Longman.

Fairclough, N. (2003). *Analysing discourse: Textual analysis for social research*. London: Routledge

Fielding, M. (2004). Transformative approaches to student voice: Theoretical underpinnings, recalcitrant realities. *British Educational Research Journal*, 30(2), 295–311.

Foucault, M. (1991). On the genealogy of ethics: An overview of work in progress. In M. Foucault & P. Rabinow (Eds.), *The Foucault reader* (pp. 340–372). Harmondsworth: Penguin.

Goodson, I. (1991). Sponsoring the teacher's voice: Teachers' lives and teacher development. *Cambridge Journal of Education*, 21(1), 35–45.

Goodson, I. (1997). The life and work of teachers. In B. J. Biddle, T. L. Good, & I. F. Goodson (Eds.), *International handbook of teachers and teaching* (pp. 133–152). Dordrecht: Springer.

Gore, J. (1993). *The struggle for pedagogies. Critical and feminist discourses as regimes of truth*. New York: Routledge.
Habermas, J. (1987). *The theory of communicative action*. Boston: Beacon Books
Hodkinson, P. (2016). *Media, culture and society: An introduction*. London: Sage.
Jackson, A. Y., & Mazzei, L. A. (Eds.). (2009). *Voice in qualitative inquiry. Challenging conventional, interpretative and critical conceptions in qualitative research*. London: Routledge.
Jordan, K., & Weller, M. (2018). Academics and social networking sites: Benefits, problems and tensions in professional engagement with online networking. *Journal of Interactive Media in Education*, 1(1), 1–9.
Kemmis, S., & McTaggart, R. (Eds.). (1988). *The action research planner* (3rd ed.). Geelong: Deakin University.
Koh, A. (2006). Working against globalisation: The role of the media and national education in Singapore. *Globalisation, Societies and Education*, 4(3), 357–370.
Krotz, F. (2017). Explaining the mediatisation approach. *Javnost - The Public Journal of the European Institute for Communication and Culture*, 24(2), 103–118.
Lingard, B. (1997). The Disadvantaged Schools Program: Caught between literacy and local management of schools. *International Journal of Inclusive Education*, 1(3), 1–14.
Lingard, B., & Rawolle, S. (2013). *Bourdieu and the field of education policy. Understanding globalisation, mediatisation, implementation*. London: Routledge.
Loader, B. D., & Mercea, D. (2011). Networking democracy? *Information, Communication & Society*, 14(6), 757–769.
Lowe, R. (2007). *The death of progressive education: How teachers lost control of the classroom*. London: Routledge.
Lupton, D., Mewburn, I., & Thomson, P. (Eds.). (2017). *The digital academic. Critical perspectives on digital technologies in higher education*London: Routledge.
MacDonald, B., & Walker, R. (1976). *Changing the curriculum*. London: Open Books.
McCollow, J., & Graham, J. (1997). Not quite the National Curriculum. Accommodation and resistance to curriculum change. In B. Lingard & P. Porter (Eds.), *A national approach to schooling in Australia?* (pp. 60–75). Canberra: Australian College of Education.
McConaghy, C. (1997). Containing diversity. The national Aboriginal and Torres Strait Islander education policy. In B. Lingard & P. Porter (Eds.), *A national approach to schooling in Australia?* (pp. 122–139). Canberra: Australian College of Education.
Rancière, J. (1999). *Disagreement: Politics and philosophy*. Minneapolis, MN: University of Minnesota Press.
Rizvi, F., & Lingard, B. (2009). *Globalising education policy*. London: Routledge.
Sachs, J. (1997). *The challenge of school-university partnerships: Walking the tightrope between theory and practice*. Paper presented at the Negotiating the Curriculum: Whose Agenda?, Sydney.
Sachs, J. (2000). The activist professional. *Journal of Educational Change*, 1(1), 77–95.
Savat, D. (2013). *Uncoding the digital: Technology, subjectivity and action in the control society*. Basingstoke: Palgrave Macmillan.
Schon, D. (1983). *The reflective practitioner. How professionals think in action*. New York: Basic Books.
Smyth, J., & Hattam, R. (2001). 'Voiced' research as a sociology for understanding 'dropping out' of school. *British Journal of Sociology of Education*, 22(3), 401–415.
Somekh, B. (1994). Inhabiting each other's castles: Towards knowledge and mutual growth through collaboration. *Educational Action Research*, 2(3), 357–381.
Stenhouse, L. (1975). *An introduction of curriculum research and development*. London: Heinemann.
St John, E., Griffith, A., & Allen-Haynes, L. (1997). *Families in schools. A chorus of voices in restructuring*. Portsmouth, NH: Heinemann.

Thomas, S. (2006). *Education policy in the media: Public discourses on education.* Teneriffe: Postpressed.

Thomson, P. (2007). Making education more equitable: What can policymakers learn from the Australian Disadvantaged Schools Programme? In R. Teese, S. Lamb, & M. Durubellat (Eds.), *International studies in educational inequality. Theory and policy. Vol 3* (pp. 239–256). Dordrecht: Springer.

Townsend, L., & Wallace, C. (2016). *Social media research: A guide to ethics.* www.gla.ac.uk/media/media_487729_en.pdf: University of Aberdeen.

Tripp, D. (1993). *Critical incidents in teaching: Developing professional judgement.* London: Routledge.

Veletsianos, G. (2016). *Social media in academia: Networked scholars.* New York: Routledge.

Warren Little, J. (1994). *Teachers' professional development in a climate of educational reform.* www.ed.gov/pubs/EdReformStudies/SysReforms/little1.html. Accessed February 13, 2006: US Education Department.

Weller, M. (2011). *The digital scholar. How technology is transforming scholarly practice.* London: Bloomsbury Academic.

Young, I. M. (1997). *Intersecting voices. Dilemmas of gender, political philosophy and policy.* Princeton, New Jersey: Princeton University Press.

Young, M. (2010). The future of education in a knowledge society: The radical case for a subject-based curriculum. *Journal of the Pacific Circle Consortium for Education,* 22(1), 21–32.

Young, M. (Ed.) (1971). *Knowledge and control.* London: Collier-MacMillan.

8

MUDDLING THROUGH WITH THE MEDIA: LESSONS FROM THE INTRODUCTION OF KIWI STANDARDS

Martin Thrupp

Introduction

This chapter speaks to the question of how best to engage with social and traditional media when we communicate our research. It draws on the case of media coverage of a system for assessing primary school achievement launched in New Zealand in 2009. This system was confusingly named 'National Standards' as if national standards in education are the same the world over, but actually it was a very particular and idiosyncratic policy. I shall refer to it as 'Kiwi Standards' to distinguish it from other national standards systems. The Kiwi Standards policy was the most contested New Zealand educational reform for decades. I have written about it in detail in *The Search for Better Educational Standards: A Cautionary Tale* (Thrupp, Lingard, Maguire & Hursh, 2017) and Chapter 8 of the same book also provides more background to the politics of research discussed here.

Initially it was difficult for teachers, principals and academics opposing the Kiwi Standards policy to get much traction with the media. Media companies such as Fairfax Media pursued the public release of Kiwi Standards data in their newspapers and websites. Those opposing Kiwi Standards were subjected to conservative attack blogs that became known as 'Dirty Politics' (Hager, 2014). But the public release of data never took off and over the years the media gradually became more critical of the Kiwi Standards, as part of a wider disenchantment with the National-led Coalition Government that had introduced them. Eventually (October 2017) the Kiwi Standards policy was thrown out after a change of government to a Labour-led Coalition.

The chapter starts by providing some discussion about the Kiwi Standards and the media treatment of them over the lifetime of the policy, including Dirty Politics. I then reflect on my own experiences with media whilst undertaking research on the Kiwi Standards. I discuss issues such as research 'independence', the reporting of research findings and the tensions between being a researcher and an activist. My experiences suggest that challenges to the legitimacy of research and academic involvement in public debate through media are best anticipated and addressed by educational researchers as part of their work. But not all such challenges can be managed and my experiences are also a salutary warning to educational researchers about the forces they might come up against when working 'against the grain' of government policy. Reviewing *The Search for Better Educational Standards: A Cautionary Tale*, Thompson suggests that this case:

> speaks to an emergent concern about the role of the academic speaking in an area of their expertise where that expertise contradicts government policy and ministers... and the pressure that can be brought to bear on an individual by the media, their institution and politicians. What is the future of expertise, given so many structures explicitly mediate against it?
>
> *(Thompson, 2018).*

Educators' concerns about Kiwi Standards

New Zealand's Kiwi Standards (Ministry of Education, 2009a, 2009b) were introduced in 2009 and involved schools making and reporting judgements about the reading, writing and mathematics achievement of children up to Year 8 (the end of primary school). These judgements were made against a four-point scale ('above', 'at', 'below' or 'well below' the standard). The policy matched up existing curriculum levels and assessment stages and progressions with the Kiwi Standards. Teachers were supposed to consider students' achievement against what is required for those levels, progressions and stages and use that understanding for then making overall teacher judgements (OTJs) about achievement against the Kiwi Standards. OTJs were therefore intended to be 'on-balance' judgements made by using various indications of a child's level of achievement, such as teachers' knowledge of each child from daily interactions, exemplars (examples of the quality of work required to meet each standard) and assessment tools, tasks and activities. The Kiwi Standards policy also required schools to report to parents, twice a year, about a child's achievement against the Kiwi Standards.

One reason why the Kiwi Standards were controversial was that they represented a sharp break from earlier approaches to primary assessment. During the decades prior to the election of the National-led Government in 2008 there had been an emphasis on formative assessment, backed up after 1995 by the National Educational Monitoring Project (NEMP), which provided a national overview of achievement by sampling all areas of the curriculum over consecutive four-year assessment cycles. There had also been a tradition of sector representatives such as teachers and principals being heavily involved in curriculum and assessment policy development. However, the Kiwi Standards were legislated for and developed by the National-led Government with little consultation. This reform can be seen as a New Zealand response to global pressures towards both high stakes national assessment systems for student achievement and international large-scale assessments such as PISA, the Programme for International Student Assessment run by the OECD, the Organisation for Economic Cooperation and Development (see Thrupp et al., 2017, chapter 2). It seemed to be taking New Zealand on a path towards curriculum narrowing and the commodification of children found in other national settings (e.g. Lingard, Thompson & Sellar, 2016).

It is not surprising then that teachers, principals and others found numerous ways to campaign against the introduction of the Kiwi Standards. They included publicity campaigns, public meetings, social media, submissions and boycotts (Thrupp et al., 2017, Chapter 4). The intent of much of this campaigning was to inform and persuade the public through the media that the Kiwi Standards should be reviewed and replaced with a better policy.

Media and Kiwi Standards

Whether New Zealand journalism promotes a genuine competition of ideas and opinion has long been debated. Comrie and McGregor (1992) wrote:

> The news media are dangerously under-debated in New Zealand society. There is a worrying absence of critical scrutiny about such issues as ownership and control, the role of the news media, what values they employ and the relationship between politics and the news media.
>
> *(p. 9)*

Certainly, the New Zealand media were largely uncritical during the initial phases of introducing the Kiwi Standards policy. New Zealand is a small country and it was feasible for the author to monitor and record national media coverage, especially print media coverage of the Kiwi Standards, fairly comprehensively from 2008 until they were thrown out in October 2017. By 2008, New Zealand's national and regional newspapers were publishing on websites as well as hardcopy and the same was often true of radio and TV. Monitoring and recording national media coverage was therefore achieved mainly through regular Google searches on the phrase 'National Standards', limiting this by country and by time periods, and collecting the articles as pdf files.

At least in print media there was no substantive coverage of concerns about the Kiwi Standards prior to the 2008 election, around the passing of the legislation or in the period leading up to the launch of the policy on 23 October 2009. Rather, most newspaper editors and commentators across the country seemed to think that the story to be highlighted was one of teachers refusing to be accountable. As the following examples will show, the arguments were often ill-informed, but they had the effect of removing any sense of public support for the concerns of teachers and principals. As Lee and Lee (2015, pp. 119–120) argue, there was 'a remarkable show of solidarity' for the Kiwi Standards policy from New Zealand's print media.

A repeated theme of *The Dominion Post* was that teachers were more responsible for achievement than socio-economic conditions. One editorial, 'Better to Make it Plain', argued that 'research project after research project shows that it is teacher expectations and teaching methods that have a greater effect on children than the homes they were born into and the decile rating of the school they attend' (Better to make it plain, 2009). Another editorial claimed that research in the year before '...showed that 90 per cent of prisoners are "functionally illiterate"... Yet most of these inmates passed through a New Zealand primary school ... How can these teachers live with themselves knowing they have failed so many children?' (Listen and learn, teachers, 2009). A repeated theme of the *New Zealand Herald* was that the unfairness of social polarisation between schools and poorly contextualised test results could be overlooked. One *Herald* editorial suggested that:

> educationalists ... are not looking at tests in the same way that parents do ... League tables are a perfectly legitimate tool from the parents' point of view. A good school for their child is one where high standards are maintained and if the pupils come with advantages, so much the better.
>
> *(Govt mustn't give way on league tables, 2009)*

A later one maintained that parents 'take variables into account. They are aware, for example, of the benefits to a school of social advantage and will incorporate that into their assessment of performance information' (Trust parents with the facts about schools, 2011).

The case of Paul Heffernan led to a particular burst of editorial wrath. Heffernan was a primary principal who had written a tongue in cheek account of how he would 'play to win' under the Kiwi Standards. *The Dominion Post* asked 'Why has this public servant still got a job?' (Listen and learn, teachers, 2009) after Heffernan had written:

> Awesome, awesome, awesome — by crickey we are going to teach to the easiest test we can find. We are going to reteach and reteach baby. We will even fudge the results big time. My school is going to be top school on the league table so that my community will know I run a brilliant school — an outstanding principal — parents will flock to my door.

This was part of a spiel posted on a forum on a Ministry of Education website for education leaders. The forum had been taken over by principals expressing their concerns about the Kiwi Standards.

It was not until the launch of the Kiwi Standards policy that an editorial of any of the larger newspapers seriously questioned the policy (Let teachers teach, not count, 2009). For a while media coverage around the launch of the Kiwi Standards started to settle. But it came to life again around the publication of Kiwi Standards data online and in newspapers in 2012. The intended release of the Kiwi Standards data was generally supported by newspaper editorials, (e.g., Publish league tables,

2012) and newspapers also began to seek data directly from schools in order to publish it themselves.

This started with *The Dominion Post* newspaper (Fairfax Media group), but its letter to schools in the Wellington region elicited only ten replies after the union representing primary teachers, principals and support staff, the New Zealand Educational Institute Te Riu Roa, (NZEI) and the professional association representing primary principals, the New Zealand Principals' Federation (NZPF) both advised schools not to respond. This led, in turn, to Fairfax Media complaining to the Office of the Ombudsman, which resulted in a ruling from the Ombudsman that schools must release their data under the Official Information Act and advice from the Ministry to all primary and intermediate schools in the country that they must comply (Brown, 2012). Nevertheless, Fairfax was eventually only able to obtain data from about half of the approximately 2000 primary schools in New Zealand. It was John Hartevelt, a Fairfax journalist who had been reporting on developments around the Kiwi Standards for several years, who became the person to lead Fairfax's publication of these data. The *New Zealand Herald*'s request to schools for these data came later and did not evoke the Official Information Act. As a result, this newspaper was only able to publish data on around 600 schools. Some principals and boards refused to give their Kiwi Standards data to the media. Many principals also made comments in the media and in school newsletters despite having been warned by Education Minister Hekia Parata against using school newsletters for political comment (Sutton, 2012).

The Fairfax release of the Kiwi Standards data was on 22 September 2012 through its 'Stuff' website that reports news in digital form and in its various regional newspapers. There was no ranking of schools but rather an approach that allowed easy comparisons, through both a searchable online database and tables of data from local schools in the newspapers. The accompanying commentary on the website provided both assertive justifications of the release and frank concessions around the flawed nature of these data:

> If there are problems with the National Standards—and it's pretty clear that there are—the Government, teachers, parents and education leaders are going to have to figure out how to fix them. If they have to be scrapped, then those that would have them scrapped will have to win the argument. In the meantime, the public should expect that the media will work to turn over National Standards information and report on it as best it can.
>
> *(Hartevelt, 2012)*

The Fairfax approach included case studies (of 'higher' and 'lower' achieving schools), 'health warnings', tips for choosing schools, the facility to download these data, statements from various of those opposed to the release of these data and some contextual data such as school socio-economic decile and links to reports by the Education Review Office (New Zealand's school inspection agency) on the searchable database.

The *New Zealand Herald* (APN media group) published its data and commentary the next day. The *Herald*'s approach did not include a searchable database or put these data online. Its tables were organised by socio-economic deciles and regions and again there were various justifications, qualifications, tips and some (in this case shorter) case studies and professional and other perspectives. Some of the professionals and academics cited supported the public release of the Kiwi Standards data but most were against. The *Herald* made up for its inclusion of fewer schools with larger claims, particularly that 'children in bigger classes and bigger schools get better grades'. Its editorial praised the president of the Waikato Principals Association who, unlike all the 'tunnel-visioned ideologues', was '…courageous enough to listen to the arguments' and 'on discussion, had accepted it was better to talk through school results with parents than hide information from them' (Won't someone please think of the children, 2012). In a slightly bizarre but apt twist, this editorial was called 'Won't someone please think of the children', a phrase that had been parodied by character Helen Lovejoy in the television programme *The Simpsons*.

The schools that were most obviously devalued by the way the Kiwi Standards data were reported were special schools for children with various kinds of intellectual disability. As the *Herald* put it, 'despite being told they would be exempt from national standards … many show a line of noughts for the numbers of pupils achieving at or above standards' (Wynn & Jillings, 2012). This was referring to a change of Ministry of Education policy in late 2011 that saw all students at state (public) schools, regardless of background characteristics, having to be entered for Kiwi Standards. The newspapers expected that qualifying commentary such as school case studies, school socio-economic decile and links to reports by the Education Review Office would make the publication of such data acceptable.

Yet the National-led Government's plan to get the public interested in Kiwi Standards data never really took off. As it turned out, opposition to release of these data had an impact as it became widely recognised that the Kiwi Standards were difficult to compare across schools. There was also the continuing problem of what to make of these data even if one took them at face value. After several years of trying to make hay off the annual release of the Kiwi Standards data, the annual release became less eventful and there was not much other media coverage either. In 2016 the *Herald* was asking 'Is the $250m policy working?' (Johnston, 2016) and again by 2017, 'National Standards: Are they working?' (Collins, 2017).

In 2014 a book called *Dirty Politics* written by Nicky Hager exposed the way in which the Government was using the services of right-wing bloggers, especially Cameron Slater and David Farrar, to attack its critics (Hager, 2014). In this way the National-led Government could marginalise its opponents, while still maintaining the kind of friendly and relaxed public image that appealed to the New Zealand public. Principals and education academics who had publicly opposed the Kiwi Standards were amongst those who found themselves subjected to ridicule or abuse on Slater's 'Whaleoil' site and/or Farrar's 'Kiwiblog' site. As discussed by Hager (2014):

Other ministers' offices began feeding information to Slater, such as Gillon Carruthers, press secretary for Education Minister Anne Tolley. 'I got those stats out of Tolley's office, seems Gillon has worked out that feeding the whale might help.' Slater wrote in early 2011. 'Yes, they should have all worked it out now', Lusk replied.

The prime-minister's office used the bloggers to launch attacks on anyone they saw as a political challenge. Each example is not earth shattering on its own but the cumulative effect is intended to wear down their opponents. This is reminiscent of the politics associated with US president Richard Nixon.

(p. 43)

The issue was not only the bloggers themselves but how their blogs provided an outlet for followers to make comments, often venting abusively under the cover of anonymity.

My experiences with media around the Kiwi Standards

Over 2011–13 I undertook a research project, Research, Analysis and Insight into National Standards (RAINS). This study was funded by education union, the New Zealand Educational Institute Te Riu Roa (NZEI), an organisation opposed to the Kiwi Standards policy. The research was sometimes attacked or dismissed in newspapers and by bloggers, but there were also significant accomplishments in reporting the research. Here, I discuss and reflect on my positioning, experiences and responses as the RAINS research got underway, providing a sense of an academic 'muddling through': trying to respond to media challenges as they arose, occasionally being blind-sided and sometimes enjoying unexpected successes.

As soon as the RAINS research was announced in February 2011, there was criticism of its 'independence' by the right-wing bloggers, 'Whaleoil' and 'Kiwiblog', as discussed previously (Slater, 2011; Farrar, 2011). Unfortunately, a press release had been written up by a media outlet (a TV station – 3News) as the NZEI funding 'independent' research although this was never claimed in the project press release or on any other occasion.

There were two parts to the 'independence' criticism. One was that I had previously been publicly critical of the Kiwi Standards, raising the problem of an academic beginning to research something that they have already shown a strong stance on. The other was that I was 'in the pocket' of the NZEI as I had been previously supportive of its campaigns against the Kiwi Standards. The bloggers 'outed' some of this work by providing weblinks and used it to argue that the findings of the RAINS research could be dismissed as a foregone conclusion. There was an editorial in the *Waikato Times* regional newspaper in April 2011 which described me as a 'union hired gun' ('Hired gun' in crossfire, 2011).

In fact, I had approached the NZEI about funding the RAINS research rather than the other way around and was publishing concerns about the Kiwi Standards long before any involvement with the NZEI on the matter. The criticisms also ignore the particular difficulties around 'independence' in a small country like New Zealand. New Zealand's few educational researchers create networks within which it is impossible to be very independent and these networks are heavily influenced by the only major educational research funder, the Ministry. Criticisms of 'independence' are predictable when researching in areas that are politically contested, but they are often easy criticisms that misrepresent complex issues. Researchers might choose to ignore such arguments but unpacking the ways in which they are counterproductive, unrealistic or hypocritical will often be the most constructive and educative way forward.

A related development was criticism of my university teaching. The *Waikato Times* editorial, mentioned previously, followed an article in the same paper in which my teaching was criticised by the then Minister of Education, Anne Tolley. The article mentioned my involvement in the RAINS project and criticised me for 'biased' teaching about Kiwi Standards in one of my university classes, claiming it had led to students being 'let down', 'clearly distressed' and 'deserv(ing) to be treated with respect' (Tolley slams biased course, 2011). There can be little doubt the comments in the article set a dangerous precedent, as they involved a Cabinet Minister publicly smearing an academic's work on the basis of scant evidence. There were 86 students in the class and Minister Tolley was criticising my teaching on the basis of hearsay evidence from four students. Other senior academics scrambled to my defence with supportive public comments, but the leadership team at our university thought it pointless to respond through the media and I had to concur.

Perhaps surprisingly, none of this adverse media coverage caused any problems for carrying out the RAINS research in schools. No one in the schools raised any concerns or withdrew from the study on account of the coverage and where the media coverage was mentioned, it was dismissed as 'political mischief' rather than something that needed to be taken seriously. The role of practitioners involved in research as advocates and allies when a researcher comes under political attack is not often considered but worth noting here. Theirs is usually a trusted perspective from within an organisation; whether or not a researcher has this support can really make a difference when 'in the field' at times of adversity.

The political context of the research also had implications for writing up the research. The first RAINS report (Thrupp & Easter, 2012) needed to be armoured against both the criticism of a forgone conclusion that had been levelled against the project and against potential misuse of the findings. One response to these concerns was to provide plenty of background about the Kiwi Standards and the nature of the research. Hence, the first report provides much more context than most do, including being explicit about the politics of the research. Another response was to say much more about the authors than most reports do: more like a disclosure statement than any typical 'About the authors'. In terms of the substantive content of the report, the case studies were checked and confirmed by the schools before being included and the findings were presented in an assertive way but one that was also open to further findings and other possibilities.

While these could be seen as features of any good research report, there is little doubt that the media coverage of the research heightened concern with clarity, transparency and rigour. As strategies for reporting a controversial research project, they were quite successful. The first RAINS report was welcomed or ignored but not criticised. It is as if those who levelled criticisms at the mere idea of the project were unable or unwilling to get purchase on the detail of it. The second RAINS report was also very well received (Thrupp, 2013a). The way this report illustrated it, it was impossible to usefully compare Kiwi Standards across schools, which struck a chord in the sector (Thrupp, 2013b). It was fascinating to hear through my networks that policymakers were agreeing with the report but were unable to say so publicly.

The third and final RAINS report (Thrupp & White, 2013) saw a lot of media coverage even though it was dismissed by the Minister:

> First of all, it's a three-year study of six schools only, [and] it's paid for by the NZEI, who have a public position of opposing National Standards ... So it's hardly unbiased and balanced research, and its sample is extremely small.
>
> *(Kirk, 2013)*

Of course, an easy retort would be that the Government has public positions on policy also but is the funder of nearly all New Zealand educational research. And that the Ministry has often commissioned small-scale studies. Such logical arguments could never prevail, however, when the National-led Government was unwilling to engage with critics.

Another telling comment came from a senior manager at my own university. Responding to a briefing that RAINS would recommend that Government abandon the four-point Kiwi Standards scale, he emailed the Dean of my Faculty:

> Total respect for independent thinking / research / professors / provocative etc.
> But how you announce / release information?
> Independent (?) research and Professor (?) funding source teacher's Union?
> Brave from a usually meek University
> Words like 'abandon' how not to win friends and influence people at Cabinet and Ministry.

Fortunately, I was able to respond that this manager should discuss the matter with our university communications team, with whom I'd been working for the previous week. But such comments illustrate the pressures on academics when they release comments, findings or recommendations that are likely to be unpopular with governments.

As well as dealing with perceptions arising from involvement in public debate about the Kiwi Standards prior to starting the RAINS research, I also had to make decisions about how much to subsequently speak out on matters related to the

Kiwi Standards. There were a multitude of specific decisions involved. For instance, in 2011 I turned down speaking engagements in areas where the RAINS research was being undertaken. There was no specific requirement to do so, but it seemed sensible from a research perspective to avoid my views dominating the discussion space in the RAINS schools.

In 2012 there were new announcements around the public release of the Kiwi Standards data that I considered needed my urgent response as an academic and also something that would be taking effect long after the RAINS research finished. For the two months leading up to the release of these data I was again frequently in the media. I appeared on 'CloseUp', a popular TV current affairs programme, spoke at three public meetings and published my speaking notes as opinion pieces (Thrupp, 2012a; Thrupp, 2012b, see also later) and was put in my place by a *New Zealand Herald* editorial (Flawed school data no reason not to publish, 2012). I also jointly organised a large group of academics who publicly opposed the release of the Kiwi Standards data through an open letter (Thrupp, O'Neill, & 105 other signatories, 2012) and there was a lot of media coverage of this. Yet it did not seem prudent or appropriate to pull out in-progress findings from RAINS during this campaign, so I tended to avoid talking much about RAINS, or kept my comments about it to passing references.

During 2012 it also became clear that my involvement in the RAINS research might be used as an excuse to try to undermine my contributions to the wider debate around Kiwi Standards. An article in the *New Zealand Herald* about league tables that quoted me as an 'expert' (Tapaleao, 2012) was criticised on *Kiwiblog* for not reporting that I was 'funded by NZEI and a prominent campaigner against the Government on education policy' (Farrar, 2012). The Whaleoil blog picked up the same point (Slater, 2012). These blogs and the comments by followers generated what New Zealand's Tertiary Education Union (2012) later described as a 'torrent of ill-informed blog abuse'. However, the argument that a disclosure statement should always accompany my public comments seemed to have little impact as the *New Zealand Herald* and other outlets continued to readily publish my comments.

What did become a problem over this time was being quoted accurately. The print media, in particular, was keen to publish league tables and probably saw financial gain through increased circulation. The papers seemed to prefer to engage in relatively general and abstract arguments about whether or not parents had the right to the information rather than focus on the important issue of harm, of why releasing these data was likely to be destructive. An example was a *New Zealand Herald* editorial that started off by pointing out that I had argued that 'schools will use tricks to portray themselves in the best possible light in Kiwi Standards results that will be published next month' (Flawed school data no reason not to publish, 2012). By leaving out the details of what had been reported previously, this carried the implication I was criticising those in schools, which I certainly wasn't. What I was consistently saying was that if the aim was for schools to be honest and authentic then we shouldn't incentivise them to be otherwise by making the Kiwi Standards data public. To counter the problem of being misquoted I began to prepare written scripts to speak from and then quickly had them released as opinion pieces on 'Scoop', an independent news website. The main advantage of doing this was to make it harder to be misquoted as the public could quickly read the whole argument online.

Conclusion: Implications for educational research

New Zealand's Kiwi Standards were a signature or headline policy of an ascendant, widely supported government that was also making unscrupulous use of attack blogs to discredit any opposition. The RAINS research was therefore always likely to be political in some obvious sense because it was raising questions that the government of the day was unwilling to consider.

My experiences with this project suggest that challenges to the legitimacy of research and academic involvement in public debate through media are best anticipated and addressed by educational researchers as part of their work.

While not all political challenges are apparent at the outset, it is clear that some approaches and stances leave researchers and academics less vulnerable than others. Consideration of such issues should probably become part of the preparation of researchers alongside other aspects of research methodology.

More than just media training, this preparation could involve consideration of the political and media landscape within which educational research is being carried out and will be disseminated in any particular national setting at a particular time. The preparation, using resources such as this book, could encourage researchers to consider and become more aware of likely allies and opponents when dealing with the media and to write in ways that avoid providing the latter with material that is easily misused.

I have discussed some problems with the media while researching Kiwi Standards in New Zealand but many researchers around the globe could share similar problems, or worse. Attention to the context and potential media pitfalls of any time or place would make it less likely that educational researchers are taken unawares, allowing us to be more confident about publicising our work and engaging in public debate. To close on a positive note, my work on the Kiwi Standards has probably been the most stimulating part of my academic life to date, leading a nation's academic push-back against a problematic education policy and ultimately with great success. I was just muddling through but remained committed over the years and helped lay the groundwork for the dumping of the Kiwi Standards as soon as the political winds shifted.

References

'Better to make it plain' [Editorial]. (2009, July 8). *The Dominion Post*. Retrieved from www.stuff.co.nz/dominion-post/comment/editorials/2572806/Editorial-Better-to-make-it-plain

'Flawed school data no reason not to publish'. [Editorial]. (2012, August 10). *New Zealand Herald*. Retrieved from www.nzherald.co.nz/nz/news/article.cfm?c_id=1&objectid=10825836

'Govt mustn't give way on league tables' [Editorial]. (2009, July 1). *New Zealand Herald*. Retrieved from www.nzherald.co.nz/nz/news/article.cfm?c_id=1&objectid=10581711

"Hired gun' in crossfire' [Editorial]. (2011, April 7). *Waikato Times*. Retrieved from www.stuff.co.nz/waikato-times/opinion/4858816/Editorial-Hired-gun-in-crossfire

'Let teachers teach, not count' [Editorial]. (2009, October 25). *Herald on Sunday*. Retrieved from www.nzherald.co.nz/opinion/news/article.cfm?c_id=466&objectid=10605223

'Listen and learn, teachers' [Editorial]. (2009, September 2). *The Dominion Post*. Retrieved from www.stuff.co.nz/dominion-post/comment/editorials/2823857/Editorial-Listen-and-learn-teachers

'Publish league tables' [Editorial]. (2012, June 21). *The Press*. Retrieved from www.stuff.co.nz/the-press/opinion/editorials/7142962/Editorial-Publish-league-tables

'Tolley slams biased course'. (2011, April 6). *Waikato Times*, p. 3.

'Trust parents with the facts about schools' [Editorial]. (2011, November 22). *New Zealand Herald*. Retrieved from www.nzherald.co.nz/nz/news/article.cfm?c_id=1&objectid=10767804

'Won't someone please think of the children' [Editorial]. (2012, September 23). *New Zealand Herald*. Retrieved from www.nzherald.co.nz/opinion/news/article.cfm?c_id=466&objectid=10835838

Brown, R. (2012, August 15). And so it begins [Web blog post]. *Hard News*. Retrieved from http://publicaddress.net/hardnews/and-so-it-begins/

Collins, S. (2017). National Standards: Are they working? *New Zealand Herald*. Retrieved from www.nzherald.co.nz/nz/news/article.cfm?c_id=1&objectid=11898617

Comrie, M. & McGregor, J. (Eds.). (1992). *Whose news?* Palmerston North, New Zealand: Dunmore Press.

Farrar, D. (2011, March 14). The independent research into National Standards. *Kiwiblog*.

Farrar, D. (2012). An independent expert [Web blog post] *Kiwiblog*, 20 June. Retrieved from www.kiwiblog.co.nz/2012/06/an_independent_expert.html

Hager, N. (2014). *Dirty politics: How attack politics is poisoning New Zealand's political environment*. Nelson, New Zealand: Craig Potton Publishing.

Hartevelt, J. (2012,September 22). Our standards for school report. *Stuff*. Retrieved from www.stuff.co.nz/national/education/7715002/Our-standards-for-School-Report

Johnston, K. (2016, May 2). Primary schools in NZ: Is the $250m policy working? *New Zealand Herald*. Retrieved from www.nzherald.co.nz/nz/news/article.cfm?c_id=1&objectid=11631750

Kirk, S. (2013, November 11). National Standards 'doesn't make much difference' *Stuff*. Retrieved from www.stuff.co.nz/national/education/9457009/National-Standards-doesnt-make-much-difference

Lee, G. & Lee, H. (2015). New Zealand: The politics of national standards in primary schools, pp. 112–141 In *Education in Australia, New Zealand and the Pacific*, ed. M. Crossley, G. Hancock and T. Sprague. London, England: Bloomsbury Academic.

Lingard, B., Thompson, G., & Sellar, S. (Eds). (2016). *National testing in schools*. Oxon, England: Routledge.

Ministry of Education. (2009a). *Mathematics Standards for Years 1–8*. Wellington, New Zealand: Learning Media.

Ministry of Education. (2009b). *Reading and Writing Standards for Years 1–8*. Wellington, New Zealand: Learning Media.

Slater, C. (2011, March 11). Independent? [Web blog post] *Whaleoil*. Retrieved from www.whaleoil.co.nz/2011/03/independent

Slater, C. (2012, June 20). League tables and the media. [Web blog post] *Whaleoil*. Retrieved from www.whaleoil.co.nz/2012/06/league-tables-and-the-media/

Sutton, J. (2012, July 17). Parata's newsletter tip defied. *Manawatu Standard*. Retrieved from www.stuff.co.nz/manawatu-standard/news/7291470/Paratas-newsletter-tip-defied

Tapaleao, V. (2012, June 20). League tables 'for sport, not schools' *New Zealand Herald*. Retrieved from www.nzherald.co.nz/nz/news/article.cfm?c_id=1&objectid=10814185

Tertiary Education Union. (2012, June 28). Ministers need to protect academic freedom [Media release]. Retrieved from http://teu.ac.nz/2012/06/ministers-need-to-protect-academic-freedom/

Thompson, G. (2018). Review of The Search for Better Educational Standards. *Policy Futures in Education*. doi:10.1177/1478210318774688

Thrupp, M. (2012a, August 23). The release of primary school achievement data: disingenuous, destructive, deluded. *Scoop*. Retrieved from www.scoop.co.nz/stories/ED1208/S00132/release-of-primary-school-data-disingenuous-deluded.htm

Thrupp, M. (2012b, September 23). The public release of National Standards data: Which children and schools will be harmed most? *Scoop*. Retrieved from www.scoop.co.nz/stories/ED1209/S00182/national-standards-which-children-and-schools-will-be-hurt.htm

Thrupp, M. (2013a). *Research, analysis and insight into National Standards (RAINS) project: Second report: Understanding New Zealand's very local National Standards*. Wellington: NZEI.

Thrupp, M. (2013b, May 21). National Standards comparisons impossible. *New Zealand Herald*. Retrieved from www.nzherald.co.nz/education/news/article.cfm?c_id=35&objectid=10884899.

Thrupp, M. & Easter, A. (2012). *Research, analysis and insight into National Standards (RAINS) project: First report: Researching schools' enactments of New Zealand's National Standards Policy*. Wellington: NZEI.

Thrupp, M. & White, M. (2013). *Research, analysis and insight into National Standards (RAINS) Project. Final report: National Standards and the Damage Done*. Wellington: NZEI.

Thrupp, M., O'Neill, J. & 105 other signatories. (2012, 16 July). '100 education academics sign letter against league tables' [Media release and briefing note]. Retrieved from www.scoop.co.nz/stories/ED1207/S00054/100-education-academics-sign-letter-against-league-tables.htm

Thrupp, M., Lingard, B., Maguire, M. & Hursh, D. (2017). *The search for better educational standards: A cautionary tale*. Cham, Switzerland: Springer.

Wynn, K. & Jillings, K. (2012, September 23). Why teachers are furious (and parents are curious). *New Zealand Herald*. Retrieved from www.nzherald.co.nz/nz/news/article.cfm?c_id=1&objectid=10835874

9

TWEET THE 'PHALLIC TEACHER': EARLY CAREER FEMINIST EDUCATION RESEARCH, ALTMETRICS AND ALTERNATIVE PEER REVIEW

Lucinda McKnight and Linda Graham

Introduction

> OMG, today's newspaper is about Trump and his fight with Turnbull[1], and then a tweet from the 'phallic teacher' Altmetrics links right back to @realDonaldTrump… It feels like he is close – he is literally in the room, there is this huge sense of bulk, weight, like he was behind Hilary in the debates. I feel frightened. It's as if I'm up against something like a cliff. How do you fight a cliff? Why assume you have reason, or human rights on your side? He's said he will pull the US out of human rights treaties. The world has tilted on its axis and I could be maligned by him and his millions of supporters. Breitbart. They know where I work.
>
> *Entry in Lucinda's academic journal, 2017*

In September 2016, The Australian Educational Researcher (AER) published an article titled, *Meet the phallic teacher: Designing curriculum and identity in a neoliberal imaginary* (McKnight, 2016a). This article was a revised version of the conference paper that had won the Australian Association for Research in Education (AARE) Early Career Researcher (ECR) Award in 2015, as the result of a double anonymous peer review process. In this chapter, Lucinda and Linda, respectively as author and journal editor, give accounts of the publication process and the negotiation of personal and professional risks involved in publishing in the contemporary mediascape with its new social ecologies and 'democratic' review processes around academic labour.

We then consider the article's Twitter impact, represented by Altmetric's digital curation service, and the discursive themes emerging in this space. In doing this work, we write into the identified gap in the literature around the abuse of academics in social media, particularly on Twitter (Campbell, 2017; Lupton, Mewburn & Thomson, 2018). We call for greater institutional attention to more nuanced affective, personal and professional impacts of public engagement that cannot be displayed by metrics, yet are created *by* them. In concluding, we will argue for much more timely, skilful, strategic and specific institutional support for those communicating research via social media. We need to engage with new media publics in creative, strategic, critical and political ways.

The 'phallic teacher' article links British sociologist Angela McRobbie's (2009) concept of the hyperfeminised phallic girl compliant with resurgent patriarchy and contemporary teachers compliant with neoliberal demands. Lucinda's article describes a case study in which the researcher worked with teachers to design curriculum at a coeducational secondary school outside Melbourne and outlines their concerns about mandated curriculum and instrumentalism in both language and policy. These are not controversial opinions, but the article does take a feminist poststructuralist approach to data analysis and argues that metrics, measurements, benchmarks and standards are features of a masculinist neoliberal education.

Ironically, within months, metrics rocketed the article into the social media stratosphere. By October 2017 – just over a year since its publication – the article had been mentioned 205 times by 191 Twitter users with an upper bound of 339,872 followers, and was #1 of all outputs from AER, as well as being in Altmetric's top category for attention. Having tracked well over eight million research outputs, Altmetric determined this article to be in the 99th percentile and in the top 5% of all research outputs they had ever monitored. These figures ostensibly represent institutionally desirable impacts of the article, but we offer our perspectives as author and editor here, so that our analysis may be read through and contextualised by these accounts.

Lucinda's account

I was working at my desk in my office when the email from AER's editor arrived, to advise me of the anxiously awaited outcome of the review process for my submitted article. I was shocked, however, to read the following from Linda. While the peer reviews had been positive, she told me:

> you should know the title of your AARE conference paper was singled out by a well-known blogger who used it as an example of 'silly' research in Education, see:[link removed] There is also a new Twitter account @RealPeerReview[2] that is posting similar examples of research published in peer reviewed journals… Whilst I'm not suggesting that academics curb their creativity (that would be hypocritical!), I do have a responsibility to advise academics (ECRs particularly) of what's going on out there…

To have my work so publicly and prematurely judged on the title of the paper, for an audience of thousands, seemed excruciatingly compromising. As I did not have a Twitter account and knew little about the platform, this ignorance contributed to a sense of losing control. I began to wonder why female and/or feminist academics should begin their careers dealing with both defamatory threats and potential editorial censorship. I acknowledge here that intersectionality may intensify such restrictions on others, for example those who are also from minority groups in relation to race or ability, or who may be attacked for other kinds of 'identity politics'. I have experienced only a slice of the hate pie aimed at those who challenge further norms through diverse abilities, cultural backgrounds, genders or sexualities.

My university's seminars on researcher profiles and dissemination of research had not covered the risks and challenges of social media exposure; such presentations were given to romanticising voice, reach and impact and ignoring the gendered nature of online threats. This performative drive does not calculate or minister to personal costs or to the affects of being a public intellectual today. Nor does it take into account particular vulnerabilities, that some academics – including myself as a mature age ECR with additional needs – may experience, such as crises of confidence and identity conflicts in becoming orientated to academia (Ivanic, 1998).

After publication of the article, I watched the Altmetric score grow with mingled delight and horror and followed links down rabbit holes to topsy turvy worlds, in which I was maligned for trying to turn children gay or squander public money on narcissistic pursuits. I was even reported directly to Donald Trump, via Twitter, as described in the opening quotation from my journal. It seemed astonishing that a critique of neoliberal curriculum design should be co-opted and put to work in the service of social ills such as homophobia and misogyny, without commentators having read my work, as the full article is behind the publisher's paywall. A mere title, along with the abstract made available on publication in the journal, had been enough to incite a vicious response.

In my defence, I wrote a blog post for the Gender and Education Association (McKnight, 2016b). This was duly discovered by my Twitter audience and incorporated into further tweets. I had been glad to have the chance to argue for the article's credentials, yet found that I had merely incited the trolls, who considered my awards as further evidence of the incestuous corruption of academia. As I became more confident on Twitter, I tried to redirect the discussion, tweeting, for example, the link to the 'phallic teacher' conference paper (not behind a paywall) and suggesting critics read it before tweeting, but to no avail.

Hostile social media backgrounds to academic work are noted by other feminists too (Campbell, 2017) and form part of the context in which we research and publish. Then there is the political context, in which Donald Trump has seemingly licensed a renewed postfeminist sexism. As a mother I've become aware of my 11-year-old son's peers in Grade Six playing pussy-grabbing at lunch time – the boys chase the girls and try to grab them between the legs, just as the US president recommends. The personal and political are intertwined in this account of trying to be a scholar-mother-woman-tweeter-citizen negotiating amorphous hostility in the Twitterverse and blog-o-sphere.

Linda's account

During my three-year term as AER Editor, I introduced a number of initiatives to improve the journal's quality, lead times, ranking and impact, which is in part determined by Twitter-dependent Altmetric scores. When Lucinda submitted her paper to AER, I knew immediately which reviewers to send it to: three leading scholars with expertise in gender and education, and feminist theory. In the meantime, however, I had become aware of Twitter activity deriding the title of Lucinda's paper in the 2015 AARE conference program, along with mentions via a new handle, @RealPeerReview representing a group account purporting to expose flawed research.

Not surprisingly, I agonised over what to do and what to say when it came time to send the reviews to Lucinda. Despite what Twitter devotees may think, Twitter does not have the coverage of other social media sites (e.g. Facebook), and most Australian academics are not familiar with it. As such, I suspected that Lucinda had no idea that her work (well, really, the title of her paper!) was being used to discredit Australian educational research in toto. The whole saga reminded me of the witch-hunt that the Australian Federal Liberal Party has conducted at various times in relation to projects funded by the Australian Research Council, where Ministers have vetoed grants that had been recommended for funding after rigorous review because of 'silly' sounding titles (Woelert & Yates, 2015). That Lucinda didn't know about this trend was no protection, and – given that I and other colleagues knew what was going on – I believed I had a responsibility, as both an editor and a mentor, to alert her that she could be (as I put it later) 'heading into a shitstorm'.

Lucinda's paper was published in AER with the original title and I supported her decision. I would have understood if she – as an ECR – wanted to tone it down but I never suggested that and was pleased that she chose not to. As editor of AER, I was happy to wear whatever criticism came along because I was satisfied that her paper had withstood the scrutiny of three highly respected feminist scholars and I believed that her work would make an original and interesting contribution to the research literature on teachers' work. As a university academic, I also strongly believe in academic freedom and freedom of speech, which would have been the victims if Lucinda had modified her work. I did worry for her though because I knew how vicious those involved could be.

Locating this work

These two accounts position us as authors and researchers in relation to the article. Returning to consider the commentary on the 'phallic teacher' as a case study of a media phenomenon, we draw on a number of academic fields researching the use of social media by academics, including sexism in the academy, early career research in the neoliberal university, platform capitalism, Twitter misogyny and ethical debates about social media research. The way we position this work is influenced by our own backgrounds in gender and media studies (Lucinda) and inclusive education (Linda) and we attempt to briefly and selectively describe the discussions to which we seek to contribute, as well as how they overlap and intertwine as complex discursive entanglements.

From blogging to microblogging

Gender had little salience in early, idealised work on academic participation in social media (see for example Davies & Merchant, 2007). The performance of academic identity through writing (Ivanic, 1998) and publishing started to shift online as part of a rhetoric of apparent democratisation (Beer & Burrows, 2007) with academics potentially being in generative dialogue with each other and their publics. Academics could potentially shape narratives of researcher identity for new media audiences, in the manner extolled by Anthony Giddens (1991), launching and managing online projects of the self.

This optimism was based on neoliberal fantasies of control, partnership and choice and, by the advent of microblogging, some of the issues with online interaction had already emerged. For those participating in the hyperpublic realm of internet exposure, the digital self was increasingly understood to be fundamentally 'coarser' and the environment colder (boyd, 2008, p. 129). Fast forward five years, and there were calls to move beyond 'simple advocacy' (Thomson & Mewburn, 2013, p. 1106) in relation to academic blogging. More recent studies explore the extent of verbal abuse experienced by women on Twitter (Bartlett et al., 2014; Cole, 2015) and feminist digilantism in response to online misogyny (Jane, 2016). The titles of works in this field, representing quotes from tweets, suggest how idealism has been difficult to sustain: 'Get back to the kitchen, cunt' (Jane, 2014, p. 558) and 'Apparently being a self-absorbed c**t is now academically lauded' (Campbell, 2017), with the latter specifically directed at those engaging in autoethnography (also mentioned in the 'phallic teacher' article abstract as one of multiple methods employed).

This online world is not necessarily different from what takes place offline, in the academy. There is no binary between a crude and violent online frontier and an academic paradise of freedom, acceptance and agency. Universities are often hostile and hypermasculinised spaces for ECRs (Macoun & Miller, 2014), where precarity rules, particularly for those beginning their careers (Gill, 2010). Being an academic is to participate in a 'masculinist fantasy' in which female academics who argue a case are reviled (Hey, 2011, p. 214) and all are invited to 'libidinally refashion' (Morley, 2015, p. 34) their personae to fit neoliberal performance objectives. The irony with the 'phallic teacher' article is that the tumescent Altmetric score is largely fashioned from masculine derision, with misogyny propelling gender critique to metric success! What was intended to extinguish feminist analysis has created a much wider audience than imagined, both within the academy and the Twitterverse.

Both spaces are demonstrated to be profoundly gendered (Savigny, 2014) and sources of 'toxic shame' (Gill, 2010, p. 232) no longer limited to the often-humiliating rituals of formal peer review. The general public, so courted by early academic social media fans, is transformed by the anonymity and flashfire of Twitter into a force vastly expanding the disciplinary gaze and normative expectations already directed at ECRs (Rusch & Ledingham, 2016). These spaces, in fact, mirror each other in enacting and reinforcing tenacious and structural exclusion (Morley, 2015). This ethical vacuum of Twitter commentary, minus the mediating influence of journal editors, has heightened the way we ourselves are attuned to an ethics of conducting Twitter research and our determination to work responsibly and with integrity in this process, so as not to create further harm.

Twitter commentary does not operate independently, but in this particular case, is aggregated and amplified by Altmetric. Literature contemplating the rise of alternative metrics for measuring scholarly impact (Priem et al., 2010; Wouters & Costas, 2012; Hammarfelt, 2014) limits critique to concerns about whether data can be manipulated, systems can be gamed, or mentions may be superficial. Discussion of the gendered nature of social media commentary and the questionable ethics of hosting misogynistic and defamatory reviews is absent yet urgently needed.

An ethics of Twitter research

In seeking to study the discursive features of commentary around the 'phallic teacher' article, we considered close study of individual tweets and Twitter accounts, to attempt to explore and clarify what was meant by each tweet. We are aware that the collection of Twitter data without informed consent is considered acceptable (Markham & Buchanan, 2012), as it is public (accessed without registration or membership required) and, in this case, not sensitive, even if crudely expressed. Twitter, more than other platforms such as Facebook, is understood by users to be 'inherently public' (Beninger et al., 2014, p. 29). Yet this is contentious, and we wish to err on the side of caution; even if tweets are in the public domain, analysing them as data shifts the context for consumption and publication (Sveningsson Elm, 2009).

There are numerous issues with using Twitter data and the ethics in this field are continually evolving through praxis (Anderson & Jirotka, 2015), so that what seems acceptable today may be unethical tomorrow. For example, it may be difficult to contact pseudonymic avatars (Sveningsson Elm, 2009), who may be individuals or groups. There is also no way of knowing if the person contacted is the person who tweeted and a prerequisite for ensuring voluntary informed consent is being certain of the identity of the person giving consent. There would be no way of knowing if participants were over 18 years of age and therefore able to give consent, and further information, such as gender, would be difficult to confirm as well.

Engaging directly with tweeters who have already expressed hostile or negative attitudes to the researchers may also expose the researchers to harm and further abuse or reputational damage. This contact may also be thought of as a form of 'feeding the trolls', validating their views and rewarding their comments by confirming that they have been read and considered. Recent work (Beninger et al., 2014) has emphasised the views of social media users in this evolving area of ethics and we recognise that ethics are always a balance of risks, needs and potential harms. Ethical decisions are also indivisible from conceptual frames and research design. In seeking to respect others and ourselves, to conduct research with integrity, and to minimise harm to all, we have chosen to:

- make the focus of this study text-based, rather than person-based (McKee & Porter, 2009). This fits with our interest in Foucauldian multimodal discourse analysis, rather than persona or identity analysis, and on what discourse does, rather than says (Foucault, 1972). In this context, with the intention to discuss broad trends experienced through digital ethnography, not individual posts or users, we believe informed consent is not required.
- avoid the mention of Twitter handles/identifiers associated with individuals, acknowledging that handles may be traced back to offline identities, and that views expressed on Twitter may be exaggerated by anonymity: digital context shaping content (Baym, 2009).
- avoid reproducing tweets in their entirety (Ahmed, 2015) as this may facilitate tracing. Instead we paraphrase or use parts of tweets without associating them with/near handles (Beninger et al., 2014), or use an interpretive collage method to represent tweets (Campbell, 2017).
- be reflexively aware of our own desires to 'name and shame' detractors and to be alert to places where these desires may surface and result in risk to the reputations of commentators.

Design for researching social media

Researching social media is the world of sentiment analysis and Twitter analytics, of large data sets imported into programs such as Nvivo, or analysed by combined automated and human methods (Ahmed, 2015), machine intelligence and the training of classifiers for natural language processing (Bartlett et al., 2014). For this study, considering our interest in commentary on the 'phallic teacher' article, and a small data set incorporating the 'flow of communications' (Gill, 2010, p. 229) mentioning the article title or link, we have chosen what might now be considered as 'traditional' human-enacted methods of empirical research into social network media (Nentwich & Konig, 2012): internet inquiry and multimodal discourse analysis. This flow of communications includes emails between the article author and journal editor, the published online article, the Altmetric details pages framing, re-publishing and contextualising related Twitter data (Altmetric, 2017c), further threads in Twitter linked from Altmetric, and Lucinda's institutional repository page badged by Altmetric.

Boundaries can be difficult to define in internet inquiry (Hine, 2009), yet this is important for any research project. It can be helpful to begin by focusing on an online culture (boyd, 2012) and so we have thought about the culture of 'democratic' review around this particular article *as represented by data science*, as a case study. We are interested in how the effects of discourse are shaped by textual assemblages including the tracking, monitoring, collating and visualising functions of alternative metrics and the role of such assemblages in reifying a neoliberal imaginary for ECRs. This is the new environment for the dissemination of research.

With academic identity increasingly understood not just to confront 'metric assemblages' (Burrows, 2012, p. 355) but to be actively constituted by them, we seek to describe how this might happen in relation to publication and review metrics. This should reinforce that we have not been driven by curiosity about individual tweeters, their motivations, beliefs and concerns, and the desire to *find out what they really think* (as if a *they* could actually be identified) and to pursue their truths. Instead we explore how various visual and textual statements made by both avatars and institutions 'coagulate to form strategic discursive practices which work to (re)secure dominant relations of power' (Graham, 2007, p. 197) in relation to this particular article.

To achieve this, we draw on Foucauldian theoretical resources to develop a discourse analysis appropriate to this project. This involves attention to rhetorical constructions shaping strategic readings of texts (in this case, the 'phallic teacher' article) and the statements (both visual and textual) that:

- produce, formulate and interpellate (Althusser, 1971; Butler, 1997);
- constitute a locatable and specific object of discourse (Graham, 2011);
- classify, particularly through a process of abjection (Kristeva, 1982) in which an exterior to acceptable or normative subjectivity is defined.

A Foucauldian or feminist poststructuralist approach to discourse analysis also suggests awareness of intertextuality, unresolved tensions, diverse perspectives, ambiguities and contradictions (Baxter, 2003; Rose, 2007). By writing collaboratively, with different perspectives on the article and experiences of the publication process and effects of commentary, we hope to call our different perspectives into play and also, through our own productive research work in determining an object of scrutiny, acknowledge the perspectives of others as formulated in discursive themes. There is a plurality of voices even in the article commentary and we wish to foreground the ways power is negotiated, rather than create a dualism of 'good' researchers and 'bad' critics. Instead of defining, exposing or discrediting tweeters, we construct an argument around what is being put to work by the convergence of multiple discursive statements and multiple platforms.

Achieving these aims has meant spending time immersed in materials selected for study through repeated re-reading and participatory observation online, allowing the material itself to offer insights, leads and themes, and searching for connected keywords and recurring images (Rose, 2007). Foucault's (1972) advice seems particularly pertinent to Altmetric's visual aggregate of tweets, as he suggests studying:

> ...relations between statements (even if the author is unaware of them; even if the statements do not have the same author; even if the authors were unaware of each other's existence); relations between groups of statements thus established (even if these groups do not concern the same, or even adjacent fields; even if they do not possess the same formal level; even if they are not the locus of assignable exchanges); relations between statements and groups of statements and events of a quite different kind (technical, economic, political, social).
>
> (p. 29)

As both Twitter and Altmetric are technologies of visual display that we have become intimately familiar with through our everyday work, discourse analysis in this instance is not the detached and formal micro-analysis of print language (as per Fairclough, 2003), but multimodal analysis that is not detached from our embodied subjectivities (Koivuren, 2010). While we are familiar with and draw on semiotic resources for visual analysis (Kress & van Leeuwen, 2006), this work is more attuned with Foucauldian discourse analysis (Baxter, 2003; Rose, 2007). We would like to move beyond a micro/macro binary, however, to understand that the 'everyday professional' and the 'global political' are inextricably linked. In this approach, affect as a bodily experience of pre-verbal intensity (Shouse, 2005), along with emotion and feeling are also important, and here our narratives come into play.

Discussion of findings

Tweeters commenting on the 'phallic teacher' article create their tweets within the microblogging platform, Twitter, and send them out to be read by their followers. Altmetric markets itself as a real-time curation service, tracking online mentions of a particular item as 'a new and better way to understand all the impacts of research' that reveals what was 'hidden' before (Altmetric, 2017b). This is in comparison to traditional methods, such as impact factors and the h-index, hence the term 'alt-metrics' or alternative metrics. The Altmetric donut, a multi-coloured circular graphic (blue for Twitter impact) contains the attention score; an algorithmically calculated number representing the attention an item has received. This is displayed to the left of the item's Altmetric details page. On the right are the tabs showing a summary, with a global map shaded to show geographic impact and demographic details of commentators or an aggregate of actual mentions. It is this aggregate, created through an application programming interface (API) with Twitter that creates a readily accessible overview of how a publication is ostensibly being received.

Institutions such as publishers and universities licence the Twitter donut and can program or embed it into their own pages and platforms. Springer, for example, which published the 'phallic teacher' article, began including a 'Shares' button linked to Altmetric in 2014, to make each article's research impact more 'visible' and 'add more value not only for users, but also for authors' (Springer, 2014). We suggest the nature of this 'value' is complicated at best.

Altmetric reformats the collected Twitter data to display multiple tweets in two wide rows, each showing the profile picture, handle and full text of the tweet. The screen scrolls, and displays 100 tweets per page, so a user can read ten or so tweets at a time, depending on individual screen display settings, creating a bulk review effect, of accolades and/or abuse. In the case of the 'phallic teacher' article, many of the hotlinks in these tweets are to @RealPeerReview, the anonymous group account. This data is accessible to anyone who clicks on the Springer 'Shares' link or the donut embedded in the article's institutional repository record, in stark contrast to traditional processes of peer review, in which 'data' remains in the anonymised author-publisher-reviewer loop. Tweeters will have agreed to this distribution and modification of their intellectual property when accepting the Twitter terms of service (Twitter, 2017), but the process for authors and employees understanding and consenting to the addition of these links to their stored papers is much more opaque.

Altmetric's sourcing and framing are part of the digital media assemblage forming public commentary on this article, and part of the discursive coalescence acting to make particular claims, including claims to truth. It is worth noting that the claims made by Altmetric and Springer, cited earlier, are based on assumptions about the truthfulness of data, when it is known that data are always generated, and algorithms designed, with intent (Kitchin, 2014). Altmetric's claims to truth are called into question, however, if readers scroll down below the fold, to where they acknowledge that the volatility of social media means attention scores can only be compared against outputs published at exactly the same time, and that the algorithm used to calculate this score is frequently being updated, so that comparisons are mathematically illogical (Altmetric, 2017b). Numbers for comparison are only meaningful if generated by the same formulae.

Similar claims to truth are made by the alternative and unqualified reviewers Altmetric hosts, including @RealPeerReview, a group Twitter account dedicated to 'exposing' (Mali, 2017) research perceived to be flawed. This group has had a number of iterations, having been closed down by Twitter in 2014 following complaints. All these iterations, however, perform the same function, making the truth claim that only they can conduct 'real' peer review, by operating outside of the academy. Members are pseudonymous and the group's Twitter background banner image is a photograph of a large blue eye, inside a lens motif and foregrounded against lines of binary code. This code and the Altmetric attention score, themselves phallic tools, represent numerical 'accuracy' and positivist certainty. The @RealPeerReview profile picture is a winged blue cartoon eye over a pyramid, symbolising both reach and power; these panoptical iris motifs rhyme visually and semantically with the article's Altmetric donut, all making claims to augmented surveillance of research. The irony here is that, as other commentators have noted (Mali, 2017), @RealPeerReview's comments are based on reading titles and abstracts of articles, not full articles. In comparison to traditional peer review, this form of surveillance and judgement is demonstrably superficial.

The ocular metaphor has been argued to be a sexist and ableist construct (McKnight & Whitburn, 2017). Here it serves to constitute an ignorant or recalcitrant academic cohort as an object requiring surveillance. Altmetric, in one of neoliberalism's skilful twists, markets this monitoring as being more inclusive and fair, incorporating all fora for comment, to better serve individuals' promotion and tenure projects (Altmetric, 2017a). More specifically, the cohort particularly requiring policing, according to the 'phallic teacher' tweeters, is scholars with an interest in gender, including those who align with feminist, queer and postcolonial thinking. This is ironic in relation to the original 'phallic teacher' conference paper, which was not submitted in the AARE category of 'Gender, Sexualities and Cultural Studies', but in 'Teachers' Work and Lives', and the subsequent article's main argument is that teachers need more autonomy and respect. The mere mention of a gendered concept in the title and abstract serves to place it in @RealPeerReview's sights, as part of a purportedly out-of-control, burgeoning body of academic work about gender that is corrupting and defiling education.

In thinking about what is produced, constituted and classified by this discursive assemblage around the 'phallic teacher' article, the concept of the abject (Kristeva, 1982; Butler, 1993) is useful in representing what must be rejected through normative masculine subject formation. The tweets in Altmetric and linked threads invoke metaphors of excrement and expulsion; this is the figurative 'shitstorm' Linda feared for Lucinda. The unread 'phallic teacher' article creates disgust, is denounced as 'shit' in more than one language, and alleged to have been pulled out of nether parts of Lucinda's anatomy. Reading these comments the first time around was personally shocking, but repeated readings reveal their broader cultural politics. Kristeva (1982) links disgust to fear – fear of disintegration of the subject – and it may be surmised that the article's mostly masculine Twitter commentators are motivated, at a basic level, by fear, and fear of gender and sexual diversity in particular. 'Trolls' here come to mean not only those who deliberately post inflammatory material online, but those who disparage as an act of gendered provocation.

Just as these diversities are viewed as distortions of nature and biology, so diverse mental health is externalised and demonised in these tweets. Lucinda is denounced as insane, crazy, mad and a danger to children. Men and boys are considered to be particularly imperilled, and anger about this filters across the Altmetric screen, through text language of explosive rage, handles such as @thefuryofbigfoot[3], and avatar images of ninjas and skulls. Scrolling down the Altmetric pages, the screen is filled with profile pictures of knights, bulls, arrows, soldiers, pirates, beards and 'head and shoulders' shots of men possibly using their own images. The eggplant emoji, which is a common device used to depict an erect penis on social media, appears frequently, as do direct links to Lucinda's Twitter profile page and her university staff profile page.

The thread throbs with testosterone. It is sobering to remember that this commentary is accessible via a direct link from both the published article and Lucinda's professional institutional repository, therefore being officially sanctioned and instrumental to her prospects of promotion. The most retweeted comment is one made by @RealPeerReview, about the way the 'phallic teacher' denounces those who are not feminist poststructuralists. This chimes with other comments that work to define the field of education as neutral, apolitical, rational, based on truth and 'real' binary biological sex differences. This is part of the ongoing masculinising project of dominating both research and education with a narrow, positivist and empiricist version of science that excludes diversity and all that is culturally coded as feminine (Harding, 1986; St Pierre, 2004; Lather, 2004).

Each time the link to the article is shared on Twitter, the journal image is rendered visible in the thread, associating the AER with the work within. However, the journal is never implicated or criticised and the attacks are always directed at the female author who is defined as a fantasist and paedophile obsessed with sex, promoting porn and using fraudulent credentials. She is outed as a repeat offender, as further articles that do not fit positivist expectations of educational research come to the attention of the keyboard warriors who follow @RealPeerReview.

Kirsti Cole (2015) has claimed that the goal of disciplinary Twitter rhetoric is 'to silence women participating in public as feminist' (p. 356), through the establishment of sexist cultural logics. Ultimately, all the spurious claims described previously, to truth, visibility, democracy, purity, sanity and rationality, have the same disciplinary purpose, in relation to women participating *in academia* as feminist. This silencing is attempted not just by individuals, or a single group, but by a complex assemblage of networked digital social media agencies with which the performance of academic identity is inextricably linked. Yet there are still recognisable actors within these assemblages.

The question of what responsibility platforms should take for the activities they host cuts across media ecologies, implicating Facebook, Twitter and services such as Altmetrics that curate other content. There are public calls for acknowledgement that algorithmic decisions facilitate workplace discrimination (Sample, 2017), based on research indicating that legal protections, such as rights not to be evaluated by automated decision-making, are inadequate (Wachter et al., 2016). Altmetric's algorithms make the decision that the crude and abusive social media commentary on the 'phallic teacher' is appropriate for re-publication and assemblage into a professionally valid numerical assessment. Altmetric's shareholders take home their profits based on new rituals of public humiliation that are particularly harsh for junior female academics who are the targets of groups such as @RealPeerReview. It is an ethical imperative for such companies to recognise that 'attention' is never neutral.

Conclusion: Disinfectant or abuse?

@RealPeerReview claims that 'sunlight makes the best disinfectant' (Mali, 2017). Yet this sanitary action is taken against imaginary filth, in articles that have not been read. This is a minor detail, however, when compared to the cumulative power of this discursive media assemblage to generate the potential silencing effects of 'toxic shame' (Gill, 2010, p. 232). This is what these discourses seek to do and they create, particularly for the early career academic, an intensified disciplinary gaze. The socially constructed academic self (Ivanic, 1998) must now participate in rhetoric of professional and performative empowerment via social media, while being made vulnerable to global publics and critiques that themselves make no recourse to reason. Hopes for new transparencies between academics and environments (Nentwich & Konig, 2012) seem naïve when said academics cannot respond to attacks, or attempts to interpellate them as scum, without feeding the trolls.

We ask where the institutions, employers, journals and platforms' responsibilities lie, in the cultural media phenomenon of 'democratic' or 'alt' peer review driven by data science. This phenomenon trades in defamation and insult, yet institutions license data science companies' visual aggregates of these attacks and proudly display their badges, facilitating the dissemination of discursive formulations undermining their own staff and/or authors. There was no institutional support provided for the author of the 'phallic teacher'. No acknowledged duty of care, no legal backing, no pastoral interest or counselling offered. Experiencing 'real' review, courtesy of Altmetric, has been a solitary, alone-at-a-desk, heart-thumping vigil, giving rise to diary entries like the one opening this chapter.

As academics and especially as ECRs, when we engage with social media to disseminate, discuss or receive feedback on our research, we need carefully conceived institutional support. The necessary expertise to provide this is likely to be located across universities and includes library staff, marketing departments, experts in academic branding, legal services and media studies academics. This is a university-wide issue that taps into global movements supporting the rights of women and diverse peoples; management must acknowledge that leaving staff (who publish to fulfil their roles) to endure social media attack as isolated individuals contravenes any policy supporting inclusion.

Specifically, we need the time allowance and skill development to:

- participate in social media platforms so we understand how they work and their affordances and threats.
- collaborate with expert mentors to develop strategic social media plans that address both dissemination *and* risk management in relation to every publication.
- speak out at every opportunity about the ways apparently neutral data science threatens to inhibit academic freedoms and to reinforce sexist academic cultures.
- engage with social media commentary creatively and politically, as we demonstrate here, putting it to work in ethical and theoretically informed ways that serve those who are targeted for abuse.

As we finalise this chapter, Australia's annual national Stay Safe Online Week is starting, with warnings from our universities about passwords, data back up and anti-virus software. The kind of academic identity crime that lurks in the digitised mediascape is much more insidious, with control ceded to algorithms, metrics and Twitter punters. It is not possible to retreat to the cloisters. Could it be that more, rather than less, engagement with these publics can shift conversations? This is a question for our times, those who are under attack in broader society where vocal majorities have far-reaching discursive media assemblages at their service.

Notes

1 Australian Prime Minister
2 This account has operated via several iterations and is currently titled New Real Peer Review.
3 Indicative pseudonym used here to protect identity.

References

Ahmed, W. (2015). Challenges of using Twitter as a data source: An overview of current resources. Retrieved from http://blogs.lse.ac.uk/impactofsocialsciences/2015/09/28/challenges-of-using-twitter-as-a-data-source-resources/

Althusser, L. (1971). *On ideology*. London: Verso.

Altmetric (Producer). (2017a, 30 October). Beginner's guide to Altmetrics. [Video] Retrieved from www.altmetric.com/about-altmetrics/tips-tricks/#prettyPhoto

Altmetric. (2017b). How is the Altmetric Attention Score calculated? Retrieved from https://help.altmetric.com/support/solutions/articles/6000060969-how-is-the-altmetric-attention-score-calculated-

Altmetric. (2017c). Meet the phallic teacher: Designing curriculum and identity in a neoliberal imaginary details page. Retrieved from https://springeropen.altmetric.com/details/10040883

Anderson, R., & Jirotka, M. (2015). Ethical praxis in digital social research. In P. Halfpenny & R. Procter (Eds.), *Innovations in digital social research* (pp. 271–296). London: SAGE.

Bartlett, J., Norrie, R., Patel, S., Rumpel, R., & Wibberley, S. (2014). Misogyny on Twitter. *DEMOS* (May), 1–18. Retrieved from www.demos.co.uk/files/MISOGYNY_ON_TWITTER.pdf

Baxter, J. (2003). *Positioning gender in discourse: A feminist methodology*. New York: Palgrave Macmillan.

Baym, N. K. (2009). What constitutes quality in qualitative internet research? In A. Markham & N. K. Baym (Eds.), *Internet inquiry: Conversations about method* (pp. 173–189). Thousand Oaks, CA: SAGE.

Beer, D., & Burrows, R. (2007). Sociology and, of and in Web 2.0: Some initial considerations. *Sociological Research Online*, 12(5). Retrieved from www.socresonline.org.uk/12/5/17.html

Beninger, K., Fry, A., Jago, N., Lepps, H., Nass, L., & Silvester, H. (2014). *Research using social media: Users' views*. Retrieved from London: www.natcen.ac.uk/media/282288/p0639-research-using-social-media-report-final-190214.pdf

boyd, d. (2008). Why youth love social network sites: The role of networked publics in teenage social life. In D. Buckingham (Ed.), *Youth, identity and digital media.* (pp. 119–142). USA: MIT Press.

boyd, d. (2012). Privacy in networked publics, podcast. School of Media and Communication, RMIT.

Burrows, S. (2012). Living with the h-index? Metric assemblages in the contemporary academy. *The Sociological Review*, 60(2), 355–372.

Butler, J. (1993). *Bodies that matter*. Abingdon: Routledge.

Butler, J. (1997). *Excitable speech*. New York: Routledge.

Campbell, E. (2017). 'Apparently a self-absorbed c★★t is now academically lauded': Experiencing Twitter trolling of autoethnographers. *Forum: Qualitative Research, 18*(3). doi:10.17169/fqs-18.3.2819.

Cole, K. K. (2015). 'It's like she's eager to be verbally abused': Twitter, trolls, and (en)gendering disciplinary rhetoric. *Feminist Media Studies*, 15(2), 356–358.

Davies, J., & Merchant, G. (2007). Looking from the inside out: Academic blogging as new literacy. In C. Lankshear & M. Noble (Eds.), *A new literacies sampler* (pp. 167–197). New York: Peter Lang.

Fairclough, N. (2003). *Analysing discourse: Textual analysis for social research*. London: Routledge.

Foucault, M. (1972). *The archaeology of knowledge*. New York: Pantheon Books.

Giddens, A. (1991). *Modernity and self-identity: Self and society in the late modern age*. Cambridge: Polity Press.

Gill, R. (2010). Breaking the silence: The hidden injuries of neoliberal academia. In R. Flood & R. Gill (Eds.), *Secrecy and silence in the research process: Feminist reflections*. New York: Routledge.

Graham, L. J. (2007). (Re) Visioning the centre: Education reform and the 'ideal' citizen of the future. *Educational Philosophy and Theory*, 39(2), 197–215.

Graham, L. J. (2011). The product of text and 'other' statements: Discourse analysis and the critical use of Foucault. *Educational Philosophy and Theory*, 43(6), 663–674.

Hammarfelt, B. (2014). Using Altmetrics for assessing research impact in the humanities. *Scientometrics*, 101(2), 1419–1430.

Harding, S. (1986). *The science question in feminism*. London: Open University Press.

Hey, V. (2011). Affective assymetries: Academics, austerity and the mis/recognition of emotion. *Contemporary Social Science*, 6(12), 207–222.

Hine, C. (2009). Question One: How can qualitative researchers define the boundaries of their projects? In A. Markham & N. K. Baym (Eds.), *Internet inquiry: Conversations about method* (pp. 1–20). Thousand Oaks, CA: SAGE.

Ivanic, R. (1998). *Writing and identity: The discoursal construction of identity in academic writing*. USA: John Benjamin's Publishing Company.

Jane, E. A. (2014). 'Back to the kitchen, cunt': Speaking the unspeakable about online misogyny. *Continuum: Journal of Media and Cultural Studies*, 28(4), 558–570.

Jane, E. A. (2016). Online misogyny and feminist digilantism. *Continuum: Journal of Media and Cultural Studies*, 30(3), 284–297.

Kitchin, R. (2014). *The data revolution: Big data, open data, data infrastructures and their consequences*. London: Sage.

Koivuren, A. (2010). An affective turn? Reimaginging the subject of feminist theory. In M. Liljestrom & S. Paasoren (Eds.), *Disturbing differences: Working with affect in feminist readings* (pp. 8–28). New York: Routledge.

Kress, G., & van Leeuwen, T. (2006). *Reading images: The grammar of visual design*. UK: Routledge.

Kristeva, J. (1982). *Powers of horror: An essay on abjection*. New York: Columbia University Press.

Lather, P. (2004). This IS your father's paradigm: Government intrusion and the case of qualitative research in education. *Qualitative Inquiry*, 10(1), 15–34.

Lupton, D., Mewburn, I., & Thomson, P. (2018). The digital academic: Identities, contexts and politics. In D. Lupton, I. Mewburn, & P. Thomson (Eds.), *The digital academic: Critical perspectives on digital technologies in higher education* (pp. 1–15). New York: Routledge.

Macoun, A., & Miller, D. (2014). Surviving (thriving) in academia: Feminist support networks and women ECRs. *Journal of Gender Studies*, 23(3), 287–301.

Mali, M. (2017, 10 January). @RealPeerReview: Their thoughts and qualms with academia. *AREO*.

Markham, A., & Buchanan, E. (2012). *Ethical decision making and internet research: Recommendations from the Association of Internet Researchers ethics working committee (Version 2.0)*. Retrieved from https://aoir.org/reports/ethics2.pdf

McKee, H. A., & Porter, J. E. (2009). *The ethics of internet research: A rhetorical, case-based process*. New York: Peter Lang.

McKnight, L. (2016a). Meet the phallic teacher: Designing curriculum and identity in a neoliberal imaginary. *Australian Educational Researcher*, 43(4), 473–486.

McKnight, L. (2016b, 1 April). The phallic blogger strikes: Denigration of feminist early career research in education. Retrieved from www.genderandeducation.com/issues/cracking-the-phallus-in-educational-research/

McKnight, L., & Whitburn, B. (2017). The fetish of the lens: Persistent sexist and ableist metaphor in education research. *International Journal of Qualitative Studies in Education*. doi:10.1080/09518398.2017.1286407

McRobbie, A. (2009). *The aftermath of feminism: Gender, culture and social change*. London: Sage.

Morley, L. (2015). Troubling intra-actions: Gender, neoliberalism and research in the global academy. *Journal of Education Policy*, 28–48. doi:10.1080/02680939.2015.1062919

Nentwich, M., & Konig, R. (2012). *Cyberscience 2.0: Research in the age of digital social networks*. Frankfurt-on-main: Campus Verlag.

Priem, J., Taraborelli, D., Groth, P., & Neylon, C. (2010). *The Altmetrics manifesto*. Retrieved from http://altmetrics.org/manifesto/

Rose, G. (2007). *Visual methodologies: An introduction to the interpretation of visual materials* (2nd ed.). London: Sage.

Rusch, R., & Ledingham, M. (2016). *Bothered bloggings and troubled tweets: Constructions of stress and concerns for early career academics*. Paper presented at the First International Conference on Advanced Business and Social Sciences.

Sample, I. (2017, 28 January). AI watchdog needed to regulate automated decision-making, say experts. *The Guardian*. Retrieved from www.theguardian.com/technology/2017/jan/27/ai-artificial-intelligence-watchdog-needed-to-prevent-discriminatory-automated-decisions

Savigny, H. (2014). Women, know your limits: Cultural sexism in academia. *Gender and Education*, 26(7), 794–809.

Shouse, E. (2005). Feeling, emotion, affect. *M/C Journal*, 8(6). Retrieved from http://journal.media-culture.org.au/0512/03-shouse.php

Springer. (2014). Springer now sharing data from Altmetric on SpringerLink: Collaboration between Springer and Altmetric lends new insight into articles' impact [Press release]. Retrieved from www.springer.com/us/about-springer/media/press-releases/corporate/springer-now-sharing-data-from-altmetric-on-springerlink/23770

St Pierre, E. A. (2004). Refusing alternatives; A science of contestation. *Qualitative Inquiry*, 10(1), 130–139.

Sveningsson Elm, M. (2009). Question three: How do various notions of privacy influence decisions in qualitative research? In A. Markham & N. K. Baym (Eds.), *Internet inquiry: Conversations about method* (pp. 69–87). Thousand Oaks, CA: SAGE.

Thomson, P., & Mewburn, I. (2013). Why do academics blog? An analysis of audiences, purposes and challenges. *Studies in Higher Education*, 38(8), 1105–1119 doi:10.1080/03075079.2013.835624

Twitter. (2017, 2 October). *Twitter terms of service*. Retrieved from https://twitter.com/en/tos

Wachter, S., Mittelstadt, B., & Floridi, L. (2016). Why a right to explanation of automated decision-making does not exist in the General Data Protection Regulation. SSRN. Retrieved from https://papers.ssrn.com/sol3/papers.cfm?abstract_id=2903469

Woelert, P., & Yates, L. (2015). Too little and too much trust: Performance measurement in Australian higher education. *Critical Studies in Education*, 56(2), 175–189.

Wouters, P., & Costas, R. (2012). *Users, narcissism and control: Tracking the impact of scholarly publications in the 21st century*. Utrecht: Surf Foundation.

10

SCHOLARSHIP OF THE CYBORG: PRODUCTIVITIES AND UNDERCURRENTS

Deborah M. Netolicky and Naomi Barnes

Scholars born from the global mediascape

Changed and changing media are transforming the ways that educators and education researchers interact with knowledge and with the world. Journalists and researchers are no longer the guardians of social truths, but part of the democratised sphere of knowledge that Bunz (2014) calls the digital public. Social media, in particular, provides communication that is viral, digital, and immediate, encompassing voices that are at once plural and that come together with a sameness of experience (Bunz, 2014). Academics are being increasingly drawn into the polyphonic global mediascape, which brings with it both possibilities and challenges. Oakes (2018) challenges education researchers to engage in public scholarship in collaboration with policymakers, education professionals, activists, and community organisations. She notes the importance for researchers to translate their research for non-scholarly audiences and to utilise traditional and emerging media as ways to move research into the mainstream. Crandall (2010) contends that academic research has been transformed by networked and computing systems and by mobile devices. On the one hand, the fast immediacy of new media, in which anyone can have a say on a digital platform, provides possibilities for the academic: increased readership, amplified engagement with scholarship, and new professional connections. It also, however, produces noise, a constant media cycle of blame and crisis, and a relentless stream of contradictory and sometimes aggressive or abusive voices clamouring for relevancy and audience.

We authors are educators who in this chapter explore how we create and make sense of knowledge in this changed and changing media landscape. Deborah is a high school English and Literature teacher, and school leader, who continues to teach and lead in a school alongside her research and academic writing, which she works on in the cracks of her life (between a full-time school job, and parenting young children). Naomi is a high school Humanities and Social Sciences teacher who moved into the realm of educational scholarship and is immersed in a university role. We therefore see ourselves simultaneously as teachers, educators, scholars, and academics. We are early career researchers whose scholarship was born amongst the mediatised landscape of academia. Like Rainford (2016) our online musings were part of our separate experiences of doctoral becoming. While we did not initially know each other, our PhDs—completed in 2016 and 2015—were both influenced by our immersion in social media and blogging during our candidature. In particular, our own blogs and the disordered vortex of Twitter were our companions, and these were the vehicles that eventually brought us together as collaborators. Both of our doctorates also included content about social media. Educators' use of Twitter for professional learning and community emerged in Deborah's PhD interview data. Naomi's PhD was concerned with how first year university students engaged with Facebook as a vehicle for community, belonging, and identity.

In this chapter we draw on Donna Haraway's theorisation of the cyborg (Haraway, 1991; Haraway & Goodeve, 2000) in order to develop our conceptualisation of the digitally connected scholar as intentionally engaging in *cyborg scholarship*. According to Haraway, cyborgs are about serious and humorous play. They are a rhetorical and political strategy that we wish to see more of in educational dialogues. We see ourselves both humorously and seriously as cyborg scholars whose relationship developed as part humans (teachers, researchers) and part technology (social media identities, keyboard collaborators). We claim we are cyborgs as a rhetorical move to spark a provocative understanding of our relationship and a political metaphor for ensuring that our machine parts are central to how we choose to relate to each other. We also take up Brophy's (2016) challenge to utilise the figure of the cyborg as a way into deep understanding of self-technology relationships. We push this further, using the cyborg as a theoretical frame that can empower the academic to at once resist, embrace, and influence the system by making transparent scholarly thinking, and inserting our voices into public online spaces. We embrace St. Pierre and Pillow's (2000) notion of a lusty confusion that interrupts and deterritorialises knowledge making. In doing so we embrace new media as a way to interrogate the mess of educators' and education scholars' being and becoming, and the sometimes-dark undercurrents of the new media world. We situate our discussion within the field of feminist cultural studies of technoscience, one open to inappropriate and impossible connections, and to explorations of theoretical in-between spaces where it is possible to think differently (Lykke, 2008). Since our birth as scholars, we have been cyborgically melded with our devices, our keyboards, and our online accounts. We have projected avatars, handles, tweets, blog posts, images, hashtags, GIFs, memes, and online bios alongside our academic writing. We have been entwined in the theory and practice of identity work, scholarship, and writing that fuses the human with the machine. In this chapter we bring intentionality to that theory and practice.

Our dialogic duoethnographic perspective shifts between the first person 'we' and the third person 'Deborah/Naomi' in order to present our shared and individual experiences, showing our connectedness, and also our separateness. We present records of our own digital experiences as human-machine-writer-blogger-scholar-collaborators. These data offer insights into the ways cyborg scholarship can make sense of online practices, and how digital media offers a collaborative platform, identity testbed, and productive sphere for the cyborg scholar. The liminal space of cyborgs is a metaphor for a realm of future possibility, and the cyborg can also be seen as the soldier of a dystopian future. While our experiences have been largely positive, we acknowledge that a narrative of innovation is a double edged sword, the usefulness and ethic of which is dependent on the people wielding it.

Academic as cyborg

Embracing the cyborg (Haraway, 1991, 2006) means simultaneously embracing production, possibility, mess, ugliness, technology, and humanity. The cyborg is partly about transgressed boundaries and bringing disparate elements together. As writing is the technology of the cyborg (Haraway, 1991, 2006), it is also about writing. We merge with our devices (Stiegler, 2007)—laptops, keyboards, tablets, smart phones, audio recorders—and with our online identities written into being on social media biographies, blog posts, likes, clicks, search histories, Google Scholar profiles. These non-human actors become our active partners, with agential and communicative abilities of their own (Crandall, 2010). We are each person and machine, simultaneously flesh and technology, tangible and digital. As humans operating as scholars in a technical world, we become cyborgs through our tools—Twitter, blogs, Google Docs, email—to push at the borders of accepted scholarship, of who the academe suggests we be, and how it encourages us to behave. We take up the postqualitative challenge to allow our cyborgic scholarship to invent (Lather, 2016) new ways of being and knowing and to disrupt what we thought we knew about education through the 'practice of the plunge: letting go, diving, freefall, surfing, swimming, waving *and* drowning' (Taylor, 2016, p.20). Our story echoes with that of Grebowicz and Merrick (2013) who refer to themselves as fellow adventurers whose cybernetic writing partnership has unfolded entirely in cyberspace. Their description of their collaboration as messy and polyvocal resonates with us, as we reflect upon the layers of conversation and collaboration that occur simultaneously in multiple modes via multiple platforms.

The story of a co-cyborg relationship

Our own experiences of new media have been part of our becoming and our connecting with others. They have allowed us to produce thoughts, words, and writing with immediacy and messiness. Online is a place we think out loud, and in doing so, we have become connected with individuals, which in turn become webbed networks of scholars and educators. Our organic-flesh bodies meld in this collaboration with our physical devices and our online digital selves. We are simultaneously human and machine, body and device. We outline our own story of this cyborgic collaboration below, via data mined from our online activities, with timelines to illuminate the way our relationship grew from two separate humans who did not know each other, to cybernetic co-writers who had never met, and finally to identifying as cyborgs. This story demonstrates our organic, fluid, and human use of the cyborgic technologies of social media, email, and online collaborative documents, through the cyborgic devices of our keyboards, computers, and smart phones.

Our story began in May 2013 with the following Twitter exchange. Here we use @Deborah and @Naomi to stand in for our Twitter handles:

> @Deborah: The right to roam. Why children need wild, unstructured freedom. <link> #elc #childhood #parenting
> @Naomi: Great! More research about a utopia designed to make parents feel bad when all they are doing is their best #phdmum
> @Deborah: Really? Or a reminder of the importance of outdoor play, childhood freedom & encouraging self-confidence and self-reliance?
> @Naomi: Learn through play is my most passionate subject. Freedom is tough when the only park is near a busy road

It was our first exchange, and one that demonstrates how Twitter can be a place of challenge and dialogue. We did not know each other, nor did we follow each other on Twitter, but Naomi engaged with Deborah's tweet and challenged her on its underlying assumptions. In this brief interchange, our then online identities are revealed: Deborah as romantic idealist and Naomi as provocateur and cynic. This type of interaction would be unlikely to happen in a public space outside of social media. Social norms would suggest that it is impolite to jump in on another person's conversation with unsolicited opinion, advice, or opposition. Social media, however, works differently to other third spaces, the places between work and home where people come together to discuss both the professional and the private (Soukup, 2006). The open platform of Twitter is where our cyborgic transformation began. Shedding the niceties of polite social norms, our thoughts and the tensions between us were shared with the global community. Hashtags, the first technic in a process of becoming cyborg, activated algorithms that might draw others into the conversation. And like algorithms, they made us uncomfortable.

Unsurprisingly, after such a bristling first interaction, we did not interact online again until June 2015 when we connected over professional learning and our PhDs. Our exchange went as follows.

> @Deborah: My other really transformational PL is my PhD. Pretty sure it has rewired & rerouted my brain! #satchatoc
> @Naomi: Me too. Taking responsibility to explore learning by myself. Rewired is a good word. But shouldn't need to be formalised IMO
> @Deborah: Doesn't need to be formalised but supervisors support & help shape quality of thinking & writing at an academic level #satchatoc

> @Naomi: That definitely helps but it shouldn't be that you need to do a phd to get access [to academic resources]
> @Deborah: Yes – wondering what I'm going to do for journal access when I'm finished!
> @Naomi: Apply to be an adjunct. That's what I did. Also sessional work keeps your library account open. Join a SIG.
> @Deborah: Thank you!
> @Naomi: No probs

Again, it was a tweet from Deborah that began the exchange, and Naomi who responded. This time, rather than disagreeing, we connected over a shared experience. Again, Naomi took on the role of agitator by challenging Deborah, although more subtly than in the first exchange. In both exchanges, Deborah is not visibly concerned with Naomi's abrasiveness and continues to engage with the conversation. As with the first exchange, Naomi's discomfort is apparent as she takes on the senior role, mediated through the language of PhD completion rather than occupation (Deborah being a school leader and Naomi a sessional tutor). Naomi, having completed her PhD, angled the conversation to give Deborah advice about what to do next, illuminating possibilities for next steps of which Deborah, as a non-academic pre-PhD-completion, was not aware. On this occasion, Deborah was open to the advice, taking on the role of grateful novice: 'Thank you!', and Naomi softened into the informal 'No probs'. Our cyborgic selves were still in their infancy as we had not yet fully connected a human to the words we were reading on our screens, via our devices. However, the humanness of shared experiences initiated the first cognitive bond between our physical and technical selves (Stiegler, 2007).

Once we had connected the humanity of the other to the technical production of text and clicks, our Twitter exchanges began to increase. Our next exchange was a month later, in July 2015. Naomi provided Deborah with support around the PhD.

> @Deborah: Full draft of thesis due to supervisor in 2 days. Up to page 229. Crawling. Through. The. Words. Send. Help. #phdchat #acwri #phdlife
> This is why I've put the #phdchat community in my acknowledgements. Solidarity, advice, inspiration.
> @Naomi: One word after the other. The end is in sight! Go girl! I only did two chapters a day at that stage. Otherwise my brain went haywire & stopped working.

Naomi's language, that originally asserted a senior role in the relationship, is beginning to flatten in this exchange. The raw humanity of the affective realms, where success and failure are located and shape our interactions with others (Ahmed, 2014), became a part of our technical interactions. Naomi's encouragement of Deborah now comes before the sharing of her own strategies for coping at this stage of the PhD. Naomi is beginning to share her own experiences as a form of advice rather than providing strategies, indicating more comfort in the relationship. The colloquial and enthusiastic 'Go girl!' demonstrates increased familiarity and Naomi's easing into the relationship.

We continued to engage with one another on Twitter, but at the same time our engagement with one another, and other academics, moved onto the longer-form cyborgic space of blogs. In July 2015, Deborah wrote a blog post as part of an online blogging challenge. Another researcher, Helen Kara from the UK, responded with her own blog post response. Naomi responded to Helen, and then Deborah jumped in to respond to both Naomi and Helen, which in turn prompted another response from Naomi. This first blog exchange included the following excerpts, from the openings and closings of each blog post.

> Deborah's blog: This blog post is part of the #blimage (blog-from-image) challenge ... I love the idea of #blimage, so to end this post I'm throwing out another image, to 'pay forward' the challenge. So, bloggers, do your worst with this pic (just attribute the image back to me).
>
> Helen's blog: Last week I received a #blimage challenge from Deborah. When I came to the photo she had posted to inspire her challengees, it only took me a moment to link those overflowing hands with the data we researchers love to gather. ... Now, a #blimage challenge for Naomi: I look forward to seeing what she makes from this picture. And if anyone else would like to use it for inspiration: help yourself!
>
> Naomi's blog: One of the things I love about reading blogs by PhD candidates and more experienced researchers is that I get a glimpse into the messiness of what it is to be a researcher. Through blogs I begin to understand that ideas do not come forth perfectly formed, logical, thought provoking and publishable. In reality, research often goes through several manifestations, partly formed and tenuous, tangented, better formed but still gauzy. I have been thinking about how to respond to Helen's #blimage challenge for a few weeks now. ... I'm going to stop and pass the #blimage challenge along to <another scholar and blogger>
>
> Deborah's blog: This image was passed from Helen to Naomi, after I had challenged Helen with an image for the #blimage (blog+image) blogging challenge (see how messily interconnected that is?). You can read Helen's post here and Naomi's post here. ... Helen's image spoke to me. ... Are we better alone or together? Can our individual voices be heard in amongst the noise of social media?
>
> Naomi's blog: How do we utilise online spaces to change the way we learn? My suggestion: we stop being experts and start being co-learners. We have part of the knowledge. Not all of it and not necessarily true. We break the teacher-student archetype and become networked learners. Use the Web, the network, the connections, to create new knowledge. Crowd sourced, collaborative knowledge. Wikipedia on steroids. It could start small. We don't

need to be in full blown Renaissance mode just yet, but it could be around the corner. A small example, I have been involved in a scholarly conversation with Deborah and Helen. ... Deborah jumped in (not out of the blue, out of the network) and wrote a post about the spiderweb, breaking the linear rules and beginning a circle of networked learning that inspired the post you are currently reading. This would not have been as easily done before the Web. I wonder what would happen if more bloggers wrote about the same image? What type of knowledge could we begin to generate as a networked collective?

Months later, in November 2015, Naomi dipped back into the blogs, describing the extended exchange as 'a relaxed scholarly conversation'. She noted that she did not know Deborah or Helen outside of our Twitter and WordPress accounts. In this post Naomi pointed out that we inspired each other to continue a non-linear conversation, and that others were drawn in too. 'Each participant', she wrote, 'broke the linear rules of the exercise and started weaving a circle of networked learning'. This, in turn, inspired another response from Deborah, who continued to play with the (now very) extended metaphor of the networked web of learners online, ending her post with an offering of 'another post, another moment of my thinking suspended in time, another layer, another thread, another voice, another tendril reaching out to others'. This exchange between three bloggers demonstrates the potential of online writing to develop human academic relationships, complete with excitement, fear, enthusiasm, and messiness, through technical computational modes of communication. The movement of the techne to becoming more human allows cyborg interactions online to shape thinking in collaborative ways.

Yet another cyborgic conversation about qualitative research occurred that November. It was this time sparked by a blog post in which Naomi discussed qualitative methods. Helen responded. Naomi responded to Helen's response. Katherine Collins—a UK academic who had been engaging with Deborah, Naomi, and Helen on Twitter—responded to these blogs with her own blog post, titled 'I'm crashing your writing party'. Katherine begins her post with 'I'm crashing Naomi and Helen's party. They've been blogging and tweeting about autoethnography this morning: writing about writing as a way of knowing, a creative and generative process with epistemological validity in and of itself'. Deborah then, having been following along, found herself thinking about method thanks to these blog posts, and wrote a response of her own. Deborah wrote that 'this post emerges out of a blog and Twitter conversation with three academics around writing and autoethnography', linking to all other posts in the thread, and noting that 'here, I offer my own thoughts to this conversation'. A fourth researcher, a PhD candidate, tweeted that she was 'really enjoying reading these blogs' and that they had 'sparked thoughts (not yet connected or coherent!)'. Deborah responded on Twitter: 'Mine didn't feel coherent either, but I put the words down to see where they went! :P'. Blogs used in this networked way, and subsequent engagement between authors and readers via social media, show how scholars can use technology, public scholarship, and open networks to embrace incoherence and unformed thinking. They can make the thinking of scholarship transparent, and reveal scholars' vulnerabilities. In each exchange the cyborg is apparent as authors from disparate parts of the world work to make the technological more human, leveraging machine and network to connect humanness to academic thought across times and spaces.

Our experiences, recounted previously, challenge the view of Tamas (2014), who presents concerns about collaborative scholarship, including that the growth of digital communities and the blogosphere have resulted in the academe being 'relationally over-fed and under-nourished' (p.371). Tamas argues that while voices have multiplied, they have become meaningless noise, empty of reliable means of analysis. We have found, however, like offline collaborations, these scholarly conversations, mediated by Twitter and WordPress, took work, interest, and commitment from all involved. The connection was cognitive seduction rather than being in the same place at the same time. The earlier interactions between Naomi and Deborah indicate Naomi did not fully consider that humanness of Deborah's techne presence online. Naomi's early tweet responses border on rude, arrogant, and dismissive, a feature often highlighted about Twitter in the scholarly literature (Owen, Noble & Speed, 2017; Campbell, 2017). As the relationship began to develop, Naomi visibly thawed, mediated by a third party (Helen). This thawing could be related to suspicion of strangers or contextual frustration finding an outlet on social media. Regardless, scholarly interactions on social media between people who do not previously know each other appear to take a different collaborative arc to offline collaborations which often develop from being pleasant in the not knowing of each other to the frustration and betrayal of knowing. In the case of Naomi and Deborah's collaboration, the ideal was not the origin story. Our relationship emerged slowly from online conversations that initially involved terseness, power imbalance, and awkwardness. We needed to see the co-cyborg in the other, and discover that through the keyboards and along the network another human was connected to a device.

Positives and productivities: Collaborative cyborg scholarship

In January 2016 our relationship moved to the more intimate direct message channel of Twitter, the Twitter back channel where users can send private messages to one another, individually or in groups. While our first messages were about a Star Wars film, we continued to use Twitter's direct messages to discuss writing together, education research conferences, job opportunities, peer review, writing technologies such as Scrivener, managing time, parenting, popular culture, and literature. In February and March of 2016 it was in the direct messages of Twitter that our academic writing collaboration began:

> @Deborah: I've been thinking about how you and I might co-write a paper ... Thinking maybe we could use blogs, tweets & emails as data &

dialogue. Maybe on collective writing as inquiry / writing as identity work / writing as heutagogy ... Do you fancy sketching something out together?
@Naomi: Love to. I would suggest we do more than just professionally learning using online spaces. I reckon we mine our blogs for the 'data'.
I just thought of what we could write together! We both developed methods for our PhDs. We could write about that. Thoughts?

And so, our first academic writing collaboration was born (Netolicky & Barnes, 2017), which we enacted via the cyborg technologies of typing, emailing, word processing, and direct messaging. As it happened, we did not then mine our blogs for data, as Naomi had suggested, but we do that for the first time in this chapter. While the direct message channel was a more intimate and personal one, our relationship was fully cyborgic, fully online. We still had not met, or even Skyped or spoken on the phone. Our conversations and writing occurred simultaneously across multiple platforms. We wrote in Word and tracked the changes, made comments via email, dumped links to references and theoretical epiphanies into Twitter direct messages. In October 2016 we used Twitter direct messaging to discuss a chapter for a book on metaphors of early career scholars, and subsequently began a new direct message group with a third co-author. For that chapter (Netolicky, Barnes & Heffernan, 2018), we used the collaborative cloud computing space of Google Docs to write together as a trio, layering our words together into a single amalgam.

Once we had fully realised the cyborg in the other we could not see each other in any other way. Being cyborgs also opened up new possibilities for knowing in the world (Haraway, 1992). In December 2016, Deborah thanked Naomi, in a Twitter direct message, for the encouragement to move into new theoretical spaces thanks to their online discussions about Haraway and Deleuze and Guattari:

@Deborah: It's the first time for me going quite theoretical in a solo paper. With thanks to you, <another academic> and <another academic> for the nudges and encouragement in that space.

Deborah's comment shows that discussions with Naomi and others shifted the direction of her writing and research.

It was around the same time that the call for abstracts for this book came out. The idea for this chapter emerged, once again, in the Twitter direct message channel:

@Deborah: Maybe together we use the monster/cyborg to explore how we interact with the technologies / digital platforms of social media, Twitter, blogging, co-authoring. How it shapes us, we shape it, we shape each other. Maybe we draw out specific data from our social media experiences in order to explore. And/or we could do some creative writing as inquiry.

> @Naomi: I like the idea of doing something new for us. I'm writing a chapter on monstrous collaborations with other people. I'll send you the theory I wrote. Then we can think from there.
> @Deborah: We are growing theory via multiple collaborations and publications over time.
> @Naomi: Yes. Like a growing orchestra of many parts.
> @Deborah: That's a cool image. Coming together to form a richer, harmonious sound, but the instruments are individual and unique.

Here there has developed a notion of the scholarly 'us' or going beyond the individual cyborg; Naomi and Deborah have plugged into each other on many occasions and developed an integrated identity of themselves as a writing duo. Our collaborative relationship had begun to resemble that of an academic reading group or book club. The metaphor of the cyborg sparked both authors' theoretical imaginations and we have produced academic outputs together and apart. Deborah wrote on cyborgs by viewing scholarly identity through the lens of *Westworld* cyborg characters (Netolicky, 2017). Naomi theorised cyborg scholarship through a London School of Economics Impact blog where she challenged other digital scholars to remember that studies conducted on the Internet should remember that these data are attached to humans. Naomi continued her cyborg theorisation into the exploration of blogging as a method of inquiry, digitally connecting researchers and the public through hyperlinks and comment capability. While these three theoretical contributions to social media and academic scholarship were published separately and about different content matter, Twitter and WordPress provided a space for both authors to discuss their emerging theorisation, despite living on opposite coasts of Australia.

In the time since we began talking about writing together in February 2016, we have co-authored two journal articles and two book chapters. We have influenced one another's thinking and writing. We have shared our voices publicly and privately online, in order to think aloud, to engage with education and academic debates, and to influence the narratives in our fields.

Dark undercurrents of new media

While we authors have found our cyborgic relationship with each other, and others, to be generally positive and productive, there are dystopian undercurrents that are often misrecognised (Bourdieu, 1990) in online spaces. Undercurrents can be dangerous; they can be hard to spot approaching, and they can pull us under. We might ask: Are our identities as open and messy cyborg scholars feeding the capitalist business model of online spaces, which monetises our words (Barnes & Davies, 2018)? Furthermore, this kind of scholarship rubs against the grain of the academe's desire for neat publishable writing of fully formed theories and elegant contributions. Rainford (2016) notes that making our private deliberations public might negatively influence career prospects. Our willingness to publish online our workings out means that we are not presenting a shiny personal brand or a façade of academic expertise. Rather, we are opening our beta selves up to online critique, public intrusion, and invasive reprogramming, with the hope that others' lines of code, whether engagement with comments, retweets or hyperlinking will, like the sometimes-brutal sting of peer review, help our thinking and writing to be stronger.

Here in this chapter we lay ourselves bare by putting our private messages, only written for one another, into public display. Likewise, on open social media platforms like Twitter, individuals reveal vulnerability by laying out their thoughts to a global audience, and can be surprised by the negativity or abrasiveness of the responses. Sharing opinion or writing online can be met with anything from banal insults to vicious personal attacks. The online landscape can be a place of opposition and intrusion (Vera-Gray, 2017). Cheng, Danescu-Niculescu-Mizil, Leskovec, and Bernstein (2017) define online trolling as activity such as name-calling, profanity, racism, or harassment that may be one-off, unintentional, or untargeted. They differentiate trolling from cyberbullying, which they define as behaviour that is repeated, intended to harm, and targeted at specific individuals. Campbell (2017) explores the outpouring of venom, mockery, and hostility towards autoethnographers and feminist academics on Twitter, including written attacks using profanity and the circulating of personal details like addresses. In this way, engaging in cyborgic scholarship opens us up to potentially unproductive or vicious engagement from those intending to disparage, censure, or harm (Carrigan, 2016). While cyborg collaboration can invite unproductive or harmful responses due to its digital nature, partnership can provide solidarity and shared resilience in the face of derision.

Cloud computing spaces such as Google Docs provide the technologies of synchronous editing and anchored commenting, but this co-authoring by multiple users has been found to blur individuals' accountability and credit of contribution, and to make some collaborators feel distracted and uncomfortable (Wang, Tan & Lu, 2017). Some collaborative writers have found their collaborators' editing behaviours to have a negative impact on how they felt about each other, such as being upset when a co-writer writes over or changes their words (Birnholtz & Ibara, 2012). We authors attempted to temper our own discomfort by writing considered comments in Word or Google Docs margins, and having transparent co-authorly conversations via email and Twitter's direct message channel, in order to support and enhance our collaborative cyborg scholarship. Even in our productive and positive relationship with one another, there are uncomfortable moments and challenging emotions. For instance, Deborah expressed uneasiness in working too closely with Naomi, in case their individual work begins to borrow too much from one another, leading to a homogeneity. Naomi expressed a level of jealousy at Deborah's academic track record. These feelings, combined with the at-a-distance nature of our cyborgic-mediatised relationship, have meant that we are hyper-aware as we work together. This hyper-awareness, that Wang et al. (2017) call 'collaboration awareness', influences the professional language we use in our emails to one another, the frank way we give each other feedback, as well as our respectful adherence to deadlines. Our relationship maintains an undertone of the tension of our first encounter and an awareness that while we collaborate closely in some ways, we are very distant in other ways. We do writing-talk and theory-talk, not small talk. We are conscious of our simultaneous closeness (in writing) and distance (geographical and personal). We wonder if we will be able to maintain this tension over time. Do we need to guard against inertia or an echo chamber of agreement, or might we outgrow each other and move on to other collaborations?

We do not present our collaborative relationship here as an exemplar to be heralded. Rather, it is one story of a cyborgic collaboration that has been ethical and productive. Our collaborative cyborg scholarship is partly about survival in the academe as new scholars, and partly about claiming our own ways of writing and ways of working. Our partnership empowered us to push at the borders of accepted scholarship, of who the academe suggests we be, and how it encourages us to behave. Maybe our ambition, our work ethic, or our socialisation to follow through with commitments has been stronger than our desire for friendship; maybe the cognitive stimulus we provide each other is enough to keep going back for more; maybe our level of associated productivity is accidental or unsustainable. Regardless, our collaborative relationship managed to navigate the complicated cyborgic space that social media has delivered—that of writing in speech, or speaking to each other in words without body language. This hybrid of organic and machine is a language that an increasingly disparate transnational academia will need to navigate in the coming decades.

Empowerment through cyborg scholarship

In presenting our co-authorly relationship, developed via technologies and the online worlds we inhabit, we have presented ourselves as a microcosm of cyborg scholarship. It is a microcosm that reveals the potential of the mediatised landscape to develop individual and collaborative scholarship. The open network of scholars active on social media such as Twitter allows the cyborg scholar to engage in ideas and writing with those with whom they might not normally come across. The polyphonic, multi-platform, and immediate nature of new media and technological tools allow writing and collaboration occurs across geographies, time zones, and multiple platforms.

In this chapter, we have addressed Tamas' (2014) warning that much collaborative writing shies away from conflict and tension, preferring to lazily sink into muddy, blunt compromise. We have found that it is through a mild level of tension and discomfort in a relationship, combined with a cognitive attraction, that a cyborg collaboration can propel academic productivity and shift individual thinking. We have shown that while we have supported one another, empathised with one another, and connected with one another through media and technologies, we have also rubbed each other the wrong way, challenged one another, and had to work to compromise. We have engaged in a courtship of sorts; pushing and pulling; finding likenesses and dissonances; seeing ourselves in one another while at the same time positioning ourselves in opposition to each other. Our differences have allowed us to write in ways that we would be unable to write alone. The niggling pressure we each put on each other, and the union of shared accountability, meant that we have influenced one another as scholars and writers, and in the process, we have produced writing and theory together. We authors did eventually meet face to face, yet our collaboration has continued via technologies, as these have become our cyborgic way of thinking and interacting: with ourselves, each other, our writing, and our thinking.

In this chapter and our writing of it, we have accepted our own edges and attempted, through this collaboration, to keep the angles of our author blades severe. As in our online interactions, reflected in this chapter's data, we have kept our separateness while allowing ourselves to create something that speaks as one. We are simultaneously Deborah and Naomi the authors and Deborah-Naomi the amalgamation. We propose that, rather than blunting one another, co-authorship can be a scholarship whet-stone that shapes and re-forms. This is a story of academics strengthening and sharpening one another, in spite of personal circumstance and an unforgiving system. It is a tale of social media and blogging as cyborgic tools for scholars to take charge of their thinking, writing, publishing, and collaboration—to become cyborg both technically and by injecting humanity into the technocratic culture of academia. Public online spaces allow scholars, including those early in their careers or those undertaking post-graduate study, to engage the public in their research and their thinking. Blogging, microblogging, and social media are democratised spaces in which the rules of academic hierarchies and the often obtuse and slow processes of peer review do not apply. These spaces allow scholars to reveal their organic, fleshy, flawed humanness through the computational, machinic, networked technologies of the cyborg.

Cyborg scholarship offers productiveness and possibilities, but also shadowy undercurrents. Haraway (1991) argues for pleasure in the confusion of boundaries and for responsibility in their construction. We have found pleasure in navigating across blurred binaries—human-machine, brain-keyboard, private-public, individual-together, corporeal-cerebral, beauty-ugliness, Deborah-Naomi—and in this chapter, we have taken responsibility for the ways we engage with the messy grey areas between these antitheses. We have embraced and explored the lusty confusion that interrupts and deterritorialises knowledge making (St. Pierre & Pillow, 2000) and embodied the 'practice of the plunge' (Taylor, 2016), in order to agitate, disrupt, and democratise ways of academic being, becoming, and engaging. We have explored how we, as early career researchers, embrace and traverse new media and digital technologies as qualitative method, collaborative platform, and productive sphere. Our cyborg scholarship is a vehicle for agency in the public sphere of education research and practice. We accept our human-machine-writer-academic selves as those that interact with Twitter, blogging, and digital co-authorship, to resist the system in which we operate and to influence our fields. Engaging publicly in the global mediatised landscape means being exposed to the glory and the murkiness of the human-technology amalgam. We propose that cyborg scholarship that focuses on mess and discomfort, not artfully curated personal brand, can deterritorialise knowledge making, and offer scholars connection, agency, and influence.

References

Ahmed, S. (2014). *Cultural politics of emotion*. Edinburgh University Press.

Barnes, N., & Davies, H. (2018). Do we (mis)recognise the political power of Twitter?. London School of Economics Impact Blog. 24 January 2018. Retrieved from http://blogs.lse.ac.uk/impactofsocialsciences/2018/01/24/do-we-misrecognise-the-political-power-of-twitter/

Birnholtz, J., & Ibara, S. (2012). Tracking changes in collaborative writing: Edits, visibility and group maintenance. Paper presented in Proceedings of the ACM 2012 conference on *Computer Supported Cooperative Work* in Seattle WA, USA, 809–818.

Bourdieu, P. (1990). *The logic of practice*. Stanford University Press.

Brophy, J. E. (2016). Connecting and reconnecting: Outfitting the figure of the cyborg for transnational coalition-building. *KOME*, 4(2), 7–27.

Bunz, M. (2014). *The silent revolution*. London: Palgrave Pivot.

Campbell, E. (2017). 'Apparently being a self-obsessed c**t is now academically lauded': Experiencing Twitter trolling of autoethnographers. *Forum: Qualitative Social Research*, 18 (3).

Carrigan, M. (2016). *Social media for academics*. Sage.

Cheng, J., Danescu-Niculescu-Mizil, C., Leskovec, J., & Bernstein, M. (2017). Anyone can become a troll. *American Scientist*, 105(3), 152.

Crandall, J. (2010). Movement, agency, and sensing: A performative theory of the event. In D. Hauptmann & W. Neidich (Eds.) *Cognitive architecture: From bio-politics to noo-politics; Architecture & mind in the age of communication and information*. Rotterdam: 010 Publishers.

Grebowicz, M., & Merrick, H. (2013). *Beyond the cyborg: Adventures with Donna Haraway*. New York: Columbia University Press.

Haraway, D. J. (1991). *Simians, cyborgs and women: The reinvention of nature*. London: Free Association.

Haraway, D. (1992). The promises of monsters: A regenerative politics for inappropriate/d others. In L. Grossberg, C. Nelson & P. Treichler (Eds.) *Cultural studies*. New York and London: Routledge.

Haraway, D. (2006). A cyborg manifesto: Science, technology, and socialist-feminism in the late 20th century. In *The international handbook of virtual learning environments* (pp. 117–158). Dordrecht: Springer.

Haraway, D. J., & Goodeve, T. N. (2000). *How like a leaf: An interview with Thyrza Nichols Goodeve*. New York: Routledge.

Lather, P. (2016). Top ten+ list: (Re) thinking ontology in (post) qualitative research. *Cultural Studies <-> Critical Methodologies*, 16(2), 125–131.

Lykke, N., (2008). Feminist cultural studies of technoscience: Portrait of an implosion. In A. M. Smelik & N. Lykke (Eds.) *Bits of life: Feminism at the intersections of media, bioscience, and technology*. University of Washington Press.

Netolicky, D. M. (2017). Cyborgs, desiring-machines, bodies without organs, and Westworld: Interrogating academic writing and scholarly identity. *KOME*, 5(1), 91–103. doi:10.17646/KOME.2017.16

Netolicky, D. M. & Barnes, N. (2017). Method as a journey: A narrative dialogic partnership illuminating decision making in qualitative educational research. *International Journal of Research & Method in Education*, 1–14.

Netolicky, D. M., Barnes, N. J., & Heffernan, A. (2018). Metaphors for women's experiences of early career academia: Buffy, Alice, and Frankenstein's creature. In A. L. Black & S. Garvis (Eds.) *Lived experiences of women in academia: Metaphors, manifesto and memoir*. Routledge.

Oakes, J. (2018). AERA presidential address: Public scholarship: Education research for a diverse democracy. *Education Researcher*, 47(2), 91–104.

Owen, T., Noble, W., & Speed, F. C. (2017). Trolling, the ugly face of the social network. In *New perspectives on cybercrime* (pp. 113–139). Palgrave Macmillan.

Rainford, J. (2016). Becoming a doctoral researcher in a digital world: Reflections on the role of Twitter for reflexivity and the internal conversation. *E-Learning and Digital Media*, 13(1–2), 99–105.

Soukup, C. (2006). Computer-mediated communication as a virtual third place: Building Oldenburg's great good places on the world wide web. *New Media & Society*, 8(3), 421–440.

Stiegler, B. (2007). Technoscience and reproduction. *Parallax*, 13(4), 29–45.

St. Pierre, E., & Pillow, W. S. (2000). *Working the ruins: Feminist poststructural theory and methods in education*. New York: Routledge.

Tamas, S. (2014). My imaginary fiend: Writing, community, and responsibility. *Cultural Studies <-> Critical Methodologies*, 14(4), 369–373.

Taylor, C. A. (2016). Edu-crafting a cacophonous ecology: Posthumanist research practices for education. In C. A. Taylor & C. Hughes (Eds.) *Posthuman research practices in education*. London: Palgrave Macmillan.

Vera-Gray, F. (2017). 'Talk about a cunt with too much idle time': Trolling feminist research. *Feminist Review*, 115(1), 61–78.

Wang, D., Tan, H., & Lu, T. (2017). Why users do not want to write together when they are writing together: Users' rationales for today's collaborative writing practices. *Proceedings of the ACM on Human-Computer Interaction*, 1(CSCW), 1–18.

11
CONCLUDING THOUGHTS, PROVOCATIONS AND SPECULATIONS ON EDUCATION RESEARCH AND MEDIA

Aspa Baroutsis, Pat Thomson and Stewart Riddle

Introduction

As we write the closing chapter to this book, the storm around the misuse of data by Cambridge Analytica is dying down. New rules about data privacy have led to lists and advertisers issuing new statements on privacy, and in the UK at least, requiring active consent for contact and for use of cookies. At the same time, alarming news comes about the amount of information being collected by 'smart house' devices, and the potential for various data sources to be joined together for frightening omni-surveillance purposes. These and other technological developments signal the advent of the 'electronic panopticon' (Lyon, 2013) in a global society prone to 'dataveillance' (Raley, 2013) through the harnessing of (meta)data, often with monetising intentions. It seems as if Orwell's 1984 is upon us, just a little later than predicted. In this context, this book makes small steps towards understanding what education research might mean and do in this kind of digital topography.

What does this book offer?

This book makes several tentative additions to the emerging field of education research and the media, with perhaps the most immediate being an acknowledgement that working in a mediatised landscape is something that must be taken seriously. This is not simply for scholars who choose to research in and on this field, as outlined by Baroutsis in Chapter 1, but for all academics who are producing and sharing research knowledge with different communities and publics. Whether it is the social media 'firestorms' and confected outrage targeting feminist scholars and their work (e.g., Veletsianos et al., 2018), or the more subtle coalescing of commercial and marketing interests in promoting 'brand' and hype through orchestrated social media events, it is clear that education researchers need to consider how these media connect and affect the work that we do.

We asked contributing authors to consider questions of public scholarship, media, and education research: 'How are academics, now expected by policy and their institutions, to take their work to wider publics?' and 'How can education researchers operate in this new and rapidly changing environment?'

Taking the collection presented in this book, it is apparent that there are multiple possible responses to these prompts. For example, universities around the world are engaging in increasing attempts to quantify and codify impact and engagement of their academic workers, such as through the *Research Excellence Framework* in the UK, and the Australian Research Council's *Excellence in Research for Australia* triennial assessment, which in 2018 included measurements of impact and engagement. There is a somewhat perverse incentive to activate the social media outrage machine, as McKnight and Graham (Chapter 9) articulate, it drives up the metrics and 'reach' of the research.

Similarly, the careful orchestration of media coverage through traditional and social media platforms to support engagement activities, such as Mockler's analysis in Chapter 3, provides potentially compelling, albeit manufactured, stories of public scholarship. The careful cultivation of public personae is expressed well in Gerstl-Pepin and Reyes' (Chapter 6) sharing of four meticulously curated education guru profiles. There is little doubt that the appeal of broader influence and networking is strong, including with teachers, as Thomson and Riddle describe in Chapter 7. However, the question of whether social media afford teachers, researchers, and others who are interested in education, a public 'voice' is very much left open. It seems that there are as many constraining as enabling factors at play in a mediatised world.

In contrast to tales of social media platforms providing space for branding, self-promotion, networking, and sharing of outputs, both Zarabadi and Ringrose (Chapter 4) and Jeffries (Chapter 5) explore the detrimental impacts of remediating practices and indoctrination potential from traditional and social media on public perception and, by extension, influencing policy making, research, and practice.

At the same time, there are revolutionary possibilities made available to scholars through these media. One example of this is Thrupp's account (Chapter 8) of commitment to collective activism in order to effect change. Of course, such public scholarship does come at some cost. Yet we would argue that Thrupp demonstrates how imperative such commitments are to the democratic potential of researchers engaging in public scholarship. Similarly, the analysis provided by Baroutsis and Lingard (Chapter 2) provides a small glimmer of hopeful potential for social media as a site of democratic and civic participation. But perhaps the most hopeful moment in terms of democratic possibility is in Chapter 10, where Netolicky and Barnes provide a reflective account of the be-comings and comings-together of two emergent feminist scholars facilitated by their collaborative engagements in social media.

It would be too easy for us to make some trite claim that if only researchers would engage more with social media, or if only they would engage better, then naturally things would improve. Yet, as our authors have demonstrated in their contributions, there is always a double-edge to encounters of education research and the media.

We decided that rather than write a conclusion that attempts to arrive at some kind of certainty and finality, it was more reflective of an emerging research area, and a rapidly changing context, to try to raise issues, ask questions, and pose problems. It also seemed desirable that we engage in a respectful dialogical response, of the kind very often lacking on social media, as several of the chapters attest. One of the challenges we can immediately identify is how asynchronous conversation might take place. As such, we agreed that we would write these final words as a three handed dialogue, using a number of questions, suggesting in form as well as argument that what is desperately needed is serious well evidenced conversation.

How are academics, now expected by policy and their institutions, to take their work to wider publics?

Pat

When we get to the question 'where to now?', I find myself heading back to the past. In 2002 I presented a paper at the European Conference on Educational Research held in Lisbon. The paper was called 'Poverty, education and Radio Gaga: the politics of evidence'. I rediscovered the paper recently. The abstract still makes sense some 16 years later:

> Federal policy in Australia has rendered poverty invisible. In education, those who attempt to bring poverty back onto the agenda are dubbed excuse makers. The educational community concerned with social justice can draw little joy from a recent radio 'debate' between poverty 'experts' which focussed on techniques of measurement rather than on the everyday lives of people with low incomes. At stake was not a moral purpose, but 'administrative poverty', that is, how many people were to receive additional support from the state in the form of welfare benefits. I use an analysis of this debate to suggest that even in the 'quality' media disposed to take up poverty research, professionally oriented journalists mostly produced neutral syntheses, or simplistic summaries of confrontations.
>
> I then show how this media practice plays out in education research. I explore media treatment of a recent study by the Australian Council for Educational Research (ACER) which suggested that while parental education, wealth and occupational status are all important factors in successful tertiary entrance, performance in literacy and numeracy at Year 9 significantly mediates those effects. This was interpreted by the national daily (*The Australian* 19/01/02, p. 16) as 'evidence' that 'theorists of "progressive education" in the 70s and 80s' had 'overstated the importance of socio-economic background' and that meritocracy was just around the corner.

I consider how educational researchers might use the media to debate this and other data and make two tentative suggestions for ways in which research associations might promote productive media-ted discussions.

The paper received a very mixed reception in the policy special interest group. Some researchers were of the view that media had nothing to do with 'education science' and that this kind of paper had no place in the conference. They—all senior white men of a certain age—were certain that this kind of research was both trivial and a distraction. I was somewhat shaken by the hostility and afterwards a handful of women approached me to say that I ought not to be put off by the bluster. They too thought that policy was not unrelated to media. I should go ahead. Because two other Australian education researchers, Sue Thomas and Jill Blackmore, were also working on media, I was reassured that media were not a blind alley for inquiry. But the conference incident, and the ill-fated Radio Gaga paper, was the genesis of the first special issue on education policy and media – fortunately the *Journal of Education Policy* was interested in the development of media research.

I tell this story not to stake a claim in the field as some kind of founding mother, but rather to suggest that it was something of a struggle to get media taken seriously as an area of education research – and I don't think that we have come that far since 2002. Despite the enormous corpus of education work that goes on around pedagogies, e-learning, and multimodal literacies for instance, and despite the body of work around mediatisation in other disciplines, there is still not much focus on media in the education research community. On a bad day I am prone to think that we are happy to talk a lot, often on social media, about how media shapes and frames academic labour and the ways in which we design conduct and communicate our research. But we just don't want to research it. As a community, we still have to see education research on and through media as an *emerging field*. There is so much that remains 'blank space'.

Stewart

I'd like to pick up on Pat's point on the notion of emergence and consider how my own experiences as an early career researcher were shaped by my interest, not so much in researching on and through media, but certainly taking up my university's exhortations to embrace this Brave New World. As well as signing up for all of the usual research profiles and networking sites, I joined Twitter and became an author for *The Conversation*. After writing my first piece for *The Conversation* in 2013, I was invited onto a couple of radio shows, republished in various media outlets, and became a momentary blip in eduTwitter. It was enough to hook me and before I knew it, I had published 37 articles for *The Conversation* with nearly 500,000 readers and 2,500 comments. I was invited onto national radio and television shows for interviews and thought that I was doing *all the right things* as a beginning public scholar.

In the middle of 2014, things took a turn, when a piece that I had penned was used as fodder for a short campaign by *The Australian*, where I became the target of several pieces opining on how I was the very thing that was wrong with contemporary academia, which in turn spawned a number of right-wing hate bloggers setting their sights on me, as well as the predictable Twitter firestorm. My university did their best in supporting me through the experience, which is to say, they suggested that I leave it alone and not pay attention to the haters. However, it was a steep learning curve and taught me two very important lessons: 1) when universities encourage engagement with traditional and social media, the public scholarship work comes at very real personal and reputational risk, which the institution might not have the capacity to support; and 2) as an education researcher seeking to engage in public discourse, the media are not your friend.

Enough time has passed for it to mostly be a bad memory, but several of the chapters in this book resonate with my own experiences in various ways. I am convinced that we are only just beginning to understand the complex interplays between education researchers' lives and work, and the deep commitment to engaging with communities and publics, alongside the contradictory tensions that come with commercial interests in the mainstream media world and social media platforms.

I have not written for *The Conversation* for some time now, I have turned down several requests for interview as I was not convinced of the honest commitment for engagement rather than production of media fodder, I have shut down most of my public research profiles, including Academia and ResearchGate, and have a more careful cultivation of my Twitter persona, including a regular purge of my tweet history – something Donald Trump should perhaps consider.

For me, this book comes at an important time, because many of the education researchers who I speak with share similar stories and concerns. How might we engage productively in public scholarship work, especially given the contemporary landscape of metrics and measuring research impact and engagement? By choosing to not have Academia and ResearchGate profiles, am I really engaged in 'brand abuse' as one speaker at a Powering Up Your Academic Profile workshop described it? What are some of the pathways for engaging with media, including researching on, with, and through media, that might become available to us? How should our universities and institutions encourage us to activate these opportunities? What support mechanisms should be available when things go awry?

Aspa

As we engage in this dialogue, I am reminded of my reasons for researching in the field of education and media. The excerpt from my thesis gives a sense of my concerns:

> A newspaper story caught my eye. It was about teachers. 'What have we done wrong, this time?' I thought to myself. I read on. The story is about an enterprise bargain pay claim and proposed industrial action by Queensland

teachers. I do not recall the headline or who wrote it but I think it was an opinion piece. I recall the effect it had on me. Apparently, based on what I read as the sub-text, teachers were greedy, selfish, arrogant, lazy, incompetent and unprofessional people. I remember the word 'craven' was used in the article. The Oxford dictionary defines craven as 'contemptibly lacking in courage'. I mentally added that to the list of teachers' flaws described in the newspaper. My reaction to this article was one of disgust and frustration. The words evoked a physical response. I was unsettled by what I read. No, it was more than that. It was visceral abhorrence at the lack of respect this person had for teachers. This person could be talking about my colleagues. I am a teacher. This person could be talking about me! Why do newspapers print these stories?

Some time later, I was reading a teachers' union magazine. The title of the article was 'Nine til three! Not likely!' It was a catchy title so I kept reading. The article challenged the 'popular' perception that teachers work short hours, have long holidays and get paid too much money, something I have read many times in mainstream newspapers. The author wrote about research conducted into teachers' work and the teachers' perceptions of their workload. The lived experiences of the teachers in this study were not like the popular perception of teachers' work seen in newspapers. The teachers in this study referred to working long hours, the lack of support and the constant reforms initiated through frequent policy changes. Mentally, I added the voice of my personal experiences of teaching, and the comprehension of my own workload challenges. Teaching is not a 'nine to three' job! So, why don't I read about this in mainstream newspapers?

While this is not the forum for a detailed discussion about democratic societies, the notion of 'parity of participation' (Fraser, 2009) is important in this context. Participation in this instance is about *inclusion*. In the previous excerpt, I was looking to find representatively just accounts of teachers' work in the newspapers I was reading; however, the newspaper version marginalised teachers and framed education negatively. Teachers were not able to actively have their say in the account that was presented about their work, except by adding comments to the online version of the news articles. Similarly, as seen in Pat and Stew's reflections, a mixed reception would certainly warrant a rethink of public *engagement* with media which is another aspect of participation. However, it would be equally problematic if such negative experiences cause academics to disengage with research and public issues about education.

A democratic public sphere, and a democratic media, are often charged with the responsibility of providing a forum for pluralistic debate and mobilising public participation (Norris & Odugbemi, 2010). However, media and education institutions rarely organise themselves within such utopian fictions (Benhabib, 1996) and as we have seen in the narratives throughout this book, there are both possibilities and challenges to education research and public engagement with traditional and social media.

Therefore, the notion of inclusive media and civic participation can frame future education research and media agendas by asking: Are social media more inclusive and therefore more democratically useful than traditional media? Does social media mean the end of education research that draws on traditional media? How can educators and researchers, who are not a part of media institutions, better participate in public scholarship through traditional media? When participating in public scholarship and education research with and about media, how can educators enrich public knowledge about education?

How can education researchers operate in this new and rapidly changing environment?

Pat

To become something other than emerging, a field needs to develop understandings of the object of its study, understandings that are researchable. I think for instance of the work done by Stephen Ball in the field of policy sociology. His work on policy as texts and discourse, and on policy trajectories (Ball, 1993), opened up ways for people to design and conduct policy sociology research. Post his paper, the researchable object of policy was able to be understood through ethnographic case study to discourse analysis to mixed method designs. Taylor et al.'s (1997) formulation of policy as context, texts, and effects is similarly researchable. Ball, Maguire, and Braun's (2012) more recent work on policy 'enactment' also opens up ways of designing research projects which focus on both patterns and differences in local responses to policy.

I don't see an equivalent of these kinds of theoretically informed researchable formulations of the mediatisation of education research. If I had to make a first pick of what area needs work then I'd suggest it is thinking a lot more about the very idea of mediatisation. While there is research going on, and there is some kind of agreement about the idea of mediatisation per se, we haven't yet worked out what we mean by this. Do we see media as something that is produced, textualised, and then received, drawing on literary reception theory? Or do we simply see media as representations? Or perhaps discourse? Or do we see it as something productive, something that makes things happen in the world, drawing both on genre theory and on notions such as assemblage? Does the idea of assemblage point us towards a way of mapping who and what comes to be assembled together, lines of thinking and activity becoming knotted together with particular consequences? Do we think of the texts themselves as actants, and track their work within networks?

Aspa

The concept of mediatisation is certainly a core concept for theoretically informed education research, but as Pat has suggested, it is sometimes difficult to identify what a scholar means by this when communicating their research. While it is understandable that there are likely multiple interpretations of mediatisation for education research depending on specific paradigm approaches, it would be useful for scholarship in education research to theorise and build on this body of literature. Particularly within individual publications, it would be beneficial for education scholars to theorise their understandings of mediatisation.

Pat

I notice that as a field we education researchers haven't been quick to bring our own bodies of knowledge to social media research. Like any other form of broadcast text, social media is public pedagogy. Sandlin, O'Malley, and Burdick's (2011) typology of public pedagogies as (a) citizenship within and beyond schools, (b) popular culture and everyday life, (c) informal institutions and public spaces, (d) dominant cultural discourses, and (e) public intellectualism and social activism – offers one way to begin to think about how education research on, in, and through social media might be understood and researched. The focus on purposes and practices (a), sites of learning (b)–(d), and (e) the pedagogical agent herself offer some helpful beginnings. Various understandings of pedagogy might be brought to the table, for instance, feminist, queer, and activist perspectives. And if social media is understood as public pedagogy then it might also be analysed for its socially reproductive, resistant, affective, and counter reproductive dimensions.

The distinction made by Sandlin, Burdick, and Rich (2017) is a helpful reminder to an emerging field about its purpose. These authors suggest that there is a fundamental difference between enacting policies about academic work on media – doing public engagement work – and how this is researched. They argue that scholars need urgently to focus on three related areas:

> (a) power dynamics embedded in individualized versus more collective enactments of public intellectualism; (b) conflicting and complicated conceptualizations of the relationship between the public pedagogue and the public, and how that relationship should be enacted; and (c) ethical issues surrounding the framing of public engagement and activist work under the umbrella of 'pedagogy'.
>
> (p. 823)

This framing offers clear opportunities for a developing field research agenda. Some of the chapters in this collection already head in this direction.

It does seem to me that research associated with e-learning and with data-fication, the use of data for governing education systems, sites, subjects, and practices, might come together with research on academic engagement with media. Perhaps some of the topics that we might examine in order to bring these together are those that focus directly on educational politics – how teacher unions and employers use social media, new forms of teacher activism, the contestation of policy, and the formation of resistances via social media (e.g. Dennis' (2015) work on blogging as a site for creating alternative education futures). We might also then see how social media is a lens for examining ongoing education research concerns. I think for instance about questions of how education policy is made and who gets to speak, about what, to whom, and in whose interests, on questions of educational importance. Is social media a platform for a new kind of educational public sphere, or is it another site where opposition is appropriated and conservative educational ideas recuperated? Well I'm showing my biases here of course, but I agree with Aspa that the question of media as a public sphere ought to be one that education researchers take very seriously indeed.

Aspa

When thinking about future research agendas, I would add a few points about conducting research with media. In particular, there is the need to consider children and young people within education systems as there is little scholarship around their perspectives. Ironically, a very large part of education is about children and young people, while not much research is conducted in terms of mediatisation of education in relation to these groups. Additionally, as I have argued elsewhere (see Chapter 1) there is cause for education research with and about media to move beyond simplistic accounts of critique about media towards more generative accounts that offer solutions to existing problems. While this is unlikely to happen in the short-term, research that enables positive change is more valuable at this point in the history of the field of education research and media.

Some of the other points to consider are about the limitations of research with media. Some of the problems I encountered when using media texts as data are around gathering and using media data sets. Compiling these data sets using databases or data mining tools is not always as straightforward as anticipated and researchers should expect this to be a time-consuming activity. While technology assisted options are available, I have always used these in conjunction with my own reading of the entire compiled data set to filter out data that may comply with the search parameter but is not relevant to the research. For example, in a recent search for media about the Programme for International Student Assessment (PISA), the searches returned relevant data but also included topics such as the 'Leaning Tower of Pisa' and the 'Associazione Calcio Pisa' which is an Italian football association. Therefore, a manual filtering process was required. This is perhaps easy enough to do with 200 individual articles or Tweets, but significantly more labour intensive with large data sets such as 20,000 articles or Tweets. Another issue relates to the processing of large data sets as these processes are often intensive and require powerful computers and digital devices to effectively render these data. There have been more than a few times where I have become frustrated with a computer crashing mid-way through processing. Finally, there is the issue of ethics. As education research involving media is often dealing with data in the public domain, this raises the question of what is appropriate and ethical in terms of reporting the findings. For example, when quoting a Tweet, is it ethical to use a person's name? Or should scholarship work towards protecting an individual's anonymity (even if that individual has said unfavourable things) even though the information is in the public domain?

Last words

Each of these lines of thought points to different kinds of methodologies and research designs. We are not arguing for some kind of homogeneity in the education field. But we agree that it might be helpful if we had more explicit explorations of what kind of research agenda there might be about mediatisation and how we might bring theoretically informed methodologies and methods together to explore key questions. Perhaps we editors are just a little disappointed that we did not manage to do this in this book but perhaps that is because our primary interest was in the politics of mediatised education research. Perhaps we needed to get this collection together before we could move on to the next step. We hope that you will join with us in making it.

References

Ball, S. (1993). What is policy? Texts, trajectories and toolboxes. *Discourse*, 13(2), 10–17.
Ball, S., Maguire, M., & Braun, A. (2012). *How schools do policy. Policy enactments in secondary schools*. London: Routledge.
Benhabib, S. (1996). Toward a deliberative model of democratic legitimacy. In S. Benhabib (Ed.), *Democracy and difference: Contesting the boundaries of the political* (pp. 67–94). Princeton, NJ: Princeton University Press.
Dennis, C. A. (2015). Blogging as public pedagogy: Creating alternative education futures. *International Journal of Lifelong Education*, 34(3), 284–299.
Fraser, N. (2009). *Scales of justice: Reimagining political space in a globalizing world*. New York: Columbia University Press.
Lyon, D. (2013). *The electronic eye: The rise of surveillance society*. Hoboken: Wiley.
Norris, P., & Odugbemi, S. (2010). Evaluating media performance. In P. Norris (Ed.), *Public sentinel: News media and governance reform* (pp. 3–29). Washington DC: The World Bank.
Raley, R. (2013). Dataveillance and countervailance. In L. Gitelman (Ed.), *'Raw data' is an oxymoron* (pp. 121–144). Cambridge, MA: MIT Press.
Sandlin, J., O'Malley, M., & Burdick, J. (2011). Mapping the complexity of public pedagogy scholarship: 1894–2010. *Review of Educational Research*, 81(3) 338–375.
Sandlin, J., Burdick, J., & Rich, E. (2017). Problematizing public engagement within pedagogy research and practice. *Discourse*, 38(6), 823–835.
Taylor, S., Rivzi, F., Lingard, B., & Henry, M. (1997). *Educational policy and the politics of change*. London: Routledge.
Veletsianos, G., Houlden, S., Hodson, J., & Grosse, C. (2018). Women scholars' experiences with online harassment and abuse: Self-protection, resistance, acceptance, and self-blame. *New Media & Society*, 0(0), 1–20.

LIST OF CONTRIBUTORS

Dr Naomi Barnes is a Lecturer in Literacy at the Queensland University of Technology, Brisbane, Australia. Her research interests are digital sociology and literacy, specifically related to social media research. Naomi has recently published 'Blogging as a method of inquiry' in *Reconceptualising Education Research Methods*.

Dr Aspa Baroutsis is a Postdoctoral Research Fellow at the Griffith Institute for Educational Research, Griffith University, Australia. Her research interests include social justice and education; education policy and mediatisation; teachers' work and identity; and children's voice and agency. Her most recent publication in *Discourse: Studies in the Cultural Politics of Education* is about media mentalities and logics.

Dr Cynthia Gerstl-Pepin is Dean of the College of Education at the University of Massachusetts Amherst, USA. Gerstl-Pepin's scholarship employs critical perspectives to examine socially just leadership and educational politics, particularly the media's role in shaping the public's understanding of educational issues and the need for reform. Her most recent work is a co-edited book entitled *Reimagining the Public Intellectual in Education: Making Scholarship Matter*, which explores the need for educational researchers to inform decision-making on education policy and school improvement.

Dr Linda Graham is a Professor in the School of Early Childhood and Inclusive Education, Faculty of Education, Queensland University of Technology (QUT), Australia. She leads QUT's Student Engagement, Learning and Behaviour Research Group and several externally funded projects investigating the development of severely disruptive behaviour. She was Editor-in-Chief of *The Australian Educational Researcher* (AER) from 2014 to 2016.

List of contributors

Michelle Jeffries is a doctoral candidate at the Queensland University of Technology, Brisbane, Australia. Michelle researches in the area of gender and sexual diversity in education, with a specific focus on families. Her research interests also include exploring public discourses about queer-related issues across traditional and social media.

Dr Bob Lingard is Emeritus Professor at The University of Queensland, Brisbane, Australia. He is the Co-Editor of the Routledge Book Series, *Key Ideas in Education* and Co-Editor of the journal, *Discourse: Studies in the Cultural Politics of Education*. His research is situated in the sociology of education and focuses on education policy.

Dr Lucinda McKnight lectures in curriculum and pedagogy in the School of Education, Faculty of Arts and Education, Deakin University, Australia. She has a BA in English, an MA in Media, Culture and Communication and a PhD in Education. Her research interests are in gender, curriculum, media and inclusive education.

Dr Nicole Mockler is Associate Professor of Education in the Sydney School of Education and Social Work at the University of Sydney, Australia. She is the author/editor of 14 books, most recently *Questioning the Language of Improvement and Reform in Education: Reclaiming Meaning* (Routledge, 2018, with Susan Groundwater-Smith) and *Education, Change and Society* (OUP, 2017, with Anthony Welch, Raewyn Connell and colleagues). She is currently the Editor-in-Chief of *The Australian Educational Researcher*.

Dr Deborah M. Netolicky has almost 20 years' experience in teaching and school leadership in Australia and the UK. She is an Honorary Research Associate at Murdoch University, Perth, Australia, whose research and academic writing focus on professional learning, school leadership, qualitative methods and identity. Deborah blogs at theeduflaneuse.com, tweets as @debsnet, and is a Co-Editor of Flip the System Australia.

Dr Cynthia Reyes is an Associate Professor in the College of Education and Social Services at the University of Vermont, USA. Her research interests include multimodal literacy, family literacy, literacy education and school policy for English learners, and social justice and inclusion. Her recent publication is a co-edited book, *Reimagining the Public Intellectual in Education: Making Scholarship Matter*.

Dr Stewart Riddle is a Senior Lecturer in the School of Education at the University of Southern Queensland, Australia. His research interests include social justice and equity in education, music-based research practices and research methodologies. He also plays bass in a band called Drawn from Bees.

Dr Jessica Ringrose is Professor of Sociology of Gender and Education at the UCL Institute of Education, London, UK, where she leads teaching in Social Justice at BA, MA and PhD levels. She is co-chair of the international Gender and Education Association. Her work over the past decade spans media studies and education, with research seeking to transform gendered and sexualised media cultures and enlivening gender and sexual equity in schools. Her latest book is *Digital Feminist Activism: Girls and Women Fight back against Rape Culture* (Oxford University Press, 2018, authored with Kaitlynn Mendes and Jessalynn Keller).

Dr Pat Thomson is Professor of Education in the School of Education, The University of Nottingham, UK. Her research agenda is to further understandings about and practices of socially just pedagogies in schools and communities; she often focuses inquiry on the arts and alternative education. She writes, blogs and tweets about academic writing and doctoral education on patthomson.net.

Dr Martin Thrupp is Head of Te Whiringa School of Educational Leadership and Policy at the University of Waikato, New Zealand. His research interests are in education policy with a particular focus on the lived effects of policy across socially diverse and unequal communities. Most recently he has been working on the enactment of National Standards in New Zealand schools and the privatisation of schooling in Finland, Sweden and New Zealand.

Shiva Zarabadi is doctoral candidate, teaching fellow and research fellow at UCL Institute of Education, London, UK. She is the co-editor of a forthcoming book *Feminist Posthumanisms/New Materialisms and Education* for the book Series on *Education and Social Theory: Putting Theory to Work* (Routledge, 2018, with Jessica Ringrose and Katie Warfield). Her research interests include feminist new materialism, posthumanism, the intra-action of matter, time, affect, space, human and more-than-human.

INDEX

accountability: individual 175; and media 9; school 13; shared 177
achievement: gap 111; media reporting of 135, 136; national 136; PISA **34,** 40, 137; reflection of 49; responsibility for 138
activism: and change 15; collective 181; parent 17, political 39, 72; scholar 108; social 187; and social media 63; *see also* voice
advocacy 13, 100, 107, 112, 113, 129, 152
affect 68, 70, 73, 75, 76, 129, 130, 169, 187; amplify 71; as bodily experience 156; encoding 70; and media 28, 66, 70, 71, 72, 75; as mediation 72; and methodologies 68, 71; and public intellectuals 150
affective assemblages 66, 68, 70
algorithms 35, 157, 159, 160, 168
alternative facts 99, 100, 114
Altmetrics: curation service 148, 156, 157, 158, 159; definition 156, 157; donut 156; metaphor 158; scores 150, 151, 152, 157; tracking publications 149; and Twitter 153, 154, 155, 156, 157, 159
amnesia: permanent and structural 8
Appadurai, A. 29, 31–32
assemblage(s): affective 66, 68, 70; agential 66; complex 159; discursive 158; digital 130, 131, 157; elements 130; event 68; haptic-optic 70, 71; material 71; media 66, 67, 71, 159, 161; and media research 186; metric 155; pedagogical 72; social 75; terrorist 66, 68, 69, 72, 75; terror jarring 74, textual 155; quiltingveil 75
Australia(n): headlines 38, 52; journalists 43, 84; media coverage of international assessments 13, 27, 29, 32, 33, 35, 37, 38, 41, 43, 52; media coverage of inequality 43, 44; media coverage of national assessments 12; media debates 130; media and teachers 15, 120, 123; media ownership 5–6; media research **10–11**; *Melbourne Declaration* 90; newspapers 28, 29, 33, 37, 44n5, 63n2; 83, 182; politicians 123, 151; vlogger 125
Australian Association for Research in Education 148
Australian Broadcasting Corporation 47, 62; @ABCTV 54, 57, 58
Australian Educational Researcher (AER) 148, 149

backchannel 47, 48, 54–55, 57, 58, 62; *see also* Twitter
Ball, S. J. 31, 122, 186
Barad, K. 17, 67, 70, 71, 73
Barnes, N. 173, 174
Baroutsis, A. 1, 7, **10**, 12, 13, 14, 29, 30, 32, 37, 41, 43, 48, 82, 84
Bauman, A. 30
becoming 66, 73, 91, 166, 167, 168, 171, 177, 186
Blackmore, J. 2, 7, **10**, 48, 123
Blog(s) 124, 125, 126, 131–132n4, 144, 166; attack blog 135, 145, 150; cyborgic

170; and education research 128, 172–173; platforms 125
bloggers 107, 109, 110, 141, 166, 167, 170–171; attack of 141; edu-bloggers 130; right-wing 140, 141; teacher bloggers 16, 124, 125, 126
blogging 41, 62, 100, 101, 103, 104, 119, 125, 127, 152, 177, 188; cyborgic 174, 177; exchanges 131, 170, 171; as inquiry method 174; microblogging 16, 152, 156, 177; vlogs 124
blogosphere 104, 150, 172
Boolean 3, 32
bots *see* internet bots
Bourdieu, P. 8, 29, 130, 174
Bruns, A. 48, 61–62, 80, 84
Butler, J. 17, 155, 158

Castells, M. 30–31
Chi-square goodness of fit test 55, 60–61
circular circulation 8, 29–30, 39–40
circulation 8, 29–30, 39, 67, 75, 144
coding 57–58, 103; overcoding 131
Common Core 12, 13, 28, 110
complexity: narratives of 50, 61
conservative orientation **85**, 87, 89, 90
content analysis 8, 33, 50, 57–58; media 101, 102, 103, 109
credibility: in research 103; of scholars 104, 106, 109, 110
crisis: narratives of 13, 49, 52, 59, 61
critical discourse analysis 8, 128
critical orientation **85**, 88, 90, 93
critique: of academics 160, 175; of Common Core 110; editorial 38; lack of 29; of education 129, 150; of PISA 13; in research 17, 18; of research 103; simplistic 188; of television 8; in tweets 58, 59, 60; of voice 120, 121
cyborg; academic as 167; cyborgic relationships 167–168, 171, 172, 174, 175, 176; technologies 168, 173, 177; selves 169, 173, 174, 177; scholar/ship 166, 167, 172, 174, 175, 176, 177, 178; space 170, 176; theorisation of 166, 174

damage: narratives of **34**, 36, 39, 40, *42*, 43
data mining 33, 35, 54
data visualisations 33, 35, 36, 41, 45, 55, 57
data visualisation software: Gephi 55; Leximancer 33, 35
datafication 7, 187
decline: narratives of 49, 52, 54
Deleuze, G. 66, 71, 76, 120, 130, 131, 173

democracy: claims 159; and media 2, 7, 29, 99, 185; participation 185; and policy 27, 44; and the public sphere 101, 185; and review process 148, 155, 160; and social media 44, 100, 102, 181, 186; and voice 120, 121, 126; weakened 99, 114
digital age 8, 31
digital assemblages 130, 131, 157
digital citizens 80, 84, 92, 93
digital curation service 148
digital ethnography 154
digital images 71
digital media 32, 41, 42, 44, 48, 102, 139, 157, 167; communication 100
digital public 166
digital text 31
digital traces 42
digitalisation 6, 7, 124
discourse analysis 102; Foucauldian 154, 156; multimodal 154, 155, 156
discourse: accountability 15; crisis 13, 49, 52, 59, 61; damage **34**, 36, 39, 40, *42*, 43; decline 49, 52, 54; diversity 81, 82, 83, **85**, 86–88, 92–93, 159; indoctrination 81, 82, 84, 88–92; PISA results 29, 33, 37, 38, 52; redemption 52–53, 61; school improvement 49, 50, 52, 53–54, 60, 61; teacher quality 15, 16, 59; standards 12, 13; eduTwitter 128
diversity: narratives of 81, 82, 83, **85**, 86–88, 92–93, 159

education systems: data governance 187; failure of 49; in media research 9, **10–11**, 14–15; problems with 14–15, 49, 111; reforms 14
edu-scholar(s): effective 114; 150 top 105; internet searches about 103; and mediatisation 187; and the political fray 101; as public influencers 104; and social media 110
Edu-Scholar Public Influence Rankings 103, 104, 105, **106**, 107
education policy *see* policy
education stewardship: and research 101, 113; maintaining 104
effects: damaging **34**, 36, 39, 40, *42*, 43; dangerous 93, 114, 121, 123, 37, 142, 174
Entman, R. M. 8
epistemological equivalences 44
ethics 91; Deleuzean reading of 131; and social media 153; and social media research 153–154, 188

ethnography 102; auto 152, 171; digital 154
equity: in education research 113; and PISA 27, 29, 33, **34**, 38, 40–41, 43, 44; programmes 122
event(s): acute 61; destabilising 44; hashtag 62; media 12, 14, 49, 62, 66–67, 68, 69, 70, 72, 75, 76, 81; pedagogical 73; pre-event 69; research 83; screening of *Gaby Baby* 88–89, 92; sense-event 71; social media 48, 49, 127, 181; viral 66; Wear It Purple 81; yet-to-happen 70

Factiva 32, 50
Feminism: abject 155, 158
field: academic 151, 174; education **55**, 104, 113, 159; education policy 100; education research and media 1, 3, 4, 6, 9, 15, 17, 18, 48, 80, 181, 183, 184, 186, 187, 188; ethics 153; feminist 166; feminist digilantism 152; global education policy 43; homogeneity 189; journalism 99; media 30, 43; policy sociology 186; political 43; positions 130; public scholarship 103; social 68
Foucault, M. 17, 31, 84, 121, 129, 154, 155
frame analysis 8, 47–48, 49, 50–52, 61–61
framing: alternative 62; Altmetric 154, 157; analysis 48, 52; bottom up 48, 61–62; conservative 92; data 4; devices 50, 52, 53; dominant 47; education 61, 62; liberal 90; news coverage 37; newspaper 38, 41; policy 62; politics 28; public engagement 187; re-framing 16; schools 53; sociological 120; top down 48, 61–62
Fraser, N. 88, 101, 185
future research 17–18, 44

Gaby Baby: diversity 86; documentary 81; media furore 93; ministerial directive 84, 87; online commentary 80, 88, 90, 92; radio commentary 82; school screening 83, 88–89; student choice
Gamson, W. 52
gatekeeping 84, 92
gatewatching 61
gender 80, 81, 82, **85**, 89, 93, 103, 150, 151, 152, 153, 158
Gephi 55
Gerstl-Pepin, C. 2, **11**, 14, 100, 101, 102, 113
Goffman, E. 8, 130
Google Scholar 3, 103; metrics 107, 108, 109; citations 105
Graham, L. 155

Haptic 70–71, 73, 75, 76
Haraway, D. 74, 166, 167, 173, 177
hashtag publics 48, 61, 62
hashtag(s) 27, 40, 47, 54, 61–62, 127, 166, 168; #aussieED 41; #blimage 170; #charactereducation 127; #CommonCore 12, 28; #edchat 127; #endpisa 40; #Gonski 40; #learnEnglish 127; #phdchat 169; #PISA 40; #revolutionschool 47, 54, 57, 58, 59–60, 61, 62, 63; #scied 127; #stemeducation 127; #TeachForAll 40; #ukedchat 127; #WomenEd 126, 127
Hattie, J. 49, 53, 58; @john_hattie 57, 58–59
heat maps 33, 35, 36, 45
Hepp, A. 6, 7, 30–31, 42, 43
Heteronormativity 86, 88, 90

identity/identities 67–68, 72, 105, 120, 150, 153, 167, 174; academic 152, 155, 159, 160, 174; analysis 154; politics 150; work 166, 173
image(s): academic 123; avatar 158; blog-from-image 170–171; event-time 74; female 67, 68, 70, 71, 76; haptic 71; jarring 72, 73; media 69, 70, 71, 72, 74, 75, 76; mediated 76; mediascapes 32; public 140; and research 155; social media 157, 159; terror 66; threat 72; of youth 16
image loops 67, 68, 71, 72, 76
inclusion: non-dominant knowledge **85**, 92; opposition to 93; as participation 185; policy 160; of private sector 31; promote 93; research criteria **3**, 4, 17; and school cultures 119; and sexual diversity 81, 83, 88; support of 93, 160; of voices 18
indoctrination: narratives of 81, 82, 84, 88–92
influence: of funders 142; institutional 87, 90; journal editors' 153; media 1, 7, 8, 62, 106, 130; policy 106; policy actors' 123; political 13, 29, 44, 83, 104, 106, 126, 143; public 84, 105, 106; rankings 103, 107; social services 83
influencers 104, 108
innovation: in education 111; narrative of 167
interference: patterns 72; political and religious 91
international large-scale assessments *see* PISA
internet bots 28, 33, 44n3,

intertextuality 31, 155
Israel: newspapers **10**, 13

Japan: newspapers **10**, 13; PISA 40
jihadi bride: construction of 66, 70, 75; as event 68, 69, 72, 75, 76; identity 72; in media 67–68; research 70, 71
jihadibridism 67–68, 70
Jones, T. 80, 84, **85**, 87, 88, 89, 90, 91, 92
journalism 2, 7, 8, 12, 17, 28, 30, 37, 38, 40, 43, 100, 114, 137

Kambrya College 49, 52, 53, 54, 58, 60

league tables 13
legacy media 28, 29, 30, 32, 33, 37, 39, 41
Leximancer 33, 35
liberal orientation **85**, 87, 88, 90, 92
limitations: of activism 39; of political campaigns 28; of public scholarship 104; of rankings 105, 107; of research 113, 188; of research methods 32–33, 43–44
Lingard, B. 7, 8, **10**, 13, 14, 29, 30, 32, 37, 41, 43, 122, 123, 135, 137
liquid modernity 30
logics: and activism 39; cultural 159; neoliberal 8; pre-emptive 67, 68, 69, 70, 72, 76; security 70; universal 2; *see also* media logics
Lupton, D. 66, 124, 148

maps: heat maps 33, 35, 36, 45; network maps 57; software generating 33, 35, 55
Massumi, B. 67, 68, 69, 70, 73, 75, 76
Mazzoleni, G. 7, 8
McKnight, L. 148, 150, 158
media assemblages 66, 67, 71, 159, 161
media content analysis 101, 102, 103, 109
media events 12, 14, 49, 62, 66–67, 68, 69, 70, 72, 75, 76, 81
media logics 7, 27; legacy 37; mass 8; and media events 66; network 8, 31; of practice 8, 29, 39; social 8; understanding 17
media manifold 30
media research: by country 5; by data source 4; by decade 4; empirical studies 8–16; journal special issues 2; methodological focus 8; by publication 4; theoretical focus 6–8
mediascapes 29, 30, 31–32, 93, 148, 160, 165
mediatisation 6–8, 9, 17, 29, 31–32, 120, 130, 183, 186–187, 188, 189; deep 31–32; social 120, 121, 123–124, 129, 130, 131
Melbourne Declaration 90
Melbourne Graduate School of Education 49; @EduMelb 56, 57, 60, 61
metrics 105, 149, 153, 155, 160, 184; *see also* Altmetrics
misogyny 150, 152; online 152; Twitter 151
mobilities 30
Mockler, N. **10**, 12, 48, 62
moral panic 89; definition of 14, 94n1; *see also* discourses
myth 12

NAPLAN 12
neoliberalism 2, 158
Netolicky, D. M. 173, 174
network maps 57
networks 30–31, 55, 142, 186; non-academic 127; open 172, peer 8; regional 126; social 8, 105; social media 8; webbed 167
newspapers: online 80, 84, 86; print 4, 13, 14, 15, 16, 27–28, 29, 31, 32, 33, 35, 36, 37, 38, 39, 41–43, 48, 50, 82, 83, 100, 105, 106, 126, 135, 137, 138–139, 140, 141, 185; regional 137, 139, 141
New Zealand: education reform 135, 137, 145; education research 142, 143, 145; journalism 137; media 137, 138, 139–140, 144; Prime Minister 28; standards 136; unions 141
Norway: newspapers **10**, 13
NVivo 50

OECD 13, 27, 30, 39, 40–41, 43, 44n1, 137; @OECDEduSkills 40; @SchleicherOECD 41
ontopower 68, 69, 75; pre-emption and 68, 69, 70; pre-mediation and 68
orientations framework 80, 81, 84, **85**, 92; critical orientation **85**, 88, 90, 93; conservative orientation **85**, 87, 89, 90; liberal orientation **85**, 87, 88, 90, 92; postmodern orientation **85**, 91

peer review 109, 148, 149, 153, 157, 160, 172, 175; @RealPeerReview 151, 157, 159
phallic teacher: Altmetrics 159; article 148, 149, 152, 153, 154, 158; conference paper 150, 158; hyperfeminized 149; media phenomenon 151, 152; support of 160; and Twitter 156, 157, 158, 159

PISA 12, 28, 52, 92, 137; media analysis 13, 33, 35, 37, 41; OECD and 13, 39; reporting 28, 29, 32, 42–43; as research data 32–33, 188; and social media 39–41

PISA performance: comparisons 30, *42*; decline 37, 38, 43; and GDP 37, 39; media coverage of 33, 37; of nations 13, 27, 29, 30, 32, 37; and socio-economic status 43

PISA rankings: league tables 13; slippage 37

PISA report: release of 32, 39, 40–41

PISA scores 59; measurement of 30; mean 29, 37

PISA shock 29

PISA test 37; effects **34**, 36, 39, 40, *42*, 43; first administered 43, 44n1; results 13, 27, 29, 30, 37, 40

PISA test equity 27, 29, 33, **34**, 38, 40–41, 43, 44

PISA test legitimacy: reinforced 37–39; questioned 39–41

PISA test quality 27, 29, 30, 33, **34**, 38, 40, 42–44

PISA test regime 39, 40, 42–43

policies: Controversial Issues in School 82; Excellence in Research for Australia 181; Kiwi Standards 135, 136, 137, 138, 141; Prevent Policy UK 69, 70, 71, 72, 75, 76; Research Excellence Framework 181; and women 160

policy effects 29, 41, 43, 107, 109, 110; contestation 37, 125, 136, 143, 144, 145; de and re-territorialising of 131; enactment 125, 186, 187–188; reinforcement/reproduction 37, 125, 128

policy field 43

policy sociology 124, 186

policy: agendas 126; circulation 102; control 99; debates 15, 50, 81, 99, 100, 107, 109; dialogues 101, 103, 110, 113; documents 123; inclusive 27; influencing 106, 113, 123, 124, 126; journals 2, 107, 183; media role in 1, 39, 41, 44, 66, 101, 138, 140, 183; mediatisation 8, 9, **10–11**, 12–13, 41, 62, 101, 104, 123; research impact on 112; in schools 67; and spin 7, 8; and teachers 122

policy makers 18, 29, 30, 39, 43, 44, 93, 101, 106, 119, 122; speaking to 126; use of media 124

political fray 101, 103, 104

politics: dirty 135; and social media 28, 43

postmodern orientation **85**, 91

post-truth 28

power 30, 31; and control 102; differentials 31, 43; and discourse 84, 104, 159; dynamics 187; and equity 102, 114; flow of 130–131; hierarchies 72, 122, 122; and knowledge 87, 122, 128; legitimacy 122; of mass media 75, 83; negotiated 155; onto 68, 69, 75; panoptical 157; performative 160; political 75; resistance to 120, 166; and scholarship 176; and schools 88, 91; and visibility 114

power relations 31, **85**, 101, 102, 121, 155

Premium Twitter Archiver 54

print media 4, 13, 14, 15, 16, 27–28, 29, 31, 32, 33, 35, 36, 37, 38, 39, 41–43, 48, 50, 82, 83, 100, 105, 106, 126, 135, 137, 138–139, 140, 141, 185

professional development 16

public discourse 1, 92, 93, 104, 114, 119, 120, 130, 184

public education 7, 12, 82, 83, 87, 107, 114, 122, 140

public intellectuals/ism 101, 150, 187

public scholars 99, 101, 102, 103, 104, 109, 114, 183; and credibility 109–110; and engagement strategies 110; and informing public dialogue 110–112

public scholarship 101, 108; dangers of 112–113, 142, 165, 172, 181, 184, 186

public sphere 7, 28, 39, 101–102, 112, 177, 185, 188

public: attitudes 1, 8, 12, 47; behaviours 69; commentary 80, 81, 83, 84, 85, 88, 93, 142, 144, 157; debate 119, 120, 130, 131, 136, 143, 145; dialogue 100, 101, 103, 113; digital 165; domain 49, 153; engagement 148, 185, 187; good 16; humiliation 159; imaginaries 67, 75; influence 8, 103; influencers 104–107; interests 32, 140; opinion 16, 28, 67, 83; participation 107, 185; pedagogy 187; perceptions of education 48, 100, 103; space 47, 62, 63, 119, 121, 166, 168, 177, 187; teacher 102; voice 124

publics 48, 61, 62, 101, 131, 139, 152, 153, 161, 180, 182; counter 114; global 160; hyper 152; media 149

Rawolle, S. 7, 8, **10**, 12, 43, 123

redemption: narratives of 52–53, 61

re-matter 67, 72–75

Renold, E. 67, 71, 72, 73, 75

Representation/s: amplification 62; and belonging 88; and binary thinking 76; beyond 18, 75, 76, 186; diagrammatic 41; and discourse 17, 81, 88, 89; dominant

61; and education 47, 48–49, 54, 61; mainstream 90; media 27, 102; network 55; problematic 14, 17; public 113; of teachers 126; visual 33
Revolution School 47, 49–50, 52, 53, 54–61
research gaps 17–18, 44
Reyes, C. 100, 101, 113
Ringrose, J. 67, 71, 72

Schleicher, A. 39, 40, 41
Scholar Public Influence Rankings 103, 104, 105, **106**, 107
school improvement: narratives of 49, 50, 52, 53–54, 60, 61
schooling complexity 50, 61
sexism 150, 151
social media 1, 28, 32, 35–36, 39–41; and academics 151, 152, 153; backlash 112; and campaigning 99; and collective professional voice 126; and communication 127; dangers of 114, 150, 160; and democracy 44, 102; as echo chambers 119; ethics 153–154; firestorms 180; influence 13; movements 125; platforms 35, 80, 103, 104, 174, 181, 184, 188; and privacy 128; and propaganda 28; and teachers 15, 16, 127
social media comparisons: with print media 30, 32, 36, 41, 44, 61–62
social network analysis 8, 33, 55, 57
software: Gephi 55; Leximancer 33, 35; NVivo 50; Premium Twitter Archiver 54
spectacle 12
spin 7, 8
standardised testing 110
statistical analysis: descriptive 4–6; statistical 55, 60–61
systematic literature review 2–4

teacher quality: narratives of 15, 16, 59
teachers' voice 15, 29, 41, 43, 119, 120–123, 130
teachers' work 1, 7, 9, **10–11**, 15–16, 48, 185; strikes 16, 102 *see also* discourse
terrorist assemblages 66, 68, 69, 72, 75
Thomson, P. 1–2, 7, **10**, 18, 122, 123, 124, 148, 152
Thrift, N. 30, 68, 69, 70, 71
Thrupp, M. 135, 137, 142, 143, 144
traditional media 1, 3, 5, 37, 80, 92, 99, 101, 105, 135, 186
trolls/ing 127, 128, 150, 153, 158, 160, 175

Twitter: conversations 62; inception 4; education research 1, 12, 13, 27–28, 30, 32–33, 35–36, 39–41, 42–44; and professional development 16; and professional networking 48; *see also* social media

UK: academics 171; counter-terrorism 66, 68; education blogs 125; election 28; General Certificate of Secondary Education 12; hate crimes 69; Headteachers' Roundtable 126; jihadi brides 67; media 12, 16; newspapers 15, 29; Ofsted 67; Plowden report 12; Prevent Policy 66, 75; privacy 180; publications 5; regional newspapers 15; research 13; Research Excellence Framework 181; researchers 170; schools 69; teacher blog 124, 125; women and leadership 126
USA: Common Core 12, 28; economic competition 111; edu-business 127; education reform 15, 112; News & World Report 105; newspapers **11**, 13, 29; Pew Research Centre 84; president 28, 43, 100, 141; presidential election 14, 114; publications 5, 6; @realDonaldTrump 148; research 13, 15; TIMSS 12; Twitter debates 12
Urry, J. 30,
Unions: teacher 16, 29, 41, 43, 89, 122; 125; 126; 139, 141, 143, 144, 177, 187; teacher strike 16

visual representations 33, 35, 36, 41, 45, 55, 57
Veletsianos, G. 16, 100, 124, 180
voice: abusive 165; clashes of 127–129; dominant 48, 54, 55, 57; excluded 15, 18, 29, 31, 55, 87, 93; gatekeepers of 105; non-dominant 91; parents' 87; plurality of 155; professional 124, 126; public 181; social mediatisation of 124, 129–130, 131; as speaking back 16; teachers' 15, 29, 41, 43, 119, 120–123, 130; vulnerable 104

Waters, L. 50, 58; @ProfLeaWaters 57
Weller, M. 124, 127

Zarabadi, S. 67, 70